Praise for *Keeping W*

"As the lengthening shadow of Social Darwinism extends across the political landscape of America, Ruth Sidel again provides us with a vision to illuminate the darkness. Drawing not only upon some truly devastating statistics but also upon her long experience of dialogue with poor women and children, she weaves a tapestry of incisive analysis that demonstrates how much of the legacy of Franklin Roosevelt and Dr. Martin Luther King is about to be dismantled and makes clear the consequences this will have for our society."

—Jonathan Kozol,
author of *Amazing Grace:
The Lives of Children and the Conscience of a Nation*

"Keeping Women and Children Last exposes the harmful effects of this past decade's policies on our most vulnerable Americans, women and children in poverty. Noting the onslaught against single mothers, particularly those in need of welfare support, Ruth Sidel bids us hear the women's voices. The wellspring of her work is women who trust her with their stories. Sidel frames their issues with solid sociological scholarship and communicates with great passion and compassion. She has the unique gift of marshalling convincing facts and arguments for humane, constructive family policies."

—Helen Rodriguez-Trias, M.D.,
pediatrician and past president of the
American Public Health Association

"Every public official should read this book. *Keeping Women and Children Last* successfully puts to rest all of the vicious stereotypes about poor women and children—stereotypes which all too often pass as informed judgments in our policy debates.

"Hopefully—through her master work—her proposals will make a substantial difference at this critical time in our history."

—U.S. Senator Paul Wellstone

PENGUIN BOOKS

KEEPING WOMEN AND CHILDREN LAST

Ruth Sidel, a professor of sociology at Hunter College and a frequent nationwide speaker on women's issues and social policy, is the author of many books, including the classic works *Women and Children Last* and *On Her Own*. She lives in New York City.

Keeping Women and Children Last

America's War on the Poor

REVISED EDITION

RUTH SIDEL

PENGUIN BOOKS

PENGUIN BOOKS
Published by the Penguin Group
Penguin Putnam Inc., 375 Hudson Street,
New York, New York 10014, U.S.A.
Penguin Books Ltd, 27 Wrights Lane,
London W8 5TZ, England
Penguin Books Australia Ltd, Ringwood,
Victoria, Australia
Penguin Books Canada Ltd, 10 Alcorn Avenue,
Toronto, Ontario, Canada M4V 3B2
Penguin Books (N.Z.) Ltd, 182–190 Wairau Road,
Auckland 10, New Zealand
Penguin India, 210 Chiranjiv Tower, 43 Nehru Place,
New Delhi 11009, India

Penguin Books Ltd, Registered Offices:
Harmondsworth, Middlesex, England

First published in Penguin Books 1996
This edition with a new epilogue published in Penguin Books 1998

1   3   5   7   9   10   8   6   4   2

LIBRARY OF CONGRESS CATALOGING IN PUBLICATION DATA
Sidel, Ruth.
Keeping women and children last: America's war on the poor / Ruth Sidel.
p.   cm.
Sequel to: Women and children last.
Includes bibliographical references (p.   ) and index.
ISBN 0 14 02.7693 9
1. Poor women—United States.   2. Public welfare—United States.
3. Family policy—United States.   4. Women heads of households—United States.
I. Sidel, Ruth. Women and children last.   II. Title.
HV699.S527   1996
362.5'0973—dc20   95–26054

Printed in the United States of America
Set in Bembo
Designed by Jessica Shatan

*To all those women and men
who are working, individually and collectively,
to build a more just society*

Acknowledgments

First, my profound gratitude to the women who so generously spoke with me about their lives, their concerns, their hopes and dreams for the future, and their views of current policies directed at the poor. Without the wholehearted participation of these and other women over the years, this book and previous works would not exist.

I also wish to thank those who have helped me to formulate and express the ideas presented here. They have discussed and read and questioned and raised new ideas and I am enormously grateful for their time and effort. To Lynn Chancer, who read key chapters, suggested new perspectives, and is unfailingly critical (in the best sense of that word), enthusiastic, and supportive, my deep admiration and appreciation; to Laurie Kramer, who read virtually all of the manuscript and provided her unique intelligence and point of view, my gratitude; to Jerome Grossman, with whom I have discussed many of these ideas over the years and who always lends his energy, commitment, knowledge, and understanding of the political process, my love and my thanks; and to Kevin and Inge Sidel who were never too busy with their own lives to care and to cheer on the writing and completion of this effort, my heartfelt thanks.

I am grateful to the colleagues and friends who help and

support in myriad ways: Mimi Abramovitz, Alice Axelbank, Naomi Chase, Gertrude Schaffner Goldberg, Barbara Grossman, Margot Haas, Marilyn Jackson, Pauline Katz, Esther Madriz, Mary Murphree, Jan Poppendieck, Jane Prather, Margaret Raymond, Mark Sidel, Joel Spoonheim, and Richard Tresch.

Special mention must be made of those indefatigable experts who staff the research and advocacy organizations that provide essential data, analysis, legislative information, and strategy, and continue to remind all of us involved in these issues of the profound impact of social and economic policy on the lives of human beings. I want to express my particular appreciation to the Alan Guttmacher Institute, the Center on Budget and Policy Priorities, the Center on Social Welfare Policy and Law, the Children's Defense Fund, the Coalition for Basic Human Needs, the Food Research and Action Center, and the Institute for Women's Policy Research.

To Susan Hans O'Connor, Lydia Weaver, Jo Jane Pitt, and Kate Griggs, my gratitude for their caring and meticulous help with the manuscript and proofs, and to Mindy Werner, my editor at Viking Penguin, my appreciation for her unfailing concern about poor women and children, her intellectual acumen, and her friendship. And finally, to Vic, who, as always, is an integral and essential part of it all, my deepest thanks and love.

Contents

Introduction

Women and Children Last: The Plight of Poor Women in Affluent America was first published in 1986. I began research for that book in the early 1980s when the poverty rate in the United States had risen to levels higher than at any time since the early 1960s. In 1983, for example, over 35 million people, more than 15 percent of the population, struggled to survive with incomes below the poverty line. Moreover, the vast majority of these poor people were women and their children.

Much had changed in the lives of many women during the two decades between the early 1960s and the early 1980s: large numbers of women joined the paid labor market; there were significant increases in the number of women entering law, medicine, and other traditionally male-dominated fields; and, perhaps most important, women from a variety of backgrounds, particularly younger women, had come to understand that the traditional two-parent family, in which the father was the central breadwinner while the mother took care of the children and the home, was no longer working for many families. But as some women significantly increased their skills, their status, and their income, and as many women assumed greater control of their lives, including their reproductive lives, millions of other women were living in poverty.

The early 1980s was the era of Reaganomics, a time of "trickle-down" economics that in reality made the rich richer and widened the gap between rich and poor. It was a time of significant cuts in Aid to Families with Dependent Children (AFDC), in the Food Stamp program and child-nutrition programs, in maternal- and child-health programs, and in funds for family planning. Federal funds for day care were scaled back sharply as were training and employment programs such as the Comprehensive Employment and Training Act (CETA), which was eliminated. It was clear that the economic policies of the Reagan administration were exacerbating the extremely vulnerable position of poor people and were helping to propel additional individuals and families into dire poverty.

At that time the metaphor of the sinking of the *Titanic* seemed particularly apt. A magnificent ship, four blocks long, on her maiden voyage from Southampton, England, to New York, with a French "sidewalk cafe," a Turkish bath with a mosaic floor and gilded beams, and reputedly the finest concert band on the Atlantic, the *Titanic* sank in the North Atlantic after hitting an iceberg on the "bitterly cold" night of April 14, 1912.

Much of the story is common knowledge. What may be less well known is that the *Titanic*, for all of its glamour and glitter, did not have enough lifeboats for its passengers and crew. Its 20 lifeboats had space for only 1,178 people out of the 2,207 on board that night. Yet, while many women and children were indeed the first to be saved, the percentage of women and children in first and second class who were saved was far higher than the percentage saved in "steerage," or what we would now call third class. Among first and second class passengers, only 8 percent of the women drowned, three who by their own choice refused to leave the ship without their husbands; in steerage, 45 percent of the women perished. The statistics for children are even more shocking: only one child of the 30 children in first and second class died, while in steerage 53 of the 76 children, 70 percent, drowned. Furthermore, there is clear evidence that the more affluent passengers in first and second class had far easier access to the existing lifeboats than the less affluent passengers and that many in steerage were purposely prevented from reaching the decks that housed their only hope of survival.

In the mid-1980s, it surely seemed as though the United States, with its glitter and glamour, its sidewalk cafes, health clubs, restaurants, and boutiques, was protecting the lives and the lifestyles of the affluent and that it too did not have enough lifeboats for the less fortunate. With every cut in social programs, the Reagan administration appeared determined to destroy the few flimsy lifeboats that existed for a fraction of the poor. During the decade of the eighties, a time of boom for the most affluent and of increasing destitution for those at the bottom of the economic pyramid, the *Titanic* seemed to be an all-too-appropriate image.

One decade later, in 1993, 4 million additional people, over 39 million, were living in poverty in the United States. While preliminary data on poverty levels in 1994 indicate a modest decline in the percentage of people living in poverty, to 14.5, and in the number of Americans living below the poverty line, to 38.1 million, in 1993, the year for which comprehensive data are available, over 15 percent (15.1) of the population were still officially designated as poor, the same rate of poverty as a decade ago when the economy was in its greatest slump since the Great Depression of 1929. Between 1992 and 1993, during a period of economic recovery, albeit a so-called "jobless recovery," over 1 million additional people fell into poverty. In the early 1980s, a shocking 24 percent of children under the age of six lived in poverty; in 1993, even more preschool children, 26 percent—more than one out of every four—lived below the poverty line. Between 1987 and 1992, the number of preschool children living in poverty increased from 5 to 6 million. When we look further at poverty rates for specific groups, we see that the poverty rate of Hispanic children is nearly three times that of non-Hispanic white children and the poverty rate of black children is three and one half times that of white children. Today women and children make up over three quarters of the poor. Indeed women and children are still last in affluent America.

As the numbers of poor people continue to rise, the gap between rich and poor is wider than at any time since census data on income have been compiled. The greatest gains in income and wealth have come to the top one-half of one percent of the population. By 1993, the top 20 percent of U.S. households received nearly half of all household income (48.2 percent), the highest percentage ever recorded for that group, while the bottom 20 percent received 3.6 percent of all income, the lowest share ever received.

In this context of increasing economic inequality and rising poverty rates among the most vulnerable segments of the population, we are in the midst of a massive effort to drastically cut and, in some instances, dismantle programs for the poor and the near-poor. This effort has escalated sharply since the 1994 election when the Republican Party gained control of both houses of Congress. In addition to the government's efforts to alter the very nature of Aid to Families with Dependent Children and other social welfare programs that benefit poor people, single mothers, specifically welfare recipients, are increasingly being blamed for the serious problems that afflict

American society today. Politician after politician, commentator after commentator, claims that virtually every problem the American people face—from school failure to crime, from teenage pregnancy to drug addiction—is caused by the escalating number of single-parent families, particularly female-headed families.

In addition, the claim is being made that programs that help the most disadvantaged among us, particularly AFDC, have fostered dependency among the poor, encouraged teenage pregnancy and out-of-wedlock childbearing, undermined the work ethic, and seriously weakened the traditional American family. This claim is being made despite considerable evidence to the contrary: Over the past two decades, AFDC benefits in real dollars have declined significantly while the number of single-parent families has risen sharply. In addition, the states with the lowest benefits have the highest rates of teenage births. In 1994, for example, Mississippi provided a maximum benefit of only $120 per month (a yearly grant of $1,440!) for a family of three and yet in the early 1990s that state had the highest birthrate among young women ages fifteen to nineteen. With the severe structural problems that afflict American society—increasing economic inequality, diminishing jobs, particularly jobs with decent wages and benefits, growing poverty among young, two-parent families, and grossly inadequate social supports for almost all segments of the population—why are single-parent families and a diminished, tattered, and fragmented social welfare system being blamed for the ills of American society? Perhaps a personal note can offer some insight.

I grew up in a single-parent family. It didn't seem strange to me as I had barely known any other way of life. Not only did

I have just one parent but I grew up virtually as an only child since my older brothers were grown and out of the house by the time I was eight.

I was certainly aware of some of the negative consequences of having only one parent: I had no one else to go to when my parent was angry with me or when I felt unjustly treated. Equally important, my parent had no one with whom to discuss child rearing or domestic crises. Nonetheless, while I knew we were different and I sometimes felt embarrassed by being different, I never had a sense that our family—and we certainly were a family—was looked down upon by my friends, by their parents, by my teachers, or our family friends or acquaintances. I never heard or sensed any concern that I would not be appropriately socialized or disciplined; there was never any suggestion that I would not succeed academically and go on to achieve a worthwhile career and a satisfying and productive life. My parent was never, to my knowledge, criticized for working outside the home, for leaving me in the care of others, for taking occasional vacations, or for continuing to have an active social life. Of course, the major difference between my single parent and the vast majority of single parents now being criticized—some would say vilified—is that my single parent was my father. Furthermore, we were not poor, and he had become a single parent through the most acceptable route possible: my mother had died.

In fact, rather than being criticized, my father was viewed by many as a hero. He had suffered great tragedy and here he was, bringing up his young daughter—alone. How devoted he was, people remarked. How caring. And to raise a *daughter* without a mother. Of course, many encouraged him to remarry. Everyone had a woman he "must meet." But there was never a suggestion that he was subverting the American family or American society; there was never a suggestion that the absence of a second parent might cause me to drop out of school, become delinquent, have a child while unmarried, turn to drugs or alcohol. There was never a suggestion that my father alone could not love me, teach me, discipline me.

Some will say that it was a different era—and it was. But my father's image as a single parent was much more connected to his gender, his race, and his class than it was to the era in which I grew up. Poor single mothers have been seen as suspect since colonial times and poor single black mothers have been systematically excluded from financial aid as well as community support and sympathy since this country was founded. Yes, widows have been favored over women who were divorced and women who had children outside of marriage; some of the sympathy and admiration my father received was certainly due to his being a widower. But it was also due to his being male, affluent, and white. Rather than being denigrated and despised, he was admired for his courage, his steadfastness, his devotion to family.

———

Today we are in the midst of a widespread effort to denigrate and stigmatize poor single mothers, particularly welfare recipients. This effort is part of a more generalized drumbeat of criticism about one-parent families. The message is clear: the single-parent family breeds trouble, and poor single mothers breed catastrophe. "Illegitimacy," the term once again in vogue for out-of-wedlock birth, is being labeled a threat to American culture and to the very survival of our nation.

In this sequel to *Women and Children Last*, I suggest that the widespread campaign against poor single mothers is in reality a form of scapegoating, the singling out for blame and opprobrium of a group that is particularly vulnerable because of race, class, and gender. The designation of poor single mothers as the cause of America's ills deflects attention from the severe economic and societal problems we face and our unwillingness to deal with those problems: the growing gap between rich and poor; widespread employment insecurity; increasing political apathy and alienation; extraordinary levels of violence, particularly among our young people; and our rapidly deteriorating infrastructure. This strategy in effect shifts blame from the affluent and powerful to the poor and powerless.

One of the functions of designating certain people as enemies is the bringing together of the rest of society. For the first time in over half a century the United States does not have significant external enemies. The relentless rhetoric against poor single mothers has provided an enemy against whom politicians and conservative ideologues can rally and against whom they can mobilize public opinion and the voting electorate.

This book attempts to demonstrate that the causes of the sharply increasing rate of mother-only families, of the rising number of teenagers becoming pregnant, and of the growing number of families living in poverty and near poverty are, in reality, neither the moral weakness of poor people nor the benefits provided by the social welfare system. Rather, the causes are profound changes in technology, in employment, in international trade, and in family structure that are occurring in the United States and in many other countries of the world, and the inadequacy of our economic, social, and family policies. These issues must be dealt with not through scapegoating and punishment but rather through fundamental structural change.

Keeping Women and Children Last attempts to present up-to-date data, analyses, and recommendations on the fundamental issues discussed in *Women and Children Last*: The extent, nature, and causes of poverty in the United States; the impact, particularly on women and children, of being poor in an extremely affluent society; the role of social welfare programs in contributing both to the well-being and the continuing misery of the poor; and the ways in which American attitudes toward the impoverished have determined our social policies. Chapter 1 focuses on current efforts to label the poor, specifically poor women, as the enemy within. It analyzes the functions of stigma and scapegoating, especially in the current American social, economic, and political context. Chapter 2 details the attack on mother-only families and the fallacies of attributing the critical problems the United States faces to a particularly powerless group within the society. Chapter 3 raises the question "Who Are the Poor?" and attempts to demonstrate that poverty in America today is not monolithic but has many faces— urban and rural, working and not working, long-term and short term, from all races and ethnic groups. Chapter 3 also raises fundamental questions about the definition of poverty and the mislabeling of millions of poor people as the "underclass." Chapter 4, "Targeting Welfare Recipients," describes the reality of living on AFDC and focuses on recent efforts at the local, state, and federal levels to "end welfare as we know it." The potentially devastating impact of the decimation of many anti-poverty programs on recipients and on their children is explored. Chapter 5 attempts to go beyond the slogans and rhetoric about teenage pregnancy to examine the data and the results of recent research. The chapter discusses the causes of teen pregnancy and the effects of teenage childbearing on the future economic status of teen mothers and their children. Chapter 6 explores the impact of poverty on the well-being of children. From low birth weight to home-lessness, school failure to premature death, growing up poor in America has dire and long-lasting consequences. Finally, chapter 7 attempts to offer analyses of the causes of America's severe problems, to place these issues into international perspective, and to detail a comprehensive social policy that would reduce the numbers of individuals and families living in poverty, provide renewed opportunities and safeguards for working- and middle-class Americans, and offer hope and support to those currently mired in poverty. Throughout the book, the issues of gender, class, and race are emphasized, particularly the ways in which race has been used to divide Americans for political and economic advantage.

As in my other books, I have used interviews with individuals to explore and illustrate the central issues. A few of the interviews were published originally in *Women and Children Last* or in my other studies; the in-depth interviews that frame and, I hope, elucidate chapters 4 through 6 were conducted during the past eighteen months as part of the research for this book. As in all my work, names and any material that might identify the individual interviewees have been changed.

During the early 1980s, the United States—like the *Titanic* —clearly did not have enough lifeboats for the millions of women and children who were living in poverty. During the mid–1990s there are even fewer lifeboats and women and children in "steerage" are still being barred from climbing aboard the ones that remain.

What is new and even more disturbing today is the campaign of vilification being waged against poor women and children, a campaign that permits and legitimizes the destruction of remaining lifeboats in order to fuel the increasing wealth of the richest among us and to further the political fortunes of those in power. Perhaps this volume will encourage some to question the wisdom and the humanity of these policies before we consign millions of women and children for the foreseeable future to the frigid waters of deprivation and despair.

Since the original publication of this book, the Personal Responsibility and Work Opportunity Reconciliation Act of 1996 has transformed the welfare system of the United States. Repealing the guarantee of aid to poor children and ceding virtually all power over the poor to the individual states, this legislation has radically altered the lives of the impoverished throughout the country. The Epilogue, written nearly two years after the signing of this landmark legislation, attempts to describe this sea change in social policy and to analyze its impact on the millions of families who continue to subsist below the poverty line. This is clearly an ongoing story, one with serious implications for all of us but particularly, of course, for the poor women and children who continue to be last in this exceedingly rich country of ours.

Ruth Sidel
New York City
June 1998

Chapter 1

The Enemy Within

Conflict between groups is, of course, nothing new. What may be new in Western Christian tradition . . . is how the use of Satan to represent one's enemies lends to conflict a specific kind of moral and religious interpretation, in which "we" are God's people and "they" are God's enemies, and ours as well.

—ELAINE PAGELS
The Origin of Satan

THEY ARE DESPISED, DENIGRATED, OSTRACIZED FROM mainstream society. In earlier times, they were known as the "dangerous classes"; today they are labeled the "underclass." They are pictured as virtually irredeemable, lazy, dependent, living off the hard-earned money of others. They are poor single mothers. They are welfare recipients. They are the enemy within.

The demonizing of poor single mothers has been an integral part of the recent onslaught on the safety net, meager and inadequate as it is, that has existed in the United States since the passage of the Social Security Act of 1935. Poor mothers have been deemed unworthy, the "undeserving poor"; nearly 15 million welfare recipients have been painted with one brush, have been relegated to that area in society that is beyond the pale. Systematic stereotyping and stigmatizing of "welfare mothers" was necessary in order to dehumanize them in the eyes of other Americans before the harsh and tenuous lifeline of Aid to Families with Dependent Children (AFDC) and the other bare-bones social programs could be shredded. The implicit and often explicit message is: If welfare recipients are so unworthy, perhaps such harsh treatment, such punishment, is warranted, even necessary, in order to modify their social and reproductive behavior. Perhaps, it has been said, removing cash and other benefits, forcing mothers to work even at dead-end jobs for poverty wages, and denying aid to children of teenagers and to additional babies born while the mother is receiving AFDC is the only way to deal with this "deviant" and "irresponsible" group. Many politicians claim that they are promoting these Draconian measures against the poor as a form of "tough love," "for their own good." These cuts in assistance and services may be painful at first, this reasoning goes, and some suggest that this current generation of poor parents may have to be written off, but in the long run these harsh measures will enable the next generation to "stand on their own two feet." Congress, the tough but responsible parent, will force the poor, as though they were rebellious adolescents, to shape up, to reform their delinquent ways.

Just over a decade ago, social scientist Charles Murray, author of *Losing Ground: American Social Policy 1950–1980*, articulated the values, priorities, and underlying agenda of America's war against the poor:

Some people are better than others. They deserve more of society's rewards, of which money is only one small part. A principal function of social policy is to make sure they have the opportunity to reap those rewards. Government cannot identify the worthy, but it can protect a society in which the worthy can identify themselves.

Thus the government legitimizes the existing social hierarchy and safeguards the affluence and lifestyles of those whom Murray deems "better," and more "worthy." Murray continues by proposing an "ambitious thought experiment":

. . . scrapping the entire federal welfare and income-support structure for working-age persons, including AFDC, Medicaid, Food Stamps, Unemployment Insurance, Worker's Compensation, subsidized housing, disability insurance, and the rest. It would leave the working-aged person with no recourse whatsoever except the job market, family members, friends, and public or private locally funded services. It is the Alexandrian solution: cut the knot, for there is no way to untie it.

It is noteworthy that the only "knots" being "cut" in the mid-1990s are those that afford some protection to the poor. Now, there is virtually no discussion of dismantling Unemployment Insurance, Worker's Compensation, or disability insurance, programs that provide help in times of need for a broad spectrum of Americans, not just the poor. In current efforts to move toward balancing the federal budget, there is considerable discussion about cutting Medicaid (the health program that serves the poor), Medicare (the health program that serves the elderly), education, health research, and environmental protection. But while debate rages on about how and how much to cut these programs, the beneficiaries have not been denigrated and made into pariahs. In the discussion about

Medicare, older people have not been disparaged; in debate about cutting money for education, children have not been demonized. Only when the discussion moves to the drastic reduction in support of programs that primarily help poor women and their children are the recipients portrayed as fundamentally different from mainstream Americans.

The rhetoric that has accompanied and paved the way for the continuing assault on programs for poor women and children was fueled by a pledge made by then-candidate Bill Clinton during the 1992 presidential campaign. After a Clinton speechwriter consulted with political pollsters and felt that the issue would resonate with voters, the decision was made to call for stronger measures in dealing with welfare. Consequently, Mr. Clinton first stated his now-famous phrase in a speech at Georgetown University on October 23, 1991: "In a Clinton Administration, we're going to put an end to welfare as we know it." As Senator Daniel Patrick Moynihan, Democrat from New York, has stated, "The Republicans took him at his word" and went much further. But the only real way to end welfare as we know it, Moynihan continues, is "just to dump the children on the streets." And indeed that is exactly what is happening.

Today as AFDC is being decimated and other programs that serve the poor are threatened by cutbacks, the litany of criticism against poor single women is relentless. Mother-only families are being blamed for virtually all of the ills afflicting American society. Out-of-wedlock births have been blamed for the "breakdown of the family," for the crime rate, drug and alcohol addiction, poverty, illiteracy, homelessness, poor school performance, and the rending of the social fabric. The labeling of some citizens as "dependent"—that is, dependent on social welfare programs rather than on spouses, parents, or other family members, or other more acceptable federal programs—indiscriminately discredits an entire group of women and children without regard to their character or their specific work and/or family history. Whether they are receiving benefits because they had a child outside of marriage or because they are separated, divorced, or widowed, or because the father of their children deserted them, welfare recipients have been labeled as being part of a "culture of illegitimacy"; moreover, some legislators have gone so far as to equate illegitimacy with promiscuity. As the political tide has rapidly turned against the poor, particularly poor women, rhetoric has escalated to previously unimagined levels of hyperbole and vitriol. At a 1994 news conference called by the Mainstream Forum, a group of centrist and conservative House Democrats affiliated with the Democratic Leadership Council (the political organization President Clinton helped found and headed when he was governor of Arkansas), Representative Nathan Deal, a Georgia Democrat, declared that welfare was dead. He went on to state, "The stench from its decaying carcass has filled the nostrils of every American."

This scathing stereotyping and stigmatizing of poor mothers has severe consequences for them, for their children, and for the society as a whole. As sociologist Erving Goffman has pointed out,

By definition, of course, we believe the person with a stigma is not quite human. On this assumption we exercise varieties of discrimination, through which we effectively, if often unthinkingly, reduce his life chances. We construct a stigma-theory, an ideology to explain his inferiority and account for the danger he represents. . . .

The very words that are being used tell us what to think and how to feel. Poor women are characterized by their "dependence," an absolute negative, a polar opposite of that valued American characteristic, "independence." This label presumes that *they* are "dependent," that *they* passively rely on the government for their day-to-day needs while *we*, the rest of us, are "independent," "pull ourselves up by our bootstraps," are out there "on our own." These designations leave no room for the considerable variation and complexity that characterize most people's lives, for the fact that virtually all of us are in varying degrees dependent on others and on societal supports during our adult lives—that many of us have been recipients of financial or other kinds of help from family members, that many have been helped by inheritance, by assistance in finding (and sometimes keeping) a job, by tax deductions for mortgage payments, or the federal subsidy of farm prices, or by programs such as Medicare or Unemployment Compensation or disability assistance.

Dividing people into "us" and "them" is facilitated by the resurrection of terms such as "illegitimacy," that encourage the shaming and denigration of mothers and their out-of-wedlock children. It is far easier to refuse aid to "them," to people who engage in disgraceful, stigmatized behavior than to people who seem like "us." David Boaz, executive vice-president of the Cato Institute, a libertarian organization, even hopes to resurrect the term "bastard": "We've made it possible for a teenage girl to survive with no husband and no job. That used to be very difficult. If we had more stigma and lower benefits, might we end up with 100,000 bastards every year rather than a million children born to alternative families?"

Poor, single mothers, particularly AFDC recipients, are being portrayed as the ultimate outsiders—marginalized as nonworkers in a society that claims belief in the work ethic, marginalized as single parents in a society that holds the two-parent, heterosexual family as the desired norm, and marginalized as poor people in a society that worships success and material rewards.

Perhaps the most dehumanizing and degrading references to welfare recipients occurred on the floor of the House of Representatives on March 24, 1995, during the debate on a bill that would cut $69 billion in spending on social welfare programs over the next five years. Welfare recipients were compared to animals by two Republican members of the House. Representative John L. Mica of Florida held up a sign that said, DON'T FEED THE ALLIGATORS. He explained, "We post these warnings because unnatural feeding and artificial care create dependency. When dependency sets in, these otherwise able alligators can no longer survive on their own." Mica then noted that while "people are not alligators . . . we've upset the natural order. We've created a system of dependency."

Representative Barbara Cubin of Wyoming carried the analogy still further:

The Federal Government introduced wolves into the State of Wyoming, and they put them in pens, and they brought elk and venison to them every day. This is what I call the wolf welfare program. The Federal Government provided everything that the wolves need for their existence. But guess what? They opened the gates and let the wolves out, and now the wolves won't go. Just like any animal in the species, any mammal, when you take away their freedom and their dignity and their ability, they can't provide for themselves. . . .

By comparing AFDC recipients to wolves on the floor of the U.S. House of Representatives, Representative Cubin seems to be suggesting that poor mothers and their children are no better than animals, dangerous animals at that. One of the central problems with such outrageous and dehumanizing language is that, in the words of one observer, it "shatters the capacity for empathy" on the part of the majority toward the denigrated group. But perhaps that is exactly the purpose of such demeaning analogies. How much easier it is to cut aid to people who are perceived to be feared animals than to mothers and children toward whom we feel some compassion, with whom we can identify.

Representatives Mica and Cubin are also suggesting that AFDC and other programs are providing "everything" the recipients need for their existence. One of the central theses of those who are championing massive cutbacks of AFDC and other programs for the poor is that these programs have made recipients dependent, unable to function on their own. According to Ralph Reed, executive director of the Christian Coalition, an organization that describes its membership as including 1.6 million people with chapters in all fifty states, the current panoply of programs to help the poor have "enslaved the very people . . . [they] promised to protect." There is, however, no evidence that Aid to Families with Dependent Children and other programs for the poor such as Head Start, Food Stamps, and the Women's, Infants' and Children's Feeding Program (WIC) are fundamentally responsible for the increase in poverty, for the increase in out-of-wedlock births, for the shortage of jobs, for the low wages, and for the shortage of child care that characterize the lives of impoverished women. (This issue will be dealt with in greater detail in subsequent chapters.)

Since the 1994 election, attacks on other groups in the United States—particularly on criminals and potential criminals and on immigrants—have escalated sharply. This process has included verbal denigration as well as cruel and unusual treatment of those who are traditionally perceived as outsiders. There has been harsh rhetoric against documented and undocumented immigrants, as well as attempts to deprive them of essential human services. Prisoners who are mentally ill, functionally illiterate, and otherwise usually exempt from such inhumane punishment are being executed. Elementary school students, mostly children of color, were strip-searched in Patterson, New Jersey, because twenty dollars had supposedly been stolen from one student. Chain gangs and forced labor have returned to the Alabama penal system. All this has occurred over the past eighteen months. It is surely no accident that all of these groups are made up largely of low-income people of color. But the harshest rhetoric and most sweeping policy changes have been reserved for the poor, particularly poor women. It is this convergence of class, gender, and race that makes a sweeping attack on one segment of society possible.

This denigration of poor welfare recipients is based in large part on dichotomous thinking and on the repetition and reiteration of commonly held myths about poor women and their children. The dichotomous thinking underlying much of the so-called welfare debate divides people, primarily women, into "good" and "bad"; "workers" and "idlers"; those who abide by traditional "family values" and those who do not; good, caring mothers and those who have been characterized by Charles Murray as "rotten mothers." Even children are being characterized by this either/or language: "legitimate" versus "illegitimate" (or "bastards"); young people who become productive citizens as opposed to those who are truant, violent, or engage in early childbearing and other forms of "anti-social" behavior.

As Elaine Pagels points out in her recent book, *The Origin of Satan*, many cultures throughout the world and over the span of recorded human history have divided people into "we" and "they," "human" and "nonhuman." The "we" is often correlated with the "human" while the "they" are envisaged as "nonhuman." Pagels claims this kind of dichotomous thinking is deeply embedded in the Judeo-Christian tradition.

In tracing the development of the concept of Satan in the books of the New Testament, Pagels points out that Satan came to be seen not as a foreign devil, not as "a hostile power assailing Israel from without" but as an "intimate enemy," as the evil among us, the "representation of conflict *within* the community." She states that those who are perceived as the enemy are often viewed as immoral, even ungodly. The vilification of poor single mothers has taken on what might be described as an evangelical tone in which they are portrayed as the ultimate "other," the enemy within our midst who is increasingly seen as "evil and beyond redemption."

Most people, of course, do not fall neatly into one category or another. Most of us are neither "good" nor "bad"; most of us do not live entirely by traditional values or by a code that flouts those values. Most people, including the poor, live complex lives during which they make a variety of choices that are often driven by external circumstance. In fact, many of the political leaders who are most vociferous about traditional values and most critical of the lifestyles of the poor have themselves led lives filled with complex choices, moral dilemmas, and occasional, and sometimes not so occasional, missteps. Dichotomous thinking—dividing people into good and evil, "them" and "us"—does not work for most late-twentieth-century Americans. Most of us do not live either/or lives.

Such constantly repeated myths about poor women and children serve to encourage the division of individuals into those who are "worthy" and therefore deserving of societal support and those who are "unworthy" and therefore vulnerable to being ostracized from mainstream society. These myths serve as justification for the harsh views toward this segment of the population and consequently their punitive treatment. In the words of Toni Morrison, author of *The Bluest Eye*, a novel that deals explicitly with the denigration of black women in white America and their internalization of that denigration,

> Outdoors, we knew, was the real terror of life . . .
>
> There is a difference between being put *out* and being put out*doors*. If you are put out, you go somewhere else; if you are outdoors, there is no place to go. The distinction was subtle but final. Outdoors was the end of something, an irrevocable, physical fact, defining and complementing our metaphysical condition.

The most commonly held myths that legitimize putting impoverished women and children "outdoors" are that young women have children out of wedlock primarily to receive AFDC and need to be punished and resocialized to make them more responsible; that women receiving welfare have numerous children either because of their promiscuity or in order to increase their benefits; that AFDC provides ample benefits, enough for recipients to live quite comfortable lives; that recipients want to be "idlers," and are mired in a "culture of dependency," and therefore resist joining the paid labor force; and that AFDC recipients are overwhelmingly African-American.

The facts are considerably different from these myths:

- Virtually all studies indicate that over four-fifths of teenage pregnancies are unintended;
- The average number of children in families on welfare is two;
- From 1975 to 1994, the average AFDC benefit per family, measured in constant dollars, *dropped by 37 percent and in no state do welfare benefits plus food stamps bring recipient families up to the federally designated but grossly inadequate poverty line;*
- Seventy-one percent of adult AFDC recipients have recent work histories, and almost half of the families who leave welfare do so to work; and
- While black families are indeed proportionately overrepresented on the welfare rolls, in 1992 they comprised 37.2 percent of all AFDC cases while whites comprised 38.9 percent.

The persistence of these myths about welfare recipients and the resistance of policy makers to the facts despite their repeated reiteration by experts in the field of social welfare is noteworthy. It appears that the United States *needs* to have someone to blame, people to hate, a group to rally against. For nearly a half-century, Americans had a clear-cut enemy—communism. Throughout the Cold War, there existed an ideology we could despise, countries to fear, foreign leaders to demonize. We had external villains whom we could blame for many of the world's ills and whom we could identify as evil in order to define ourselves as good. There were enough countries under the banners of communism and socialism so that if the United States suddenly took a more accepting view of one—as Americans did toward China following the 1972 visit of Richard Nixon—there were always other countries on whom we could project our fear and animosity. With the worldwide breakdown of so-called communist countries (with the exception of Cuba and North Korea), who would be the enemy now? Whom could we distrust and despise? Who would be the devil that in comparison would make us feel righteous and worthy? Who would be the "them" to help us to feel more truly "us"?

Furthermore, over the past decade and a half we have seen two dramatic economic shifts within the United States—shifts that have had significant impact on the social and economic well-being and on the collective psyche of many Americans and that have placed in jeopardy the achievement of the American Dream for millions of Americans. The first has been a massive concentration of wealth and income in the hands of the richest among us. In 1977, the highest fifth of all households received 44 percent of total national income, the middle three-fifths received 51.8 percent, while the lowest fifth received 4.2 percent. By 1993, the income of the highest fifth rose to 48.2 percent, the highest percentage of income on record for that group; the income of the middle three-fifths dropped to 48.2 percent, the lowest share on record; and the bottom fifth received only 3.6 percent, also the lowest share ever recorded. Over the same decade and a half, the income of the top 5 percent rose from 16.8 percent to 20 percent. According to Kevin Phillips, author of *Arrogant Capital: Washington, Wall Street, and the Frustration of American Politics*, "the 100,000 American families in the top tenth of one percent enjoy by far and away the greatest wealth and income gains in the 1980s," but despite their enormous affluence, "the Clinton tax increases of 1993 did not concentrate on the high-income, high-political-influence, investment-dollar rich, the people making $4 million or $17 million a year." There is consequently a greater gap in income today between rich and poor than at any time since such data have been collected and, as

Phillips points out, those profiting the most are the top tenth of one percent.

If we examine differences in wealth among the U.S. population, we see an even more dramatic differential. In 1989, the top one-half of one percent (the "super-rich") owned 31.4 percent of total household wealth, an increase of five percentage points since 1983. Moreover, the top 20 percent of the population owned 84.6 percent of total wealth. Since one-fifth of Americans owned 84.6 percent of total wealth, the remaining four-fifths owned only 15.4 percent. More specifically, the top one-half of one percent owned nearly twice as much wealth (31.4 percent) as the bottom 80 percent of all Americans (15.4 percent)! Preliminary estimates indicate that between 1989 and 1992, 68 percent of the increase in total household wealth went to the richest one percent—an even greater gain than during the 1980s. According to economist Edward Wolff,

> As a result, the concentration of wealth reached a postwar high in 1992, the latest year for which data are available. If these trends continue, the super rich will pull ahead of other Americans at an even faster pace in the 1990s than they did in the '80s.

While the rich have become significantly richer both in terms of income and wealth, not only have the poor lost ground but the working class and many in the middle class have lost ground as well. If we examine education and income, we find that between 1979 and 1989 the real average hourly wages of male high school dropouts declined 18 percent and the income of female dropouts declined nearly 12 percent. Income declined substantially (nearly 13 percent for males and over 3 percent for females) for high school graduates as well.

Males with one to three years of college also experienced a significant decline in income (over 8 percent) while females with the same amount of education saw their income rise slightly (nearly 4 percent). Only when workers had completed four years of college did both men and women realize an increase in income over the decade of the 1980s—for men a bare rise of 0.2 percent and for women a significant increase of 12.6 percent. The real advantages accrued to workers with postgraduate training—nearly 10 percent for males and nearly 13 percent for females. However, as companies have downsized and restructured during the 1980s, millions of blue- and white-collar workers have been laid off and have had to scramble for whatever employment they could find—be it full-time or part-time. An estimated 3 million workers have been laid off between 1989 and 1995 as corporate profits have soared. Many workers have found it necessary to piece together two or more part-time jobs in order to earn anything like their original salaries and many have been unable to obtain work that provides income even approximating their previous salaries.

Moreover, as manufacturers have transferred semi-skilled work out of the country since the 1960s and 1970s, during the 1990s skilled white-collar jobs are increasingly being sent to other countries as well, where the work is being done at a fraction of the cost by educated locals. Texas Instruments, for example, is designing sophisticated computer chips in India; Motorola recently set up equipment design and computer programming centers in China, India, Singapore, Hong Kong, Taiwan, and Australia.

Not only have millions of Americans lost jobs, income, status, and, in some cases, their roles as workers and earners, but millions of families have seen their neighborhoods deteriorate; the quality of schools, public transportation, health care, and other services decline. They have seen crime rates and their feelings of physical insecurity rise, and their overall quality of life plummet. Whom can they blame? I suggest that during the past fifteen years when the working class and the middle class were losing ground, a period during which the rich and "truly rich" were increasing their income and their share of the nation's wealth to what many consider obscene levels, we have seen a strategy on the part of many politicians, policy makers, and conservative thinkers to encourage the middle and working classes to blame their losses on the poor and the powerless, particularly women and people of color, rather than on the rich and powerful.

It is the view of Thomas and Mary Edsall, propounded in their book *Chain Reaction: The Impact of Race, Rights, and Taxes on American Politics*, that the dual issues of race and taxes in collision with the movement for greater rights for groups that have traditionally been discriminated against persuaded

working and lower-middle-class voters to join in an alliance with business interests and the affluent. Opposition to busing, to affirmative action, to quotas, and to housing integration have given a segment of the traditionally Democratic white electorate ideological common ground with business and the affluent in shared opposition to the federal regulatory apparatus.

Using coded language that rarely mentions race explicitly but that implies race at every turn—for example, "welfare queen," "fairness," "merit," "equal opportunity," the issue of crime in general and the Willie Horton commercial in particular—the Republican Party has been successful in pitting "whites and blacks at the low end of the income distribution against each other" and "has intensified the view among many whites that the condition of life for the disadvantaged—particularly for disadvantaged blacks—is the responsibility of those afflicted, and not the responsibility of the larger society." The Edsalls point out that

> Racial polarization, in effect, helped create a political climate receptive to an economic agenda based on the conservative principle that sharply increasing incentives and rewards for those people and interests at the top of the economic pyramid and decreasing government support for those at the bottom would combine to spur economic expansion and growth . . .
>
> Insofar as those in the bottom quintile of the income distribution can be identified as disproportionately black and Hispanic—making possible the isolation of the poor as conceptually separable from the white majority—racial polarization facilitates the enactment of regressive redistributional policies. And insofar as the government programs serving those in the bottom of the income distribution simultaneously divide the poor from the working class and black from white, those programs are highly vulnerable to conservative assault.

Thus, it clearly serves the goals of the Republican Party, of many at the top of the U.S. economic pyramid, and of those who want to dramatically slash the role of the federal government, especially in protecting the rights of the most disadvantaged among us, to play the race card. To cite one example, affirmative action, or the use of "quotas," as it is often mislabeled, has been brilliantly used to persuade white workers that they are losing jobs and opportunities to people of color. In reality, few can cite specific examples of such "reverse discrimination" but nonetheless the view that unqualified members of minority groups are benefitting as white workers lose ground has become embedded in the consciousness of millions of Americans. In political parlance, race has become an enormously effective wedge issue for Republicans—splitting traditional blue-collar and lower-middle-class voters from the Democratic Party and thereby capturing the presidency for all but twelve years over the past three decades and in 1994 taking control of Congress as well.

In his book *Race and Class in Texas Politics*, Chandler Davidson gives a vivid example of the diversion of blame from elected officials to poor people of color. Davidson describes a conversation between two working-class men standing waist-deep in the swimming pool of a Houston, Texas, apartment building:

Bob stared at his beer can for a moment, and then savagely, to no one in particular, he said, "That son-of-a-bitch Reagan put me out of a job. That's who did it."

Al stiffened. "Wa-a-a-it a minute," he said. "You're talking about my man, now. You're talking about my man."

"I don't care if he's your man. That son-of-a-bitch is the reason I'm standing in this goddamn pool tonight, drunk on my ass. . . ."

"Just a minute," he said. "You don't talk about the president like that."

"To hell with the president!" . . .

"Listen, Bob," Al said, suddenly calm. "You've got it wrong. You've got it all wrong. You want me to tell you who's taken your job away? You really want to know?"

Bob glared at him.

"It's the goddamn niggers, who'll work for lower wages.

And it's these goddamn wetbacks. That's who's taken your job. You can't blame that on Reagan."

Bob was silent for what seemed like a long time, staring straight at Al. "Now you're talking sense," he said, finally. "Now you're talking something that I can relate to. You've put your finger on something now."

Common sense would suggest that working- and middle-class Americans should blame the "super-rich," since this elite group has profited enormously while the vast majority have seen their income and their quality of life deteriorate. But blaming the rich doesn't jibe with American ideology, particularly during the final decades of the twentieth century. Americans don't want to *resent* the rich; Americans want to *be* the rich. The fantasy that if only we work hard, play by the rules, get some education, and, particularly in the case of women, look the part, we will somehow make it in America is an integral part of the long-revered American Dream. Many Americans originally came to this country to share in the proverbial gold with which the streets were thought to be paved. Therefore, rather than resent the wealthy—the multimillionaire entrepreneurs, entertainers, athletes, and even those who inherit or marry into great wealth—we often revere them, emulate them, long for a touch of the glitter and glamour of their lifestyles. Rather than being seen as the enemy, the "rich and famous" are made into icons by the media. Their consumer goods are yearned for throughout the class hierarchy. Fashion models, film stars, and other entertainers are instantly recognizable and referred to by their first names (or perhaps just their initials). Designers such as Ralph Lauren have made fortunes selling the upper-class lifestyle through every commodity from jeans to sheets.

In a study I conducted in the late 1980s, young women demonstrated the most recent incarnation of this quintessentially American belief system. Until recent years, that vision was, for the most part, a male dream and women hoped to achieve affluence and success through marriage. But over the past two decades, significant changes within American society, within the family, and in women's perceptions of their roles, their rights, and their responsibilities have fundamentally altered many women's images of themselves and their relationship to the American Dream. Young women from fourteen to twenty-four repeatedly spoke of their need to transform their own lives and of their ability to do so. A sixteen-year-old high school sophomore from New York stated flatly, "I'll make myself what I am." A seventeen-year-old Midwesterner said, "I don't want to have to depend on anyone." An eighteen-year-old Latina unmarried mother from Arizona wanted to "do it, make it, have money." But perhaps a sixteen-year-old high school junior from Southern California most clearly expresses their attitudes: "It's your life. You have to live it yourself. . . . If you work hard enough, you will get there. You must be in control of your life, and then somehow it will all work out." This young woman is expressing the optimism, the belief in the individual's ability to control her destiny, and the confidence that success is there for the taking that is inherent in the ideology of the American Dream. This belief in the power of individuals to determine their future and to achieve success further isolates and stigmatizes the poor who, if we are to believe in the ideology of the American Dream, clearly must be doing something wrong.

Blaming the poor and powerless for America's social and economic problems is far more comforting and acceptable than blaming the rich and powerful. Blaming the poor upholds a fundamental tenet of the American Dream: that individuals can dramatically alter the course of their own lives, that they can rise in the class hierarchy on their own initiative. To maintain our own dreams of success we must blame the poor for their failure; if their failure is due to flaws in the structure of society, these same societal limitations could thwart our dreams of success. The notion that the failure of the poor is due to their character weaknesses enables others to blame the impoverished for their own poverty while simultaneously preserving the faith of the nonpoor in the possibility of success.

Americans who want to hold fast to their belief in the American Dream and their belief in themselves but who, at the same time, see their hopes and dreams for the future slipping away may need some group to blame for the gap between their dreams and the realities of their lives. As Howard Winant, author of *Racial Conditions: Politics, Theory, Comparisons*, has stated:

> Today, in all the advanced countries, the established working classes are fearful and resentful. In the U.S., this is the "angry white male" phenomenon; elsewhere, it focuses more particularly on immigration, or on Islam, but these are largely superficial differences. The "angry white males," the nativists, believed for a long time that their race, their gender, their religion more or less guaranteed them a middle-class standard of living, a well-paying job, a secure home in a safe neighborhood, access to quality education and health care, paid vacations, a comfortable retirement.
>
> These prospects are slipping away. Children are worse off than their parents were. The policies of the welfare state no longer appear able to fend off the unease in the heartland. Thus, they look for someone to blame. In the tradition of

American nativism and European colonialism, racialized minorities and immigrants furnish the ready scapegoat.

American society has from its beginnings harbored suspicion
and, to some extent, hostility toward the poor. But, of course,
all poor people are not equally subject to negative feelings.
Reflecting a long history of dichotomous thinking, poor people
have been classified as either "worthy" or "unworthy" since
colonial times. As Mimi Abramovitz, author of *Regulating the
Lives of Women: Social Welfare Policy from Colonial Times to the
Present*, has pointed out, from the early days of colonial settle-
ment, aid was far more likely to be given to women who were
seen to be in compliance with the "family ethic." The colonial
family was seen as the "key unit for survival, socialization, and
social stability" and "the patriarchical family [was placed] at the
center of the social order." According to this belief system,
"free white women" were expected "to marry, to bear and
raise children, and to manage a household in which they were
economically productive, but faithful, obedient and subordinate
to men." All women were not viewed as deserving of aid.
Women who were seen as unable to work and those who
complied with the family ethic received more favorable treatment than those who "appeared to choose idleness and those
who could not or chose not to conform to prescribed wife and
mother laws."

In her book *The Neutered Mother, the Sexual Family and Other
Twentieth Century Tragedies*, law professor Martha Fineman
points out the continued dominance in the United States of
the traditional patriarchal family:

. . . although the image of the traditional family has undergone
some revisions in light of the modern concerns with gender

equity and equality, the nuclear-family form, with a sexual affiliation between man and woman as the paradigmatic intimate associational bond, is still dominant. . . . Although our social circumstances have substantially altered, patriarchal concepts remain at the center of how we define and understand families in our culture.

Consequently, Fineman notes, "untraditional forms of motherhood," particularly single motherhood, are designated as "pathological" or "deviant." In other words, ". . . single motherhood is synonymous with deviant motherhood."

As sociologist Kai Erikson elucidates in his study of seventeenth-century Puritan life in Massachusetts, there is often a fine line between the behavior a society deems deviant and the behavior a society deems acceptable or even exemplary:

Definitions of deviance vary widely as we range over the various classes found in a single society or across the various cultures . . . , and it soon becomes apparent that there are no objective properties which all deviant acts can be said to share in common. . . . Behavior which qualifies one man for prison may qualify another for sainthood. . . .

Some men who drink heavily are called alcoholics and others are not, some men who behave oddly are committed to hospitals and others are not, some men with no visible means of support are charged with vagrancy and others are not—and the difference between those who earn a deviant title in society and those who go their own way in peace is largely determined by the way in which the community filters out and codes the many details of behavior which come to its attention.

Erikson elaborates on how some are selected for designation as deviant while others are not: "When the community nominates someone to the deviant class, then it is sifting a few important details out of the stream of behavior he has emitted and is in effect declaring that these details reflect the kind of person he 'really' is." William Scott Green concurs and emphasizes the way societies caricature some groups in order to more clearly "define and consolidate their own group identity":

> A society does not simply discover its others, it fabricates them, by selecting, isolating, and emphasizing an aspect of another people's life, and making it symbolize their difference.

In branding all welfare recipients "dependent," "lazy," or "rotten mothers," we are singling out an entire group of people and declaring them deviant because of their economic status at a particular moment in time. If we narrow the designated group to poor, single welfare recipients, we are adding marital status to economic status and thereby declaring those particular traits central to their character, to their functioning in society. We are, in effect, stating that those details of a person's life "reflect the kind of person [s]he 'really' is." She could be a conscientious, caring mother, a loving daughter, a hardworking student, a pious churchgoer, a loyal friend, and a concerned neighbor, but the details of her life by which we as a society are judging her and finding her wanting are her current economic status and whether or not she has participated in a marriage ceremony. The designations "dependent," "lazy," and "rotten mothers" are assumed to characterize all welfare recipients—particularly those who have never been married. They are generalizations assumed to be true of an entire group of people, regardless of their personal characteristics and circumstances. Major policy decisions are therefore being made on the basis of massive stereotyping. In other words, false assumptions about millions of poor women are being encoded into a social policy that will affect the lives and the life chances of these women and their children for years, possibly decades to come.

The irrationality and arbitrary quality of these judgments raise questions about the value and meaning to a society of branding an individual—or an entire category of people—as outside the norms or boundaries of that society. Erikson, citing the work of French sociologist Emile Durkheim, discusses how forms of deviance "may actually perform a needed service to society by drawing people together in a common posture of anger and indignation" so that they then "develop a tighter bond of solidarity than existed before." Moreover, defining deviance and designating certain individuals who have crossed the line as outcasts stipulates the boundaries of behavior for others in the society. In some sense, the boundaries a society sets create the deviants in that society. In a country such as Sweden where births to unmarried women are far more common and accepted than in the United States, these mothers are not designated deviant and ostracized from mainstream society. In the United States, however, the opprobrium associated with "illegitimacy" is once again causing those who have a child outside of marriage to be labeled deviant and, indeed, in Toni Morrison's words, to be "put outdoors."

Perhaps societies need to create deviants in order to have a stigmatized group to blame for the ills of that society, to create a sense of solidarity among the majority, and to set firmer boundaries for the population as a whole. Clearly many issues such as drug and alcohol abuse, prostitution, and even poverty are socially constructed problems. These issues are endemic in most societies. The question of why these particular phenomena become the target of major public campaigns at a specific time in a specific place must therefore be raised. What is the catalyst? Whose interests are served? Jews lived in Germany for centuries with considerable success. Why was the virulent campaign of anti-Semitism that led to the Holocaust mounted in the 1930s? Social reformers and others sympathetic to socialism and/or communism had lived and worked in the United States, many of them highly respected and honored, for decades. Why was the witch hunt of the 1950s mobilized at that particular time? Poverty, particularly among poor women and children, has been a fact of life in this society since colonial times. Aid to Families with Dependent Children, as we have noted, has been in existence in some form since 1935. Why is there a campaign *now* to treat poor women and children as pariahs and to eliminate so many social and economic supports for this impoverished, powerless group?

One theory is that societies are "subject, every now and then, to periods of moral panic." Stan Cohen, author of *Folk Devils and Moral Panics: The Creation of the Mods and Rockers*, describes the phenomenon of moral panic:

A condition, episode, person or group of persons emerges to become defined as a threat to societal values and interests; its nature is presented in a stylized and stereotypical fashion by the mass media; the moral barricades are manned by editors, bishops, politicians and other right thinking people; socially accredited experts pronounce their diagnoses and solutions; ways of coping are evolved or (more often) resorted to; the condition then disappears, submerges or deteriorates and becomes more visible. Sometimes the object of the panic is quite novel, and at other times it is something which has been in existence long enough, but suddenly appears in the limelight. Sometimes the panic is passed over and is forgotten except in folklore and collective memory; at other times it has more serious and long lasting repercussions and might produce such changes as those in legal and social policy or even in the way society conceives itself.

For Cohen, as for Erikson in his analysis of the witchcraft hysteria of the late 1600s in Salem, Massachusetts, "panics serve[d] to reassert the dominance of an established value system at a time of perceived anxiety and crisis. . . ." Or as Erich Goode and Nachman Ben-Yehuda state in their book *Moral Panics: The Social Construction of Deviance*, ". . . moral panics arise in troubled times, during which a serious *threat* is sensed to the interests or values of the society as a whole or to segments of a society."

We are indeed living in "troubled times" during which a substantial segment of the middle and working classes have lost significant earning power, have lost long-held jobs, benefits, and even, in some cases, pension funds, and have been forced to piece together alternate employment at lower salaries, with less security and considerably less status. Many have lost faith in governmental and societal efforts to solve America's critical problems, and are increasingly fearful about the future, for both themselves and their children. The phenomenon of the angry white male has been widely credited with the profound shift to the right in Congress since the 1994 congressional elections, but the anger and anxiety go beyond the white male. Millions of Americans—male and female, white and people of color, from the upper middle class to the poor—are apprehensive about their social and economic well-being, their personal safety, and their ability to take care of themselves and their family members in an environment in which little seems secure. Widespread alienation from traditional political leaders and from the political process is clearly evident: People all over the country are participating in the increasingly harsh discourse of talk radio as well as other forms of popular culture. Significant numbers of Americans are forming themselves into armed militias. Racist, sexist, anti-Semitic, and homophobic speech is increasingly heard from cultural icons such as Michael Jackson, from academicians, and from political leaders. Films celebrate violence as virtually the only solution to our problems.

As Winant points out, the rage and desire to return to earlier, "simpler" times is fed by

a vision or an ideology of community, of an "imagined community" which emerges from revulsion at late modernity and which seeks to turn back the clock toward the white supremacy of the past.

The Right still sees the nation as a "white man's country." Its patriotism is identified with "blood": with whiteness, with imperialism, with masculinity and with heterosexuality.

The times are ripe for scapegoating. Scapegoats have been used throughout history to attempt to solve societal problems. In ancient Greece, human scapegoats (*pharmakos*) were used to ward off plagues and other calamities. In early Roman law, an innocent person was allowed to take on the penalty of another who had confessed his or her own guilt. In the Old Testament ritual of Yom Kippur, a goat was symbolically burdened with the sins of the Jewish people and then sent into the wilderness to rid the nation of its iniquities.

Scapegoating has become national policy in the United States. We are heaping the sins of a violent and unjust society on the poor and sending them out into the wilderness. In so doing we are hoping to return to an era in which the rights, norms, and values of the traditional majority, the group Newt Gingrich has referred to as "normal Americans," were sacrosanct and virtually the law of the land.

Yet another way of describing and analyzing the process of blaming one individual or group for the problems of the wider community is the theory that societies create "folk devils," who are often seen as the "personification of evil." In the same vein as Pagels's work on the development of the concept of Satan, Goode and Ben-Yehuda point out that folk devils are "stripped of all favorable characteristics and imparted with exclusively negative ones. . . . In short, folk devils are *deviants*; they are engaged in wrongdoing; their actions are harmful to society. . . ."

Are welfare mothers today's folk devils? They surely have been "stripped of all favorable characteristics and imparted with exclusively negative ones," and they are surely being blamed for much of what is wrong in American society. And, of course, the subtext, often but not always unspoken, is the myth that most of these poor, single, child-bearing women are black. Even if one asks a sociology class, most of whom are themselves members of minority groups, "From what racial background are most AFDC recipients?" the answer invariably is that most of them are African-American. This image of the poor, inexorably intertwined with the long-standing baggage of racist ideology, facilitates their being perceived as folk devils. As anthropologist Leith Mullings has stated, "Women of color, and particularly African-American women, are the focus of well-elaborated, strongly held . . . ideologies concerning race, class, and gender." She goes on to state that "the images, representations, and symbols that form ideologies often have complex meanings and associations that are not easily or readily articulated, making them difficult to challenge."

Historically, African-American women have been described on the one hand by the image of " 'Mammy,' the religious, loyal, motherly slave. . . ." and, on the other hand, by the image of " 'Jezebel,' the sexually aggressive, provocative woman governed entirely by libido." As Mullings states, this Mammy/Jezebel stereotype is a variation of the widespread madonna/whore dualism but the issue of race adds an even more pernicious element to the classic stereotype. The view of African Americans as a different species, what Mullings and others have termed the "otherness of race," has "justified the attribution of excessive sexuality." That "sexuality continues to be a major theme in the discourse about race" assures that it is also a major theme in the discourse about poor women. Moreover, the Mammy image, so prevalent through the first half of the twentieth century and memorialized in popular culture by the film *Gone With the Wind*, has been replaced, according to Mullings, by the image of the "emasculating matriarch." Therefore, whether through overt sexuality or through control within the family that supposedly robs black men of their authority and power, black women are portrayed as deviant and as the primary cause of the problems within the black family and within the black community.

Patricia Hill Collins, author of *Black Feminist Thought: Knowledge, Consciousness, and the Politics of Empowerment*, analyzes the ways in which these deeply rooted images of black women underlie and buttress the harsh treatment of poor women over the past two decades and particularly during the 1990s:

Portraying African-American women as matriarchs allows the dominant group to blame Black women for the success or failure of Black children. Assuming that Black poverty is passed on intergenerationally via value transmission in families, an elite white male standpoint suggests that Black children lack the attention and care allegedly lavished on white, middle-class children and that this deficiency seriously retards Black children's achievement. Such a view diverts attention from the political and economic inequality affecting Black mothers and children and suggests that anyone can rise from poverty if he or she only received good values at home. Those African-Americans who remain poor are blamed for their own victimization.

The problems the United States should be addressing as we move into the next century are widespread poverty amidst incredible affluence, massive hopelessness and alienation among those who feel outside of the boundaries of the society, and a deeply felt despair among the poor and the working class that is increasingly expressed through violence. There is no question that the welfare system in particular and the society in general have not addressed these issues and, in fact, have exacerbated them—not through generosity but through miserliness, not through the coddling of recipients but through their humiliation, not through making poor people dependent on a panoply of services but rather by not providing the essential education, job training, child care, health care, and, perhaps most important, jobs by which families can support themselves at a decent standard of living. The central problem American society must deal with is not the character of poor women and the structure of the welfare system; the central problem is poverty, the multiplicity of ways that it is embedded in the structure of American society, and the need to find real ways of altering that fundamental structure in order to truly help people move into mainstream society. We must recognize that people are not poor due to character defects but rather that the poverty that plagues so many Americans has been socially constructed and therefore must be dealt with by fundamental economic and social change.

Before dealing directly with exactly who are the poor in America, the nature of the welfare system, the current dismantling of Aid to Families with Dependent Children and other programs essential to those who are most in need, and the impact of these changes on poor women and children, let us examine the broader assault on single-parent families of which the war on poor women and children is the central component. Single parenthood (which must be seen as a code phrase for *female* single parenthood since the vast majority of single parents are mothers) has over the past few years been defined, in Stan Cohen's words, as a "threat to societal values" and indeed social policy and "the way society conceives itself" are being dramatically changed. What is the nature of this assault on single mothers and what are the repercussions for single parents, for their children, and for American society as a whole?

Chapter 2

The Assault on the Female-Headed Family

I think this reason why girls don't do well on multiple choice tests goes all the way back to the Bible, all the way back to Genesis, Adam and Eve. God said, "All right, Eve, multiple choice or multiple orgasms, what's it going to be?" We all know what was chosen.

—RUSH LIMBAUGH

The grass-plot before the jail, in Prison Lane, on a certain summer morning, not less than two centuries ago, was occupied by a pretty large number of the inhabitants of Boston; all with their eyes intently fastened on the iron-clamped oaken door. . . . never had Hester Prynne appeared more lady-like, in the antique interpretation of the term, than when she issued from prison. Those who had before known her, and had expected to behold her dimmed and obscured by a disastrous cloud, were astonished, and even startled, to perceive how her beauty shone out, and made a halo of misfortune and ignominy in which she was enveloped. . . . But the point which drew all eyes, and, as it were, transfigured the wearer . . . was that SCARLET LETTER. . . . It had the effect of a spell, taking her out of the ordinary relations with humanity, and inclosing her in a sphere by herself.

HESTER PRYNNE MOVED FROM THE PRISON DOOR TO THE marketplace where, her sentence decreed, she must stand for "a space of three hours" beneath "a sort of scaffold" and "then and thereafter, for the remainder of her natural life, to wear a mask of shame upon her bosom." According to an observer in that Massachusetts marketplace in Nathaniel Hawthorne's novel *The Scarlet Letter*, "thus, she will be a living sermon against sin, until the ignominious letter will be engraved upon her tombstone." Not only must Hester Prynne be punished for violating the customs of her society—for having a child outside of marriage—but her punishment and her shame must serve as a warning to others that behavior outside of the mores of Puritanical New England society would not be tolerated and would be punished by powerful social sanctions.

One hundred and fifty years after the publication of Hawthorne's novel and 350 years after the peak of Puritan power in Massachusetts, an outcry is heard once again against the single-parent family, particularly against families headed by women in which children are born outside of marriage. Once again shame and stigma are being touted as methods of social control.

During the August 1995 debate on overhauling AFDC, Senator John Ashcroft, Republican of Missouri, articulated what has become a virtual litany among elected representatives and those who are featured by the media: "Illegitimacy is a threat to the survival of our nation and our culture." The same day in an Op-Ed piece in *The New York Times*, Lisa Schiffren, a former speechwriter for Dan Quayle, began her article by stating, "America faces no problem more urgent than our skyrocketing illegitimacy rate."

While the entire category—single-parent family—is often decried, in reality it is the female-headed family that is under attack. Of the children in the United States who lived with one parent in 1993, the vast majority, 87 percent, lived with their mother; 13 percent lived with their father. All female-headed families, however, are not perceived as equally reprehensible. Widows are exempt from criticism as they are perceived as victims of tragic circumstances rather than as women who have flouted the conventional moral code of society. Divorced mothers have increasingly come under scrutiny as studies and articles focus on the damage the authors feel divorce has wrought upon the children. But it is the never-married mother and, within that cohort, the poor never-married mother who needs financial assistance from the state, who has been the clearest target of criticism. While some of the discussion of the problems of mother-only families has been scholarly and has attempted to be balanced, much of the recent rhetoric has had a hostile, victim-blaming, hysterical tone reminiscent of other episodes of scapegoating in America's history.

In 1965, a confidential report to President Lyndon Johnson written by a young assistant secretary of labor, Daniel Patrick Moynihan, and entitled *The Negro Family: The Case for National Action*, was leaked to the press and caused a furor. In it, Moynihan, now a Democratic senator from New York, stated:

> At the heart of the deterioration of the fabric of Negro society is the deterioration of the Negro family. It is the fundamental source of the weakness of the Negro community. . . . In essence, the Negro community has been forced into a matriarchal structure which, because it is so out of line with the rest of the American society, seriously retards the progress of the group as a whole.

The notion that family structure is at the root of poverty and a wide variety of social ills rather than the social and economic conditions that lead to that structure is the core of the current wave of blaming poor, female-headed families for their own problems and for many of the problems of American society.

As noted in chapter 1, the argument that "deviant" values and family structure are primary causes of poverty resurfaced in the mid-1980s with the publication of Charles Murray's *Losing Ground*. Murray labeled out-of-wedlock births "the single most important social problem of our time—more important than crime, drugs, poverty, illiteracy, welfare, or homelessness because it drives everything else." He has also suggested rehabilitating the term "illegitimacy" in order to "make an illegitimate birth the socially horrific act it used to be."

In the summer of 1992, then–Vice President Dan Quayle condemned Murphy Brown, the central character in a popular television program, for having a baby outside of marriage. It is significant that the episode in which Murphy decides to have her baby focuses on her conflict between abortion and bearing the child. Could Quayle have been suggesting that she have an abortion instead of having the baby? Was he suggesting that a single woman in her early forties abstain from sex completely or that she and her partner revert to the shotgun weddings of previous eras despite the fact that the father was not interested in a long-term commitment to Murphy or to the baby? But Dan Quayle's appeal to "family values" went much further than his criticism of a fictional TV character. Quayle also suggested that unmarried women with children were at least partially responsible for the "lawless social anarchy" that erupted in the May 1992 riots in Los Angeles following the acquittal of the four police officers who so brutally beat Rodney King.

Several months after the Quayle speech, an influential and widely read article by Barbara Dafoe Whitehead entitled "Dan Quayle Was Right" was published in *The Atlantic Monthly*. In her article, Whitehead claims that studies show that children who grow up in single-parent families are at significantly greater risk for a variety of problems than children who are raised in two-parent families. These problems include emotional and behavioral difficulties, dropping out of school, becoming pregnant as teenagers, abusing drugs, getting into trouble with the law, and being victims of physical or sexual abuse. Whitehead stresses, moreover, that children of divorced, separated, or never-married parents are far more likely to live in poverty, commit crimes, fail in school, engage in "aggressive, acting-out behavior," and engage in "assaults on teachers, unprovoked attacks on other children, [and] screaming outbursts in class." The language Whitehead uses clearly indicates her point of view: The terms "stable" marriage and "intact" families are used to describe two-parent families; single-parent families are often referred to as "disrupted" or "broken." The implication of her choice of language is that one-parent families are not "stable" and two-parent families are rarely "disrupted," generalizations that are both simplistic and frequently false.

During the late 1980s, Judith Wallerstein published the results of her study, *Second Chances: Men, Women, and Children a Decade After Divorce.* Wallerstein found that divorce has significant negative implications for many children, leading some to depression, underachievement, or difficulty in forming long-term, intimate relationships of their own. Wallerstein compares children of divorced parents with those of "reasonably happy intact" families, but if we are examining the effects of divorce upon the well-being of children of divorce, does it make sense to compare them to children from "reasonably happy intact" families? If these families were reasonably happy, the parents presumably would not have divorced. Until studies of the impact of divorce on children compare children of divorced parents with children of unhappily married parents—since the parents' conflicts with one another may be at least partially responsible for the problems of the children—we will not be able to disentangle the impact of divorce from the impact of family problems.

David Blankenhorn, founder and president of the Institute for American Values, has broadened the critique of single-parent families by focusing primarily on the impact of father-lessness. Blankenhorn claims that American society has become a "culture of fatherlessness" and that we are even losing our "idea of fatherhood." Adding to the general tone of panic and imminent disaster embodied in discussions of single parent-hood, Blankenhorn's book, *Fatherless America*, is subtitled *Confronting Our Most Urgent Social Problem*. Are mother-only families really our most urgent social problem? More urgent than poverty? Than increasing joblessness and inequality? More urgent than AIDS or massive alienation or violence? Blanken-horn's response is that the critical social problems that plague the United States—"Divorce. Out-of-wedlock childbearing. Children growing up in poverty. Youth violence. Unsafe neighborhoods. Domestic violence. The weakening of parental authority"—are bound together by "the flight of males from their children's lives." While many who bemoan the death of the two-parent family focus primarily on the role of women, Blankenhorn's book is refreshing in that it at least places men in an active role and attempts to hold them somewhat account-able for the increasing number of female-headed homes.

Even thoughtful observers of American society who do not ordinarily look for simplistic answers to complex problems or try to pit one group against another find a way to blame single mothers for some of the most wrenching, deeply rooted, multi-faceted social problems of our time. In May of 1994, Senator

Bill Bradley, Democrat from New Jersey, delivered a major speech at the National Press Club on violence in America. Although Bradley decries the social, emotional, and physical cost of violence, and discusses the urgent need for gun control and the glorification of violence by popular culture as well as the issue of domestic violence, and while he does mention urban and rural poverty as well as economic depression as causes of violence, Bradley saves his most vivid rhetoric for single parents and their children. Bradley acknowledges that some single mothers raise law-abiding children but the problems produced by female-headed families—not the profound economic and social inequality that grips this land, or continuing racism or sexism—takes center stage in Senator Bradley's outcry against violence:

> In Detroit, nearly 80 percent of the kids are born to single parents. In 1991, 30 percent of all children born in America were born to a single parent. Among black children, it was two-thirds. Many single mothers do heroic jobs in transmitting values and raising their children well against great odds. Many others are too young, too poor, and too unloved, and their children at birth become 15-year time bombs waiting to explode in adolescence. If you think violence among the young is bad now, wait until this army of neglected, often abused, sometimes abandoned, street-trained, gang-tested, friendless young people reach age 15. Their capacity to have any kind of meaningful attachment will be gone. . . .

Much of Bradley's speech is meant to be a wake-up call that will move people emotionally and stir the press and the citizenry into taking action against the scourge of violence. But the paragraph about single mothers and their children contains some of the most disturbing language of the speech—"this army of neglected, often abused, sometimes abandoned, street-trained, gang-tested, friendless young people"—and of course it was this point that was picked up widely by the press.

Senator Bradley is surely correct when he states that millions of children in the United States are "neglected," "abused," "abandoned," and "friendless," but to suggest that the central cause of their debilitation and despair is that they are the children of single mothers is to isolate one factor in their background and focus on it above all others. Millions of children from single-parent families are, of course, *not* "neglected," "abused," "abandoned," and "friendless."

In a chilling article on the current prevalence of violent crime in the United States and the likelihood of a massive increase in the level of violence in the near future, Adam Walinsky, a lawyer who advocates adding citizen officers to existing police forces, focuses on the violent crimes committed by black youths from single-parent families:

> We first notice the children of the ghetto when they grow muscles—at about the age of fifteen. The children born in 1965 reached their fifteenth year in 1980, and 1980 and 1981 set new records for criminal violence in the United States, as teenage and young adult blacks ripped at the fabric of life in the black inner city. Nevertheless, of all the black children who reached physical maturity in those years, three quarters had been born to a married mother and father. Not until 1991 did we experience the arrival in their mid-teens of the first group of black youths fully half of whom had been born to single mothers—the cohort born in 1976. Criminal violence particularly associated with young men and boys reached new peaks of destruction in black communities in 1990 and 1991.

Walinsky continues by discussing future crime rates based on the number of black males born into mother-only families:

> In the year 2000 the black youths born in 1985 will turn fifteen. Three fifths of them were born to single mothers, many of whom were drug-addicted; one in fourteen will have been raised with neither parent at home; unprecedented numbers will have been subjected to beatings and other abuse; and most will have grown up amid the utter chaos pervading black city neighborhoods.

While Walinsky says that "It is supremely necessary to change the conditions that are producing such cohorts," he continues by stating that "no matter what efforts we now undertake, we have already assured the creation of more very violent young men than any reasonable society can tolerate, and their numbers will grow inexorably for every one of the next twenty years."

Has Walinsky truly given up on this generation of disadvantaged young men when he states that "no matter what efforts we undertake" the numbers of "very violent" criminals "will grow inexorably"? Walinsky's solution is to massively increase the police force—by at least a half a million in the next five years and perhaps more after that. He states that this police force is not to imprison citizens but to "liberate" them. But is it really a foregone conclusion that all of these young people will turn to crime? Are there no other ways of intervening in their environment to avert the catastrophe Walinsky describes?

Those who focus on family structure rather than poverty, joblessness, grossly inadequate education, and the lack of community resources—all of which often lead to the despair, rage, and hopelessness that are so often the wellspring of crime—are promoting the view that having a single mother is virtually the only factor of importance shaping the attitudes, behavior, and well-being of young people. What is being neglected in these analyses is that profound changes in family structure do not simply spring up in societies at a certain time but are themselves the result of profound shifts in the broader social structure. The increase in the number of female-headed families is itself caused by social, economic, and political factors that may be key in understanding current social problems.

There is no question that the number of children living with one parent has risen sharply in the United States over the past quarter century. In 1970, 12 percent (11.9) of all children under the age of eighteen lived with one parent; by 1993, nearly 27 percent (26.7) were living with one parent and, as has been mentioned earlier, 87 percent of these young people were living with their mother. If we examine the data more closely we see that, in 1993, 77.2 percent of white children under age eighteen were living with two parents while 20.9 percent were living with one parent. Among children of Hispanic origin, 64.5 percent were living with two parents, 31.8 percent with one parent. The single-parent rate for black children was significantly higher than for either white or Hispanic children. Only 35.6 percent of black children lived with two parents in 1993, a significant decline from 1980 (42.2 percent) and 1970 (58.5 percent), while 57 percent of black children under age eighteen lived with one parent.

But the rise in out-of-wedlock births and single-parent families is not a phenomenon limited to the United States; it is occurring in many parts of the world. The rise in the number of unmarried mothers is most dramatic in Northern and Western Europe as well as in the United States. Divorce rates are also rising rapidly in many other parts of the world. Thus, families in different cultures are changing in similar ways and we must look for structural causes and develop social policy measures that will strengthen all families.

Critics of AFDC and other social welfare programs claim that these very programs and the benefits they provide are the cause of the sharply escalating rate of single parenthood. They claim that the cushion provided by programs for the poor, as meager and tattered as it is, enables women to choose single parenthood and that only when that support is markedly diminished or totally withdrawn will women choose childbearing within marriage and paid employment. There is, however, no evidence that AFDC payments are a cause of increased childbearing outside of marriage. As mentioned earlier, this issue will be discussed in far greater detail in subsequent chapters, but for now it is important to note that the recent rise in single parenthood has occurred over a period of time during which welfare payments have been sharply curtailed.

Several key demographic factors have contributed to the significant number of young people living with a single parent in the United States and in other countries: the current practice of delaying marriage, the increase in never-married households, and the divorce rate. The estimated median age of marriage has continued to rise over the past quarter century. In the United States in 1970, for example, the median age of marriage for women was 20.8 years and for men, 23.2 years. By 1993, the median age for women was 24.5 and for men, 26.5. Marrying later combined with the earlier onset of menstruation and sexual activity puts unmarried young women at risk of becoming pregnant for several additional years. At the same time, the phenomenon of the never-married parent has been increasing significantly while the divorce rate has been leveling off. Between 1970 and 1981, for example, the percentage of children who lived with a divorced parent rose by 50 percent (from 30.2 to 43.8 percent) while the percentage living with a never-married parent more than doubled (from 6.8 to 15.2 percent). Between 1983 and 1993, the percentage of one-parent children living with a divorced parent declined from 42 to 37.1 percent, while the percentage living with a never-married parent continued to rise from 24 to 35 percent. In other words, a decade ago a child in a single-parent family was almost twice as likely to be living with a divorced parent as with a never-married parent; today a child is slightly more likely to be living with a divorced parent than a never-married parent.

Many factors are responsible for the rise of never-married parents. Some of the key issues include the high divorce rate that peaked in 1981 and has made many young people wary of marriage; the increasing acceptability of having children outside of marriage; women's massive move into the paid labor force and their subsequent increased sense of independence; and the substantial decline in wages of millions of male workers.

While there is no doubt that the number of single-parent families, particularly mother-only families, has risen dramatically in recent years, the central question is what does this trend mean for women, for children, for families, and for American society? *Growing Up With a Single Parent: What Hurts, What Helps* by sociologists Sara McLanahan and Gary Sandefur attempts to explore this issue. The authors begin by stating their position clearly:

> *Children who grow up in a household with only one biological parent are worse off, on average, than children who grow up in a household with both of their biological parents, regardless of the parents' race or educational background, regardless of whether the parents are married*

when the child is born, and regardless of whether the resident parent remarries.

McLanahan and Sandefur point out that growing up without a father affects young people in a variety of ways. First, children from single-parent families do less well educationally and are approximately twice as likely to drop out of high school as are young people from two-parent families. Their grades and test scores are lower, their attendance poorer, and their expectations about college lower than that of their peers. Second, young people in one-parent families are less likely to find work in their late adolescent and young adult years. And third, growing up in what these authors term a "disrupted family" significantly increases a female's risk of becoming a teen mother. As the authors state, "Finishing school, finding a job, and starting a family are events that mark the transition from adolescence to adulthood." Young people who have problems in these areas are clearly starting their adult years with a substantial handicap. But, as McLanahan and Sandefur also point out, these issues are often interrelated. Young people who leave school pre-maturely may well have difficulty finding work and those who have inadequate education and are "idle," to use the authors' term, may well look for gratification and a symbolic transition to adulthood through early childbearing. (Consider once again the use of language to communicate a point of view. The term "idle" places the onus for lack of work on the individuals—implying they are lolling around the house and perhaps not actively seeking employment; the term "unemployed" or "job-less" implies at least in part a societal contribution to the young person's lack of employment—the recognition that perhaps suitable jobs may be in short supply.) The fact that problems in these three coming-of-age tasks are interconnected may be of greater significance than that each takes place more frequently in single-parent families.

McLanahan and Sandefur themselves stress that many of the disadvantages children of single-parent families experience are directly due to low income or, in the case of divorce, a sudden drop in income. Not only must single-parent families often survive on one salary rather than two but the mother's earning power is likely to be significantly less than the father's. Also, as the authors state, "When a father lives in a separate household, he is usually less committed to his child and less trusting of the child's mother. Hence he is less willing to invest time and money in the child's welfare."

That single-parent families are frequently characterized by poverty, low income, or a sudden drop in income is intimately connected to educational achievement, job prospects, and early childbearing. Children from poor families are likely to attend grossly inadequate schools (as Jonathan Kozol has made abundantly clear in his powerful book *Savage Inequalities: Children in America's Schools*), have few job opportunities, and are at greater risk for early childbearing than more affluent young people. Due to a drop in income, children of divorced parents may well need to move from a more affluent neighborhood, in which they had access to good schools, friends, and familiar faces and surroundings, to a school that is less adequate and a neighborhood that is new and strange. A disruption in the family often sets off a series of other disruptions for all of the family members that are frequently due to abrupt and profound changes in economic status.

Many authors who extol the two-parent family and blame most of the ills of society on the increase in single-parent families compare the problems of 1990s female-headed families with an idealized image of the ways in which families might function. McLanahan and Sandefur state,

When two biological parents share the same household, they can monitor the children and maintain parental control. . . . Having another parent around who cares about the child increases the likelihood that each parent will "do the right thing" even when otherwise inclined. In short, the two-parent family structure creates a system of checks and balances that both promotes parental responsibility and protects the child from parental neglect and, sometimes, abuse.

The parenting McLanahan and Sandefur describe occurs in some families and there is no doubt that having two parents when they are both involved in parenting takes the burden off of each parent and gives the child more than one caregiver and role model. But what about the families in which the father is barely there—because of long hours of work, out-of-town travel, golf, or the notion that domestic affairs are best left to the mother? What about the family in which the father (or the mother) is alcoholic, or emotionally unavailable because of depression or disinterest? What about the family in which the father is frankly abusive—either physically or emotionally—to the mother and/or the children? Why should single-parent families be compared only to ideal two-parent families? McLanahan and Sandefur seem to assume, also, that only fathers can perform certain functions within the family. They state,

Clearly children whose fathers do not reside in the household are at great disadvantage relative to peers with fathers at home when it comes to finding a job, not only because they are less likely to know about job openings but also because *they may not know how to apply for a job and how to conduct themselves during interviews.* [Emphasis added.]

Can only fathers help young people apply for jobs and tell them how to "conduct themselves during interviews?" This sounds strangely like a 1940s or 1950s image of the American family in which the mother donned an apron, baked pies, did spring cleaning, and was relatively unsophisticated about the world of work. Don't millions of women—particularly single women—have these skills today?

I am not suggesting that being a single parent is easy or, for that matter, that growing up in a single-parent family doesn't require young people to deal with problems they might not face if they had two parents. What I am suggesting is that comparing the social, emotional, and economic status of single-parent families with idealized versions of two-parent families does not elucidate the issue.

Many of the problems these families, particularly families headed by women, face are due to low economic status, either chronic or sudden. They also suffer from other socially constructed disadvantages such as the gross inequality in the American educational system, a lack of decently paid jobs for those who wish to work, and a profound lack of community-based services that are necessary to families with two working parents and even more essential for single parents and their children. It is the many forms of discrimination based on gender and race, and the stigmatizing of single women and their children, that play a significant role in their economic, social, and psychological disadvantage.

What we are seeing here is strangely circular reasoning: Because women are disadvantaged in the labor force both in the types of jobs they hold and in their wages, because men often feel disconnected from their families and do not pay child support, because post-industrial societies have high rates of divorce that all too often leave mothers and children with insufficient resources, and because the United States has not established the widespread, first-rate services so necessary for families today, women are being blamed for the negative consequences of single parenthood. In other words, because American society has not adjusted to contemporary family patterns, to current economic realities, and to continuing racial, gender, and class inequities, single-parent families are suffering and women are being blamed—for making poor choices, for their children's problems, and indeed for many of the problems of American society. In some sense, women are being blamed because of massive "culture lag"—that is, many elements within American society refusing to adjust to the profound changes that have occurred during the second half of the twentieth century and instead attempting to revert to the norms, values, and patterns of earlier eras.

Many of these problems could have been and could still be addressed by American society, but perhaps one of the central functions of scapegoating individuals and/or groups such as single-parent families is to remove pressure from the society to adapt to present-day reality. In fact, rather than finding ways of helping parents cope with late-twentieth-century life, many leaders are trying to turn the clock back to the 1950s or even some earlier period, to the two-parent patriarchal model as the only legitimate family type.

It is clear that young women who have hopes and dreams and can see the possibility of achieving their goals are far less likely to bear children at an early age. It is clear that young men who have jobs and productive, connected roles in society are far more likely to form long-lasting familial relationships and to take seriously the social role of father. It is clear that if women earned a living wage and were at greater economic parity with male workers, their children—even if they lived in mother-only families—would suffer less economic disadvantage. And it is clear that if fathers were more strongly encouraged to provide child support and to remain a viable presence in their children's lives, the social, economic, and psychological costs of divorce, separation, and never-married parenting would be far less.

Politicians and policy makers need to recognize that the problems of American families are rooted in great part in the socioeconomic conditions of American life and that we as a society can change some of those conditions. If we want to make policy changes that will encourage parents to remain together, we can do so. And when parents choose not to live together, as millions will continue to do for a wide variety of reasons, we can make policy changes that will make life easier for single parents and their children.

Finally, what do those who so strongly deplore single parenthood feel should be done about the increasing number of children in one-parent families? Do they believe couples who have "irreconcilable differences" should remain together "for the sake of the children"? Do they feel women should remain in marriages because their jobs do not pay a living wage? Do they believe women who are battered and abused should remain in abusive relationships because children of single parents seem to do less well in a variety of ways? Or do they believe, as the Puritans of Massachusetts did some 350 years ago, that single mothers and their children should be stigmatized and shunned, thus guaranteeing that they will suffer still further from their single parenthood?

And what of women who have not found an appropriate mate? Must they remain childless? What of women who choose careers with long periods of training and then find that the eligible men are taken? Must they remain childless? What of gay and lesbian adults who want to love and nurture a child? Must they forsake the parenting experience? And what of poor women whose male acquaintances have few job prospects and therefore may make unstable partners? Or black women who have long recognized that far too many black men are chronically unemployed, in jail, or victims of drug and/or alcohol abuse? Must these women take on the responsibility of caring for these men or forsake motherhood? What indeed are the repercussions of establishing the two-parent, heterosexual couple as the only legitimate model of parenthood?

In a recent article, sociologists Christopher Jencks and Kathryn Edin have raised the important question "Do Poor Women Have a Right to Bear Children?" As they point out, in discussing the need to revamp AFDC the Clinton Administration stated that their plan "signals that people should not have children until they are ready to support them." But as Jencks and Edin state, ". . . for many poor women, that time will never come. Sad to say, there are neither enough good jobs nor enough good husbands to provide every American woman with enough money to support a family." In our zeal to discourage single parenting, particularly single parenting among poor women, are we in reality trying to limit the reproduction of low-income women? Is this a legitimate goal of social policy?

Jencks and Edin spell out three commonly heard "fairy tales" about single motherhood and poverty.

Fairy Tale # 1: "If teen mothers simply held off parenthood until their twenties, they would have enough money to raise a family." Fairy Tale # 2: "If single mothers got married they wouldn't need welfare." Fairy Tale # 3: "If teen mothers finished high school before having kids, they could get good jobs."

Jencks and Edin go on to point out the fallacies of each "fairy tale": that delaying childbearing is an extremely complex issue and that teenage pregnancy is driven by many factors, such as poor education and troubled homes, over which young women have no control; that there are not enough men who earn a living wage to go around and that "marrying a man with an unstable work history or low wages is not a good formula for avoiding welfare"; and that finishing high school is no guarantee of a job that will enable a single mother to "make ends meet" and, in fact, "only a minority [of American women] can support children on their earnings alone."

Jencks and Edin correctly point out that many critics of AFDC, including many politicians, would like to "prevent the poor from having children." Andrew Hacker suggests that the campaign to curtail the number of children poor people have is in reality a campaign to curtail black births. Many of those most vociferous about the damaging impact of the poor on their own children and on the wider society think that "most welfare recipients are irresponsible or incompetent parents living in communities that breed lawlessness and promiscuity. Perhaps equally important, they think of welfare recipients as black idlers who live off the labor of industrious whites." Do these policy makers want to prevent the so-called "underclass" from reproducing? But the issue is more complex than those who claim that the poor are the root of all evil would have us believe. Nearly half the children receiving AFDC in any month were born to parents who were married and supporting themselves at the time of the child's birth. Do they want to prevent these couples from bearing children too? And if this is their strategy, how does it jibe with the rhetoric of diminishing the role of government in the lives of the American people?

The question of whether or not a society has the right to

try to limit childbearing leads irrevocably to the next question: Does a society have the right to punish children for their parents' behavior? For that is exactly what is happening when states refuse to extend AFDC benefits to children conceived while the mother is receiving welfare, when states slash their benefits far below the level at which any family can live, or institute time limits for receiving benefits regardless of the families' economic situation. Based on these actions, a case can be made that states are, in reality, punishing children when their mothers are forced to work and leave their young offspring in the care of others, particularly when the society does not provide first-rate, accessible, affordable child care. Is the United States the kind of society that sanctions punishing the innocent in order to exact retribution against those whose behavior some politicians and policy makers deplore?

The United States may not be requiring all unmarried mothers to wear scarlet letters today but we are surely finding myriad ways of stigmatizing and ostracizing them. To avoid substantial societal restructuring and to preserve the status and privilege of the few, many politicians and opinion leaders are looking back to earlier times—both in this country and in England—to find ways of exercising social control over those who have been deemed deviant.

In March 1995, Speaker of the House of Representatives Newt Gingrich, in a speech to the National League of Cities, recommended returning to the values, norms, and social sanctions of Victorian England in order to modify behavior he considers antisocial:

They [Victorian England] reduced the number of children born out of wedlock almost by 50 percent. They changed the whole momentum of their society. They didn't do it through a new bureaucracy. They did it by reestablishing values, by moral leadership, and by being willing to look at people in the face and say, "You should be ashamed when you get drunk in public; you ought to be ashamed if you're a drug addict."

But looking backward may not always be useful. As Michiko Kakutani has written in a piece entitled "If Gingrich Only Knew About Victoria's Secret,"

> While the Victorians were grappling with problems that may appear to be familiar to us (growing urbanization, accelerating social changes, concerns about education and health) they also inhabited a vastly different world, a world that was far less heterogeneous, far less egalitarian than our own. Analogies between that age and our own can, therefore, be highly deceptive.
>
> In fact the more one thinks about the Victorians, the more one is inclined to agree with the British novelist L.P. Hartley, who once declared: "the past is a foreign country; they do things differently there."

The other era that so many critics of today's families seem to yearn for is the 1950s, that post–World War II period of economic boom and baby boom, when fertility increased and divorce declined, when the Gross National Product rose by 250 percent, per capita income grew by 35 percent, and many working class families moved into the middle class. But this was also a period of extensive governmental programs that made a dramatic difference in the lives of millions of Americans: veterans' benefits, education subsidies, housing loans, highway construction, and job training. According to Stephanie

Coontz, author of *The Way We Never Were: American Families and the Nostalgia Trap*, people were aware of the availability of low-interest home loans, expanding educational and occupational opportunities, and steady employment, and these expectations led to early marriage and childbearing. But while the Father-Knows-Best-Leave-It-to-Beaver image is what policy makers may think of when they conjure up the fifties, it was also a time in which 25 percent of the population was officially poor, a time when 60 percent of Americans over the age of sixty-five had incomes below $1,000, a time when the poverty rate of two-parent black families was 50 percent.

It was also a time of brutal segregation. According to Coontz, "When Harvey Clark tried to move into Cicero, Illinois, in 1951, a mob of 4,000 whites spent four days tearing his apartment apart while police stood by and joked with them."

It was a time when millions of women lost the jobs they had held during the war and were forced to retreat to domestic roles in relatively isolated suburban tracts. It was a time when tranquilizers were developed; by 1959, consumption, mostly by women, had reached 1.15 million pounds. It was a time when teen birthrates soared. In 1957, 97 out of every 1,000 females ages fifteen to nineteen gave birth, compared to 59.6 per 1,000 females in 1993. If the girls and young women were unmarried at the time of conception, every effort was usually made to persuade them to marry. If this wasn't possible, many middle-class white girls were sent away from home to a "distant aunt" or a maternity home where they were expected to give their babies up for adoption immediately after birth, forsaking all contact with the infant or the adoptive family from that moment on. Indeed, even the more recent past is a "foreign country" where they did things very differently.

Would we want to return to that world even if we could?

The relentless denigration of mother-only families ignores the heroic women who ceaselessly work to provide and care for their families. Barnard College sponsors an annual competition for eleventh grade girls in New York City's public high schools. The theme is "A Woman I Admire." In 1995, first prize went to Amelia H. Chamberlain of Townsend High School in Queens. Her essay, entitled "Mama's Dark World," describes one of the millions of mothers who are struggling to take care of their families with few social supports. At 10 p.m. every night, Amelia awakens her mother, who is sleeping on the living room couch. Her mother gets up instantly to go to work, sometimes after as little as four or five or even two hours of sleep. Amelia tells her mother "not to push herself," but her mother says, "We need the money."

Amelia writes that before her mother leaves, "[s]he hands me my $3.60 for school and kisses me on the cheek. As always, she tells me she loves me." Watching her mother go to work, Amelia wonders how she always remembers to give her money for school, how she always remembers to tell her she loves her, how she works all night and raises "me and my sisters on her own."

Amelia returns to her room, but before starting to study again she writes that she "silently thank[s] the Lord for Mama."

Many mother-only families have severe problems in American society but many others are cohesive, loving, supportive units in which the children, like Amelia Chamberlain, are being nurtured and prepared for a productive life in the wider society. As female-headed families are heterogeneous, so are poor families.

Let us now examine the nature of poverty in the United

States during the mid-1990s. Exactly who are the poor today? Who are the welfare recipients who are held responsible for so many of America's current problems? What situations propel women and children into poverty during the last decade of the twentieth century and what is the impact of low economic status on poor families?

Chapter 3

Who Are the Poor?

Captain John Smith's 1607 statement, "If you don't work you won't eat," is the complete opposite of today's redistribution ethic that subsidizes idleness. Nothing could be less traditionally American than the modern welfare system. It violates the American ethic that everyone should work hard to improve both their own lives and the lives of their children. If you are not prepared to shoulder personal responsibility, then you are not prepared to participate in American civilization.

—NEWT GINGRICH

IN *WOMEN AND CHILDREN LAST*, NO ONE PERSONIFIED THE enormous variation among poor women as vividly as Doreen Cullen. When I interviewed her in her rather ramshackle house in a small city in New Hampshire, she was forty-six years old and recently divorced. She and her husband had been married twenty-three years and they had eight children. She describes their marriage:

My husband was a devoted husband and father but we had very separate roles. He took care of everything outside of the home and I took care of everything inside the home. He handled all the financial matters. When I told him I wanted to get a job after twenty years of marriage, he didn't understand and told me everything had to be done around the house the same way even if I worked. No routines could be interrupted; all the meals must be ready on time and supper must be on the table at five o'clock every day.

Meanwhile, I was losing myself. Not having my hair done. I had gained weight. I was losing myself and I didn't know it.

On their twenty-third anniversary Doreen's husband sent her flowers for the first time except when she had given birth. A few weeks later he took her dancing for the first time in their married life. Shortly afterward he invited her to McDonald's for coffee and told her that he had fallen in love with a twenty-eight-year-old woman and was leaving her. His exact words were: "I love you and I love the kids but I just can't live without Sandy."

Within one month, Doreen's husband had left her and the children, walked away from his construction business and moved out of state with Sandy. Her (and the children's) income dropped from over $70,000 a year to just over $7,000 which was all she was earning as a homemaker/health aide. Doreen took her husband to court for child support; he was ordered to pay $125 a week but rarely did so. By the beginning of the following winter she was out of heating oil. She sold her dishwasher and anything else she could do without. The bank foreclosed on the mortgage so she lost their house. And perhaps most painful of all, Doreen describes how she felt: "I was devastated. I became suicidal. My self-esteem was a big, black zero."

Doreen had become a member of the "New Poor," a group

of people who did not grow up in poverty, some of whom grew up working class or middle class or even upper middle class but, because of events in their lives—divorce, death, illness, unemployment, an untimely birth, or other precipitating events—have fallen into poverty.

Another all too common group of the "New Poor" are older women. Whether they have worked outside of the home for much of their lives, for only a few years, or not at all, their money from pensions and social security is often inadequate to meet even modest living expenses. If they are married, many must spend their joint savings on their husband's health care (some must "spend down" to enable their husbands to qualify for Medicaid to pay for a long, grueling illness) and find themselves with little if anything for their own old age.

With marriage being touted today as a central route out of poverty, few critics of the choices and behavior of poor women speak about marriage as a path into poverty. When I interviewed her, Elizabeth Cameron was living with her three children in the Bronx. A former welfare worker, she became a welfare recipient through marriage:

> I originally came from Ohio and went to Ohio State. After graduation I came to New York. I got married ten years ago and it was a marriage into poverty. I married someone who came from poverty, someone who was Hispanic, a welfare client, *my* welfare client.
>
> I worked for five years in a welfare office in the Bronx and I was confused and lonely. I was away from my family structure and fell apart. I couldn't find a place for myself here. So I ended up with him, a good guy, a basically decent, loving man but one with insurmountable handicaps. He has little education, a drug problem, and an alcohol problem.

After eight years of marriage, which included his abusing her physically and, she felt, his inflicting psychological damage on the children, Elizabeth separated from her husband and applied for aid to the welfare department (the same office in which she used to work). She and her husband were apart for six months while he was in a treatment program but then, she said, "I weakened." They got back together but eventually he "switched back to drugs and became hooked on heroin. Then we separated again so I could survive economically." In other words, she needed to separate from her husband to requalify for AFDC.

Few politicians today speak of the instances in which the husbands walk out. One Maine mother of four spoke about her husband walking out on Mother's Day. "He said, 'I'm going to the store and I'll be right back,' and that was it." According to her, "He left because he couldn't take the pressures"—several small children close in age and an older child with serious medical problems. She survived by working in a textile mill and receiving supplementary welfare. Her hope is that "my children will know there is a better life."

Yet another group of poor women are the temporarily poor. Those legislators and policy makers who are slashing benefits and denigrating poor people, particularly welfare recipients, do not talk about women who move out of poverty. They do not talk about Lynn Woolsey, the Democratic congresswoman from California. When she was a thirty-year-old mother of three small children, Representative Woolsey's husband walked out and refused to pay child support. For a brief time she was a welfare recipient. She talked about that experience in March 1995 when members of the House of Representatives were debating legislation to dismantle the federal program Aid to Families with Dependent Children and replace it with block

grants to the states that would not guarantee aid to all families
who met the criteria:

> As the only member of Congress who has actually been a
> single, working mother on welfare, my ideas about welfare do
> not come from theory or books. I know it. I lived it. . . .
>
> I will never forget what it was like to lie awake at night
> worried that one of my children would get sick or trying to
> decide what was more important: new shoes for my children
> or next week's groceries.
>
> Even though I was working the entire time I was on
> A.F.D.C., I needed welfare in order to provide my family with
> health care, child care and the food we needed in order to
> survive. So my colleagues see I know about the importance
> of the safety net, and I also know about the importance of
> work. . . .
>
> We could punish our children by voting for H.R. 4, or we
> can invest in our children and their families so they can lead
> strong, productive lives.

Nor do they speak of Connecticut Representative Marie
Kirkley-Bey, Democrat of Hartford, who during the debate on
overhauling the welfare system recalled the four years she spent
living in a housing project and receiving public assistance as
"one of the hardest things I had to do." She continues, "I was
shunned, not because of the quality of my character but because
of the source of my income. Until you've walked a mile in
my shoes, don't judge me." Connecticut, one of the richest
states in the nation, has since passed one of the most restrictive
welfare bills adopted by any state.

Those denigrating the poor rarely mention the working
poor—the domestic workers, child-care workers, health aides,

and part-time fast-food employees who struggle to make enough to take care of their families. Those who stereotype poor mothers as lazy and unwilling to work do not talk about the thousands who work in unregulated sweatshops in Los Angeles or the forty-four-year-old immigrant from China who works twelve hours a day, seven days a week, in a "windowless garment shop" in Brooklyn and earns on average less than $2.50 an hour. They do not mention the twenty-six-year-old garment worker from Lima, Peru, who earns $3.00 an hour trimming finished dresses and wrapping them in plastic. She does not dare to report abuses of U.S. labor laws because, as she says, "If I claim the overtime, they will fire me."

Those who are stigmatizing welfare recipients do not point to all those young mothers who are valiantly caring for their children on meager AFDC checks while struggling to complete their education. Legislators do not point to the women who are trying to balance their responsibilities and complete their high school education, or those who dropped out of high school and then return to obtain their GED. They do not talk about women like Tanya Robinson, a twenty-seven-year-old African-American welfare recipient, the mother of a five-year-old and a student at Columbia University's School of General Studies. Just a few years ago, Tanya was homeless and begging for money in front of a supermarket in New York City. Today she is a sociology major at a major university and is thinking about the possibility of graduate school. At one point in her life Tanya knew that she "was cut out for more than scrubbing floors and welfare." She credits the Higher Education Opportunity Program (HEOP) at Columbia, and particularly its director, with making it possible for her to attend Columbia. Tanya talks about the day-to-day struggle to care for her daughter, commute from the South Bronx to Columbia, work

part-time for her financial aid and to make ends meet financially. In addition, she is constantly fearful that HEOP will be
cut back and that "welfare reform" will force her to quit school
and go to work full-time. What indeed will the cutback of
financial aid and far stricter regulations of welfare recipients
mean for Tanya and others who are trying to complete their
education? Will she be forced to drop out of college and take
whatever job she can find? Will this intelligent, highly motivated young woman be locked into a low-paying job with little
or no upward mobility because New York State, along with
other states, is more interested in getting recipients off the welfare rolls than in helping poor mothers prepare for a future in
which they can truly provide for themselves and their children?

Yet another group of poor women often ignored by politicians and those policy makers who single-mindedly blame
women for their own poverty are those battered and abused
women whose only recourse from violence all too often is the
welfare system. Joan, a twenty-nine-year-old former Texan,
describes her husband's abusive behavior:

> He used to beat me up, he drank a lot, but I stayed
> with him. . . .
> He spent a lot of money drinking and wouldn't support us
> so I had to. He became violent when he was drinking, but I
> saw the good in him when he was not. He would smash
> things; he almost choked me a few times. The only time he
> would leave me alone is when I pretended I was dead, or
> when I was pregnant.

Marilyn, a thirty-five-year-old mother of two from Arizona,
was pregnant with her third child. She describes her husband
trying to strangle her, chasing her around the apartment, ter-

rorizing the children, threatening to kill her. When she finally spoke with a social worker at a Family Violence Project she realized, "You mean, I don't have to put up with this?"

A woman from Tucson whose husband threatened to shoot her when she said she wanted a divorce discusses how difficult it is for battered and abused women to leave their husbands: "Most women are basically too afraid to leave. They're un-educated and it's mostly economic. Battered wives are kept barefoot and pregnant by their men and are afraid to leave. Ninety percent is due to economic fears."

All of these women comprise the poor. Poor women are young, they are middle-aged, and they are old. They are from rural Maine and Mississippi, from New York, Detroit, and Los Angeles, from small towns in the Midwest, from the mining towns of Appalachia, and from the suburban communities that ring the major cities. They are married, divorced, separated, widowed, and never married. They are from all backgrounds —white, African-American, Latina, Asian-American, Native American, and many others on whom the Census Bureau does not keep detailed data. They are full-time workers, part-time workers, the unemployed and the underemployed. They are high school dropouts and high school graduates; some have attended college, some have even completed college.

One of the issues that has seriously distorted our perception of poor women and our choices of appropriate social policy has been the widespread use of the label, the "underclass." According to historian Michael B. Katz,

By the late 1970s, the specter of an emergent underclass per-meated discussion of America's inner cities. . . . The word *underclass* conjured up a mysterious wilderness in the heart of America's cities; a terrain of violence and despair; a collectivity outside politics and social structure, beyond the usual language of class and stratum, unable to protest or revolt.

According to Katz, in 1977, *Time* magazine "announced the emergence of a menacing underclass in America's inner cities." The *Time* article stated:

Behind the [ghetto's] crumbling walls, lives a large group of people who are more intractable, more socially alien and more hostile than almost anyone had imagined. They are the unreachables: the American underclass. . . . Their bleak environment nurtures values that are often at odds with those of the majority—even the majority of the poor. Thus the underclass produces a highly disproportionate number of the nation's juvenile delinquents, school dropouts, drug addicts and welfare mothers, and much of the adult crime, family disruption, urban decay and demand for social expenditures.

With the publication of Ken Auletta's book *The Underclass* in 1982, the term became widely used in describing the poor in the United States. According to Auletta, the underclass (which he specifies is both black and white) "generally feels excluded from society, rejects commonly accepted values, suffers from *behavioral* as well as *income* deficiencies. They don't just tend to be poor; to most Americans their behavior seems aberrant."

As Katz points out, many scholars and social critics object to the term "underclass," claiming that it has become the "modern euphemism for the undeserving poor, it reinforces the tradition of blaming the victim. By stigmatizing them it insults those it designates." The definition of underclass has been disputed over the past two decades. Some emphasize interlocking patterns of behavior "particularly the combination of out-of-wedlock childbirth, welfare dependence, poor school achievement, and crime, which . . . co-exist in dangerous conjunction within certain neighborhoods of America's inner cities." Others focus on persistent, concentrated poverty and the attendant hopelessness and detachment from the labor force.

William Julius Wilson has defined the underclass as "that heterogeneous grouping of families and individuals who are outside the mainstream of the American occupational system." Wilson includes

> individuals who lack training and skills and either experience long-term unemployment or are not members of the labor force, individuals who are engaged in street crime and other forms of aberrant behavior, and families that experience long-term spells of poverty and/or welfare dependency.

Focusing on changes in ghetto neighborhoods over the past quarter century, Wilson claims that the "exodus of the more stable working- and middle-class segments" has left the remaining individuals and families, many of whom are long-term welfare recipients and street criminals, "increasingly isolated socially from mainstream patterns and norms of behavior." Furthermore, Wilson emphasizes male joblessness and the general unavailability of "marriageable" males as central factors in the formation of female-headed families, in the social isolation that excludes many ghetto dwellers from a job network system, and in young people's disbelief in the efficacy of education.

While many scholars agree that members of the underclass share specific behavioral patterns, the controversy around the term focuses on whether the so-called "deviant" behavior is the cause of long-standing poverty or whether joblessness and other structural problems lead to behavioral differences. Some observers claim, moreover, that the behavior of certain long-term, extremely poor, and socially isolated inner city dwellers is an adaptation to social and economic circumstances that enables them to survive with a modicum of humanity and self-respect. A persuasive case has been made that "sharing and caring," the reliance by single mothers on extended family, friends, and other members of the community who function as kin, as a support network often replacing the middle-class model of the nuclear family is in reality an adaptation to the lack of marriageable men, the lack of viable jobs, the lack of adequate education, the lack of adequate income, and, above all, the lack of options.

The most critical problem with the pervasive use of the concept and the term "underclass" is the widespread view that most poor people are members of this despised, feared, and forsaken group. This view, this stereotype, is patently false but it has, I believe, driven much of the social policy discussion in the United States in recent years and is driving the profound changes in social policy that we are witnessing in the 1990s. In addition to driving welfare policy, this view is having profound effect on health policy (the cutbacks of Medicaid), on nutrition policy, on job training and education programs for the poor, and on the criminal justice system. The willingness (some would say eagerness) to execute selected convicted criminals (most of whom are poor and the vast majority of whom are African-American), the emphasis on building jails rather than focusing on prevention, the imposition of severe mandatory sentences for a variety of crimes, not necessarily only for the most heinous, is the result of the belief among policy makers and a substantial percentage of the populace that "these people" are beyond redemption, that they are, perhaps, a species apart and must be controlled by virtually any means. The assumption that virtually all poor people are members of the underclass is a shorthand way of saying that their behavior is the central factor in their poverty, that they are dangerous, do not share mainstream values, are the "other" who must be brought into line, must be resocialized with the stick rather than the carrot, must be punished for their aberrant behavior. Above all, this broad categorization of the poor, particularly welfare recipients, as members of the underclass clouds our ability to truly understand the variety of circumstances that propel women and children into poverty and to develop a humane social policy to deal with these circumstances.

We must get beyond the slurs and stereotypes and recognize that millions of women are part of the labor force and are still poor and millions more care for their families, participate in the labor force, and study in the hope that they and their children will one day share in the American Dream. And while some families are poor for more than one generation, millions of families are temporarily poor—needing benefits for a finite period of time until they find a way out of poverty. Only if we understand clearly the complexity and diversity of American poverty can we hope to fashion social policy that will truly help families to live in dignity.

According to the U.S. Census Bureau, 15.1 percent of all people in the United States (39,265,000 people) lived below the poverty line in 1993. In that year, the poverty line for a family of three was $11,522 and for a family of four was $14,763. This rate of poverty is essentially the same as the levels in 1982 and 1983 when the unemployment rate was nearly 10 percent and the economy was in its deepest slump since the Great Depression of 1929. Between 1992 and 1993, a year in which the unemployment rate averaged 6.8 percent, over one million additional people fell into poverty. Thus, despite an economic recovery, virtually all categories of persons—working families, whites and minorities, married-couple families, and female-headed families—have experienced significant increases in their poverty rates.

It must be noted that the vast majority of poor people in the United States are women and children. In 1993, 14.7 million women ages eighteen and over were officially classified as poor; these women constituted 37.4 percent of all people living in poverty. In that same year, 15.7 million children under the age of eighteen officially lived below the poverty line; these children constituted 40 percent of all poor people in the United States. Therefore, women and children in 1993 made up over three-quarters (77.4 percent) of all Americans living in poverty.

Analyzing the poverty rate by race, we see that in 1993 blacks (33.1 percent of whom lived in poverty) and Hispanics (30.6 percent) had poverty rates three times that of whites (9.9 percent). The poverty rate of children demonstrates this disturbing phenomenon even more dramatically. The poverty rates of children will be discussed in greater detail in chapter 6, but here it must be noted that in 1993, 22.7 percent of all children under the age of eighteen lived in poverty, and among children under six, 26 percent lived in poverty in 1992. The breakdown by race and ethnicity shows a disproportionate representation of black and Hispanic children. Examining poverty by family type, we find that in 1993 female-headed families were more than five times more likely to be poor (35.6 percent) than married-couple families (6.5 percent). Consequently, the poverty rate for children living with their mothers was significantly higher than the poverty rate for children living with married parents.

But merely examining national poverty statistics is not sufficient to understand the depth of poverty in the United States. Certain parts of the country, such as many urban centers and rural areas, have particularly high levels of poverty; this concentration has serious implications for the poor living in these areas, for the economy and the provision of human services, as well as for the remaining population.

If we examine the statistics for New York City, for example, it becomes clear that New York has a far higher percentage of people living in poverty than either New York State or the country as a whole. According to a study prepared by the United Way of New York City for the City's Human Resource Administration entitled *Low-Income Populations in New York City: Economic Trends and Social Welfare Programs, 1994,* one out of every four New York City residents (24 percent) lived in poverty in 1992. The comparable rates for New York State and the United States as a whole were 10 and 15 percent respectively. Not only does New York City have an extraordinarily high poverty rate but it also has a high rate of people in "extreme poverty" (18 percent) (defined by this study as people living below 75 percent of the poverty line), and of "near-poverty," over one-third of the population (36 percent) living on income between 100 and 150 percent of the poverty line.

As in the larger society, children are the poorest group. In 1992 nearly 40 percent (39 percent) of New York City children lived below the poverty line. The other particularly vulnerable group are women. Twenty-three percent of New York City women are living in poverty; they comprise one-third of the city's poor people.

As in the rest of the country, African-American and Hispanic New Yorkers are the poorest racial and ethnic groups. In 1992, 40 percent of Hispanics and 33 percent of non-Hispanic blacks lived below the poverty line while approximately 12 percent of the non-Hispanic whites were poor. The high poverty rate of Hispanic New Yorkers is particularly startling since nation-wide African Americans generally have higher poverty rates than do Hispanics. Female-headed families also have an exceptionally high poverty rate in New York. In the United States as a whole, approximately one-third (35.6 percent) of female-headed families live in poverty; in New York City, nearly two-thirds (61 percent) of female-headed families with children were poor; among these mother-only families nearly half (49 percent) were extremely poor and 74 percent were poor and near-poor.

Clearly, New York and other major cities have a heavy burden of social services to provide for the large population living in poverty. It is virtually impossible for these urban areas to provide the income supports, health and child care services, and nutrition programs so desperately needed by these poor families without substantial assistance from the state and federal governments. As federal and state support for the cities diminishes, poor urban dwellers will become even more destitute and marginalized.

To return to the myths and stereotypes discussed in chapter 1, statistics indicate that the majority of poor children in the United States—some 61 percent—lived in families in which someone worked during 1993. Even among children under six, the majority (58 percent) lived with working parents; 38 percent of these children were supported by their parents' earnings only, with no cash public assistance. *Less than one-third of children under six who lived in poor families lived in families that relied exclusively on welfare.* Clearly, the equation of poverty with dependence on welfare is false; millions of families are working and are still poor.

In examining the issue of the working poor, it is essential to examine the poverty line. Many experts claim that the federal poverty line is set far too low and that if it were set at an appropriate level, millions of additional working people would be included in American poverty data. The poverty line, based on work by Mollie Orshansky, a research analyst at the Social Security Administration, was originally set in 1963. Orshansky took the estimate of the least amount of money required for a family of four to meet minimal nutritional requirements and, because at that time the cost of food made up one-third of the total budget for an average family, she set the poverty line at three times the cost of that minimal food budget. Political scientists John Schwarz and Thomas Volgy point out that by the early 1980s, food had fallen to approximately one-fifth of the cost of the average family budget in the United States, and by 1990, food was only one-sixth of the average budget, but the poverty line was nonetheless still calculated as three times the minimal food budget rather than six times the food budget. As Schwarz and Volgy state in their book *The Forgotten Americans: Thirty Million Working Poor in the Land of Opportunity*, if the United States Government used the same formula to establish the poverty line in 1990 as Mollie Orshansky originally used, the income needed in 1990 to support a family of four at a minimal level would be closer to $22,500, 67 percent greater than the $13,360 used in that year by the federal government. The authors examine an economy budget based on the lowest-level food budget allowed by the federal government and the rent necessary for a low-cost, two-bedroom living unit in an urban environment. Many experts question whether a family can indeed obtain adequate nutrition on this "thrifty food budget," but if one uses it and the average rent necessary for a family of four, the federal poverty line would be $20,700.

Schwarz and Volgy question what it really means to live on the economy budget. After calculating expenses they conclude that

> Members of families existing on the economy budget never go out to eat . . . ; they never go out to a movie, concert, or ball game . . . ; they never purchase alcohol or cigarettes; never take a vacation or holiday that involves any motel . . . , hotel or . . . any meals out; never hire a baby-sitter or have any other paid child care; never give . . . spending money to the children; never purchase any lessons or home-learning tools for the children; never buy books or records for the adults or children, or any toys, except in the small amounts available for birthday or Christmas presents ($50 per person over the year); never pay for a haircut; never buy a magazine; . . . and, never spend any money for preschool . . . or educational trips . . . away from home, or any summer camp or other activity with a fee.

They further point out that families living on this meager budget have no money to pay for emergencies or to help other people such as ill or elderly parents, and have no resources to buy life insurance or to pay for college for the children. None of these items are provided for in the budget. If they need money for these expenses, they would have to borrow from others or from money earmarked for other purposes.

Using these calculations, Schwarz and Volgy find that "the wide array of families in America who fail to attain self-sufficiency, despite hard work, is astounding." They found that in 1989, 5.9 million workers worked full-time year round and yet lived below the $20,700 "threshold of self-sufficiency." The households of these fully employed workers contained 18 million Americans, "the equivalent of every man, woman, and child living in the eleven largest cities on the nation's two coasts—New York City, Los Angeles, Philadelphia, San Diego, San Jose, Baltimore, San Francisco, Jacksonville, Washington, D.C., Boston, and Seattle." This number is more than half again as many people who were on welfare that year and four to five times more Americans usually defined as the "under-class." Furthermore, if we include workers who work part-time or part-year, as many as an additional 6 million employed workers cannot provide for their families. These workers, full-time and part-time, and their family members, comprise an additional 30 million people living in poverty.

Interestingly, the American public agrees with Schwarz and Volgy that the poverty line should be set at a significantly higher level. In 1989, the Gallup Organization asked a nation-ally representative sample of adult Americans what amount of income they would use as a poverty line for a family of four. The average figure reported by the respondents was $15,017, 24 percent higher than the official poverty line in 1989. If that figure had been used in that year, the number of poor Amer-icans would have been nearly 45 million instead of 32 million; the poverty rate would have been 18 percent instead of 13 percent and the poverty rate of children would have been 26 percent rather than 19 percent.

A recent report by experts convened by the National Acad-emy of Sciences, the Panel on Poverty and Family Assistance, also recommended significant changes in the way poverty is defined and measured in the United States. The group, which included economists, sociologists, and other social scientists rec-ommended that the government count not only cash income but also noncash benefits such as food stamps, school lunches, subsidized housing, and home energy assistance in calculating family income. It also recommended deducting taxes, the cost of child care, work expenses, and medical costs paid directly by consumers from cash income. The net result would be "higher poverty rates for families with one or more workers and for families that lack health insurance coverage, and lower rates for families that receive public assistance." The panel further suggested adjusting the official poverty line for geographical differences in the cost of housing. Today the poverty line is the same across the country despite the wide variation in housing costs, for example, between rural Mississippi and New York City.

These changes in the poverty line would have significant implications not only for AFDC but for eligibility for a wide variety of government programs such as Medicaid, Head Start, and food stamps which are all linked in some way to official poverty levels. In trying to estimate the effect of modifying the poverty line on the numbers of people who would officially be considered poor, the panel estimated that the official number in 1992, 14.5 percent of Americans officially considered poor, would rise to 15 or 16 percent or possibly to as much as 18 percent of the population.

Who are these breadwinners who, while employed, are nonetheless still living with their families in poverty? It is clear that any worker earning the minimum wage of $4.25, a yearly income of $8,840, is automatically earning a wage that is well below the federal poverty line. Child care workers whose weekly median income in 1994 was $158 (a yearly income of approximately $7,500), have incomes significantly lower than the official poverty level. Other workers whose incomes are well below the federal poverty line for a family of four include cashiers (median yearly income of $11,000), farm workers (median yearly income of approximately $12,000), waitresses and waiters (median yearly income of $13,300). Workers as varied as bank tellers, construction laborers, secretaries, and telephone operators would receive poverty wages if the poverty line were at the level suggested by Schwarz and Volgy. These categories include white-collar workers as well as blue-collar workers.

One of the reasons so many female-headed families with working mothers live in poverty is that, despite the substantial gains made by millions of women in the labor force, the ratio of women's median weekly earnings to men's in 1994 was 76.4 percent. The majority of women still work in the lowest paid occupations—technical, clerical, service, and sales jobs. In addition, two-thirds of all part-time workers are women, many holding more than one job. This frequently means they do not receive benefits from these jobs, no matter how many they hold. Many of the poorest paid occupations are both sex-segregated and female-dominated. Child-care workers, health workers, pink-collar workers such as hairdressers and manicurists, and other service and sales people remain among the poorest-paid workers in the United States. Nurses' aides, for example, earn an average yearly wage of $13,000; the profession is 87 percent female.

Moreover, during the 1980s as the purchasing power of the minimum wage declined and the shift from manufacturing to retail jobs continued, the number of full-time workers who were paid too little to lift a family of four out of poverty increased significantly. Among those hardest hit were men ages twenty-five to thirty-four. In 1993, over 30 percent of these men were not earning enough to keep a family of four above the poverty line. This percentage has more than doubled since 1969. In that year, 13.6 percent of male workers twenty-five to thirty-four years old earned wages below the poverty line for a family of four. By 1993, that percentage had risen to 32.2

percent. This bleak economic picture undermines the two-parent family by causing many men who cannot fulfill their roles as breadwinners to abandon their responsibilities as fathers and causing many women to see low-wage men as poor marital prospects. As the chief demographer for the Annie E. Casey Foundation noted, "I think many women may have reconciled themselves to the fact that they can't find a husband that can support them. So they have children and try to support them as best they can."

Among employed persons there are significant differences in income by race and ethnicity. In 1993, for example, the per capita yearly income of black workers ($9,860) was approximately 59 percent of white workers' income ($16,800). Contrary to the perceptions of many Americans, black families have lost ground economically to whites over the past quarter century despite affirmative action. In 1969, the median income of black families ($22,000) was 61 percent of white families' median income ($35,920). By 1993, the median income of black families had essentially remained the same ($21,550) while white family income rose to $39,310; black family income had, therefore, declined to 55 percent of white family income. One of the reasons for this decline in black family income is the high percentage of African-American families with only one wage earner. In 1994, 48 percent of black families were maintained by women with no spouse present compared to 13 percent of non-Hispanic white families. But even among black married-couple families with children under the age of eighteen nearly 14 percent were poor in 1993 compared to 8.2 percent of white, married-couple families with children.

Not only are African-American families losing ground but Hispanic families are also suffering economically. Studies indicate that the income of many Hispanic workers is lagging not only because of outmoded skills and lower levels of education, but also because they are increasingly subject to "intense suspicion, resentment and, in many cases, outright discrimination." While the black unemployment rate is traditionally more than double the white unemployment rate and generally significantly higher than Hispanic rates, in recent years the unemployment rate for black and white workers has declined while the rate for Hispanic workers has remained relatively high, particularly relative to that of blacks. In January 1995, the Hispanic unemployment rate jumped briefly to 10.2 percent, equal to the jobless rate of blacks for the first time in two decades. In California, where approximately one-third of the country's Hispanic population live, the Hispanic unemployment rate exceeded that of blacks, 11.2 percent to 11 percent, for the three-month period that included January 1995. Hispanic workers are nearly twice as likely as whites to be unemployed.

Since the November 1994 adoption in California of Proposition 187, the initiative that proposed denying welfare and other government benefits to immigrants who do not possess proper credentials, employers have become increasingly wary of hiring *all* Hispanic workers, whether documented or not. According to Juan Vargas, deputy mayor of San Diego, "There's no doubt that discrimination has increased against Latinos. Proposition 187 has created almost a crisis in the Latino community. It has employers panicked." It is noteworthy that while poverty rates have increased for all groups over the past decade and a half, rates for Hispanics have increased most dramatically from 22.4 percent in 1977 to 30.6 percent in 1993.

In the quotation at the beginning of this chapter, Newt Gingrich states that the American ethic includes the belief that "everyone should work hard." It is clear that millions of Americans are working very hard indeed and yet are still not able to raise themselves and their families out of poverty. Therefore, they, who are surely not "idle," may well need benefits from the "modern welfare system," which Gingrich designates as virtually un-American. Hard work does not assure living above the poverty line. Even adults who are not in the paid labor force may well be working hard. Caring for children, the elderly, or for family members who are ill can be extraordinarily hard work and must be respected as such. By the same token, one must question the phrase "personal responsibility." Is Mr. Gingrich limiting the shouldering of "personal responsibility" to participation in the labor force? Isn't caring for children and other family members shouldering "personal responsibility"? Aren't there a variety of ways of being a responsible human being and don't these ways deserve respect? And what if certain people do not live up to Mr. Gingrich's definition of "shouldering personal responsibility"? Do they not have the right to "participate in American civilization"?

If the United States is truly concerned about poverty and its consequences, we must be aware of the real extent of economic deprivation in this society, the variation among poor Americans, and the often heroic efforts many make to provide for themselves and their families. However, the debate in the mid-1990s has not centered on poverty but on "welfare"—more specifically on Aid to Families with Dependent Children. How have families headed by women been affected by recent economic developments? What about AFDC? Has it helped or harmed recipients? And how has it come to symbolize all that is wrong with present-day America?

Chapter 4

Targeting
Welfare Recipients

Welfare: "the state of faring or doing well: thriving or successful progress in life: a state characterized esp. by good fortune, happiness, well-being, or prosperity . . ."
—*Webster's Third New International Dictionary*
(unabridged)

"I urge my colleagues, open your eyes. Read the small print. They are coming for the children. They are coming for the poor. They are coming for the sick, the elderly, and the disabled."
—REPRESENTATIVE JOHN LEWIS
speech on the floor of the House of Representatives
March 22, 1995

MARIA ALVAREZ IS A THIRTY-ONE-YEAR-OLD MOTHER OF two and an AFDC recipient. The next-to-youngest of four children, Maria grew up in rural Texas. She describes her family:

My family is a success story. My grandfather didn't know how to read or write but he was a success. My father was a skilled worker most of his life and now he owns a restaurant. My parents divorced after twenty-five years of marriage. My mother stayed in an abusive relationship with my father—as so many women do—because of her fear of being alone and her fear that she couldn't support her children.

I had two aunts—my mother's sisters—who were on welfare and they were ostracized from our home because my father felt he was better than they. I didn't tell my family for a long time that I was on welfare.

Maria excelled in school. She got good grades and was a member of the band, the flag corps, and the chess club. Her senior year she met her future husband, started skipping classes, "went totally downhill." She states:

I wanted to have fun; I was looking for my freedom. I finished high school and felt that I had to leave my father. He wouldn't allow me to go out; he wouldn't allow me any freedom. He was a typical dominant Hispanic male.

Maria became pregnant at eighteen, married shortly afterward, and had her first child, a daughter, at age nineteen. She describes her husband as older than she (he was twenty-five at the time), and literally from "the wrong side of the tracks." Her father was totally opposed to the relationship and, she says, "he was right." Within the first year she and her husband were separated three times. Maria describes him as alcoholic and abusive:

He beat me up badly. My father came to the rescue and gave me money to get a divorce but I reconciled with my husband instead. My father was so angry he disowned me. I wasn't allowed to be anywhere near the house for a long time.

Maria moved to Houston with a girlfriend, leaving her daughter with her family. She got a job and went home on weekends. When she was twenty-one, she moved to New York City. She felt Houston wasn't far enough from her family, that she was still within their orbit. She wanted to get "as far away as possible." Also, she says she "fell in love" with the motto "If you can make it there [New York], you can make it anywhere"; she wanted to make it in New York.

Over the next few years she had a series of "bad relationships," started drinking and taking drugs. She feels she was acting on the basis of "Fire, Ready, Aim," acting first and thinking later. She found herself dependent on unreliable men who used and abused her and sometimes deserted her. Although she was working at Macy's at the time, she nearly became homeless and was saved from wandering the streets only by the intervention of an acquaintance who eventually demanded she sleep with him in return for a roof over her head.

Over the next few few years she had been in a close relationship with a man who is the father of her three-year-old son. Though she was never divorced from her husband, she and this man considered themselves married, "linked together," as she put it. They prayed for a child, a son, and were so happy when he was born. The child's father is a master craftsman, a carpenter, and Maria and he would sometimes work together making "really good money," but he has a drug problem. He can be "clean" for three to six months, but he is a "habitual relapser" and periodically goes back to using. And, as Maria points out, "It gets harder and harder to get into detox [programs]."

Maria and her partner have recently separated. When he went back to using, it was "total insanity." She would "lose total control" and his using was "putting me in danger, putting my own sobriety in danger."

Currently, Maria is a sophomore at a City University of New York college. She goes to school full-time, cares for her children, and is a welfare rights activist. She hopes to complete her education and acquire the skills necessary to help others who have economic, legal, and personal problems.

Maria is not a statistic. She is not a stereotypic, cardboard figure. She is a poor woman, a recipient of AFDC who has had many problems in her thirty-one years and is fighting to overcome them. She is a caring mother, a hardworking student, and she hopes to make a difference for others who find themselves in similar situations. As she would be the first to state, she has made some unwise decisions, has been hurt by abusive men, has endured poverty, and has been a victim of drugs and alcohol. She has also worked hard to support herself and her children, she excels academically, speaks out on behalf of poor women, and hopes one day to be in a position to help them professionally. She is one of the many faces of poverty; she is one of the many faces of the welfare system.

Before discussing in depth the massive assault on Aid to Families with Dependent Children, it is important to state at the outset that AFDC is a deeply flawed, often miserly and humiliating program that has frequently done little to help poor women and their children move from abject poverty to a decent life. It has, nonetheless, saved millions of families from hunger, homelessness, physical assault, and total despair. AFDC has frequently been racist and sexist; it has treated vulnerable and needy women as though they are worthless and contemptible, but it has also helped to pay the rent and put food on poor families' tables, although, often, unfortunately, providing such meager benefits that recipients could not simultaneously feed their families and pay their rent. It has enabled women who were battered and abused to have choices other than remain in the same dwelling with the batterer, and it has occasionally assisted recipients in acquiring some much-needed education, referred others to caring social service workers, and demonstrated in myriad other ways that there was someone out there who cared. This is the system that is being fundamentally decimated. It is a system that many of us have criticized. We have documented its weaknesses, its shortcomings, its frequent denigration of the very people it was established to serve. But AFDC has, over the past sixty years, made up a slender thread of the extraordinarily thin and frayed safety net that is commonly referred to as the social welfare system. AFDC was there for millions of desperate women when there was nothing else—no hope, no other place to go, no other way to care for their children. And now it is about to be dismantled.

The recent attack on Aid to Families with Dependent Children has been so massive, so widespread, so devoid of nuance, compassion, and understanding of the real facts, that we must ask why. Why is "welfare," specifically AFDC, the target of such massive cuts, of such a relentless campaign of vilification? Why is a program that amounts to only 1 percent of the federal budget targeted in this way? Why not target tax write-offs to real estate developers? Why not target subsidies to tobacco growers? Why not target tax benefits to the "truly rich"?

Aid for the poor, particularly poor women and children, has been problematic since colonial times. Historically, the poor have been divided into those considered "worthy" and those considered "unworthy"—unworthy of aid, of respect, of their social rights as citizens. What we now colloquially refer to as "welfare" was originally established by the Social Security Act of 1935. According to Linda Gordon, author of *Pitied But Not Entitled: Single Mothers and the History of Welfare*, a two-tier "safety net" was put into place; it was a stratified system in which "the social insurance programs were superior both in payments and in reputation, while public assistance was inferior—not just comparatively second-rate but deeply stigmatized." The higher tier consisting of programs such as unemployment insurance, workers' compensation, and Old-Age Insurance, today called Social Security, are "rights- and earnings- or contribution-based;" they are federal, they disproportionately benefit whites and men, and respect the recipients' right to privacy. The lower tier, which today includes AFDC and Home Relief, is needs-based, administered at the state or local level, disproportionately serves minority groups and women, and has always reserved the right to intrude on the recipients' private life. Originally, AFDC (which was adopted in 1935 as Aid to Dependent Children and did not even include a caretaker grant until 1950) was derived from mothers' aid programs developed during the early 1900s. These programs, which were adopted by the vast majority of states, authorized aid to "deserving" poor single mothers with children. The goals included defraying the costs of raising children in their own homes, deterring child labor, and preventing the institutionalization of fatherless children. By the second decade of the twentieth century, reformers, many of whom were women, focused on the needs of widows and in doing so, "implicitly conceded that other categories of single mothers were guilty of something. . . ." Yet, "mothers' aid was never meant to be open-armed or trusting toward those it helped. To the contrary, mothers' aid functioned—and was intended—to superintend and discipline as well as support its recipients."

As Gordon clearly points out,

Not only did mothers' aid shape the welfare state, but the debate about it introduced the themes and questions that still dominate welfare policy discussions today. These include concerns about how to help single mothers without encouraging single motherhood and about the proper role of women, as well as the most fundamental questions about what entitles a person to help. Who is deserving? Who should be required to work for wages? What if wages are too low? Does the state have an obligation to police the behavior of those who receive public funds? What is an entitlement, and what is charity? Today's welfare debates began here.

Historically, a relatively small percentage of needy single mothers and their children received aid. The relief given was so meager that the families needed additional resources to survive and aid was seen as a temporary measure until mothers could play their rightful role of caregiving within a family unit in which the male was the central breadwinner.

Today many of the same issues are central in the assault on welfare recipients but before we deal with these issues let us examine the facts about current AFDC recipients.

- In 1993, a monthly average of 5 million families received Aid to Families with Dependent Children. The average family size was 2.9 persons, typically a mother and two children, and over two-thirds of the recipients (9.2 million) were children. AFDC recipients comprised 5.6 percent of the total U.S. population.
- Nearly 39 percent (38.9 percent) of the recipients were white; 37.2 percent were black; and 17.8 percent were Hispanic.
- The average monthly benefit in 1993 was $377, a yearly income of $4,524.
- Benefits in the forty-eight contiguous states in 1994 ranged from a low of $120 per month (a yearly benefit of $1,440) in Mississippi to a high of $680 per month ($8,160 yearly) in

New York State. Alaska provided $923 per month ($11,076 yearly) but this relatively high benefit is due to the extraordinarily high cost of living in the state.

•In all fifty states, AFDC benefits are well below the poverty line, ranging from Mississippi where benefits are an incredibly low 13 percent of the poverty line to Alaska where they amount to 79 percent.

Contrary to the widespread impression in the country, AFDC benefits have *declined* 42 percent in real terms in the last two decades. In 1972, the average monthly benefit in constant 1992 dollars for a mother and two children with no earnings was $690; in 1992, the average benefit was $399. This decline has been partly offset by an increase in food stamps, so that the combination of AFDC and food stamps for the same family, a mother and two children with no earnings, has fallen 26 percent in real terms between 1972 and 1992.

While benefits have declined sharply, the number of persons receiving AFDC increased significantly between 1975 and 1992. In 1975, 11.1 million individuals received benefits; in 1992, there were 13.6 million recipients. Between the recession years of 1991 and 1992, one million additional individuals became AFDC recipients. But this increase is not uniform across the country. While rates in some states increased considerably, rates in twenty-two states declined over the same time period. Furthermore, between 1975 and 1992 the average size of families receiving AFDC fell from 3.2 persons to 2.9.

Again, contrary to public perception, real expenditures for AFDC have remained relatively constant over the past two decades. In 1975, total federal and state spending on AFDC amounted to $21.3 billion in 1992 dollars; in 1992, that amount was $22.2 billion. Furthermore, the percent of federal spending allocated to AFDC declined from 1.5 percent in 1975 to 1.1 percent in 1992.

Another fact must be stressed. Only 60 percent of all poor children are actually receiving AFDC. This means that at least another 6 million children are living in absolute poverty but are not receiving benefits. The reasons the majority of children are not receiving benefits include states' efforts to discourage applications, techniques designed to minimize the number of recipients that range from humiliation to summarily expunging poor people from the rolls, the lack of awareness of the poor about their right to assistance, their reluctance to be stigmatized by becoming recipients, and complex combinations of these and other factors. Whatever the reasons, millions of needy women and children are struggling to pay their rent, eat, and live a bare-bones existence without help from AFDC.

One issue that has fueled controversy about the nature of the current welfare system has been the question of how long recipients continue to receive AFDC benefits. Perhaps the single most important fact about the welfare population is that it is heterogeneous. One stereotypical image cannot adequately or accurately capture the characteristics of the five million heads-of-household involved.

According to Mary Jo Bane and David Ellwood, authors of *Welfare Realities: From Rhetoric to Reform* and currently members of the Clinton Administration dealing directly with welfare policy, "For most, welfare is a short-term transitional program." Bane and Ellwood continue by differentiating between a "spell" on welfare (each episode of time an individual receives AFDC benefits) and the total time individuals spend (adding up all the "spells"). They then provide the following analysis:

For most, welfare is a short-term transitional program. But for a smaller number, spells can be quite long. And these long-termers represent a very large portion of the recipients at any one time. Because long-term recipients are a large portion of the caseload, they receive a roughly equivalently large portion of the dollars we spend on welfare.

The AFDC population is made up, as Bane and Ellwood point out, of "short-termers," "long-termers," and "cyclers." The "long-termers," who have been the recipients of the greatest hostility from conservative politicians and policy makers, are often themselves "a heterogeneous and often relatively dynamic group," and are frequently, in reality, cyclers. Who are the "long-termers"? Five groups seem to be at greatest risk of long durations on AFDC: women who begin receiving welfare as teenagers; high school dropouts; women with no recent work experience; never-married mothers; and African Americans. Clearly, many of these characteristics are interconnected and those women who share several of these characteristics are at even greater risk of chronic poverty and long-term need for support. For example, many young women who become mothers as teenagers drop out of high school and thus are unlikely to obtain work experience.

While the emphasis on "long-termers" feeds the image of all welfare recipients as members of the underclass, it is important to stress that the majority of recipients leave AFDC either because of increased earnings or marriage. Bane and Ellwood emphasize that "education and previous work experience are very powerful predictors of exiting [AFDC] with moderate earnings."

A key false assumption, therefore, in the current effort to "end welfare as we know it" is that AFDC recipients are "lazy," "dependent," "passive," and resist working in the paid labor force. Virtually all studies indicate that AFDC mothers have "many faces." A study done by the Institute for Women's Policy Research (IWPR) based on a nationally representative sample of single welfare mothers generated from a U.S. Bureau of the Census Survey of Income and Program Participation, found that AFDC recipients fall into three groups, each of which have identifiable work patterns: the "combiners," the "cyclers," and the "more welfare-reliant." The combiners simultaneously work and receive welfare for at least four months and work more than 600 hours in a two-year period; the cyclers alternate between paid work and welfare benefits, do not receive money from both sources simultaneously for more than three out of twenty-four months, work more than 600 hours and receive at least two months of AFDC benefits; and the more welfare-reliant work at a paid job fewer than 600 hours during a two-year period and receive at least 16 months of AFDC benefits. In fact, four out of ten recipients worked at paid jobs either by combining work and welfare or by cycling between work and welfare.

Even among the more welfare-reliant mothers the IWPR study found that 23.4 percent are looking for work, 7.4 percent are both looking for work and working limited hours, 6.6 percent are disabled, and only 19.7 percent are not in the labor force at all. Among this last category, some are in school, others caring for a child under the age of two, and the largest group is caring for preschool children between the ages of two and five.

If we examine the characteristics of women who comprise the three groups, we find that all three types of AFDC recipients have similar marital histories, are the same average age, have similar welfare histories, and are almost equally likely to be women of color. The central differences among the groups are level of education and previous work experience. The cyclers are most likely to have a high school diploma (71 percent) and have the most previous work experience (an average of 6.5 years). Fewer of the combiners (63 percent) have a high school diploma and they have somewhat less work experience (6.0 years). Those who are more welfare-reliant are least likely to have a high school diploma (only 43 percent) and have the least work experience (three years). Having completed high school is clearly key in income-packaging (combining work and welfare benefits), and in living above the poverty line.

Those AFDC recipients who are engaged in paid labor are likely to work in the lowest-wage, female-dominated occupations and earn an average of $4.29 an hour. Their employers pay for health insurance only one-third of the time. The most common jobs are maids, waitresses, nursing aides, and child-care workers.

A central conclusion from this study is that those welfare recipients who combine AFDC and work or, even better, AFDC, work, and income from family members are more likely to escape poverty and that AFDC alone or work alone in traditionally female occupations will not lift recipients and their families out of poverty. A high school diploma and health insurance, whether through employment or through a national health care system, are essential for these families to remain off welfare and out of poverty.

It seems clear that the way to truly help women and their children out of poverty is to encourage girls and women to stay in school as long as possible—at the very least, to complete high school and preferably to go beyond high school to vocational training or college—and to raise the minimum wage, particularly the extremely low wages in female-dominated occupations. Two additional elements are essential for women and children to climb out of poverty—adequate, accessible child care for preschool children and after-school care for school-aged children, and health insurance. Without these four components—education, higher wages, child care, and health coverage—millions of women and children will remain locked in poverty.

With these considerations in mind, let us examine recent welfare legislation at both the state and federal levels. Efforts to modify AFDC (and Home Relief, the program for needy adults without children, as well) have been ongoing at both levels for several years but have speeded up significantly since the early 1990s. During the period from January 1993, when the Clinton Administration took power, through August 1995, the Secretary of Health and Human Services waived federal AFDC requirements to permit thirty-two states to implement "demonstration projects." The Department of Health and Human Services (HHS) has for many years approved such demonstration projects without clearly defining the policies and standards that led to their approval. While HHS announced a set of policies applicable to these waivers in September 1994, they are still so general that many observers have criticized the process as leaving the agency free to "invent the rules anew with each project submission, approve virtually anything, and evade public accountability for its actions."

According to Mark Greenberg, a lawyer at the Center for Law and Social Policy, an advocacy group based in Washington, "The waiver policy is being used to undercut basic safeguards of federal law, and this has contributed to the current environment in which states want no federal standards whatsoever." More than thirty states have received permission from the federal government to relax the rule that requires welfare recipients to lose $1 in benefits for every $1 earned after four months of employment. Approximately twenty states have received permission to expand Medicaid and child care for women who lose their benefits because they have found employment. Twenty-five states now require teenage mothers to live at home with parents or other responsible adults and many pay cash bonuses to recipients who stay in school.

A central theme in state applications for waivers has been the imposition of time limits on AFDC benefits. At least seventeen states have been permitted to impose such time limits. In addition, many of the applications have included requirements for stricter work obligations, generally without provisions to increase the availability of paid employment. Two of the applications included what is known as a "drop dead" time limit, an absolute limit on the provision of aid without regard to whether the family has paid employment or any other form of income.

Several states received waivers that tie aid to the recipients' behavior. Some waivers permit work requirements unrelated to time limits; other states, including New Jersey, received approval to deny aid for any child conceived while the mother was receiving AFDC; some have received approval to reduce aid if the children are not properly immunized; others were permitted to tie AFDC benefits to school attendance or performance; and still others reward marriage by increasing assistance to households with two parents.

These waivers have frequently been justified as a way of letting a "hundred flowers bloom"; in other words, permitting states to try different approaches in order to see which ones are effective. In a speech in February 1993 to the National Governors' Association, President Clinton stated that his administration planned to give states "more elbow room to experiment." The concept of "experimentation" has frequently been used by the Clinton Administration to justify waivers that permit changes in the provision of welfare benefits that clearly subvert the letter and the spirit of current AFDC law and practice.

The "experiments" being permitted by these waivers also involve the health of human beings. Refusing to provide additional benefits to a newborn infant is likely to affect that child's health and perhaps the health of the child's parents and siblings as well. If the newborn doesn't have enough to eat, if other children go hungry so that the infant can eat, this experiment has had a direct effect on their health and well-being. When states establish time limits for families receiving benefits or systematically exclude one group such as teenage mothers from aid, they surely are affecting the health and well-being of these individuals. Without welfare benefits, many may become homeless, others will go hungry.

Are these waivers truly for the purpose of experimenting with different approaches to AFDC or are they in reality a way of "ending welfare as we know it," without federal legislation? Or are they fundamentally a way of pandering to an electorate that is increasingly hostile to social programs for poor people, a way of proving that the Clinton Administration and the leaders at the state level are "tough on welfare"? If the real rationale is political subterfuge, are these waivers appropriate at all?

Mary Jo Bane, an assistant secretary of health and human services who "presides over the waiver proposals," has essentially acknowledged the political aspect of the granting of waivers: "We try to focus completely on the policy, but we are not unaware of the political consequences. It's a balancing act, but I'm quite confident that we've achieved a good balance." Making clear the Clinton Administration's sympathy with the states' desire to assume greater authority in providing AFDC benefits and their current efforts to limit the number of welfare recipients and the amount of their benefits, Bane stated, "We are not in the business of turning down waiver requests. We are in the business of helping states do what they want to do."

Mark Greenberg suggests that these so-called experiments are really ways of dismantling AFDC state by state: "It has become a backdoor way of a state to enact any policy it wants, regardless of the potential harm to families."

On October 1, 1992, the Family Development Program took effect in New Jersey. While this law had several components, the best known is the child exclusion law, also known as the "family cap" law. This section of the program stipulated that an AFDC family who has an additional child will not receive any cash assistance for that child if he or she is born more than ten months after the mother's application for AFDC. In other words, any child conceived after the mother has applied for AFDC will not be given cash assistance. There are no exceptions for cases of documented rape, incest, or contraceptive failure. Although the infant's eligibility for Medicaid and food stamps is not affected, the monetary loss is significant since the increase to the monthly AFDC grant would be between $64 and $102, depending on the size of the family.

Clearly, the goal of the New Jersey law is to limit the child-bearing of mothers receiving Aid to Families with Dependent Children. Leaving aside for the moment the question of the appropriateness of state intervention in intimate decisions around procreation, has the policy worked? Then-Governor Jim Florio asserted during the first two months of the law, August and September 1993, that births to welfare families had decreased by a monthly average of 16 percent from the same

two months one year earlier. The governor and the bill's spon-
sor, Assemblyman Wayne Bryant, announced that the Family
Development Program was an "obvious" success. The law has
since served as a model for similar policies in several other states
as well as for the bill passed by the House of Representatives.
Subsequent research indicates, however, that the law may not
have significantly affected AFDC recipients' reproductive
choices.

In the first year that the family cap was put in place, New
Jersey denied benefits to 6,267 children born to AFDC recipients. Did denial of benefits to these children prevent the births
of others? Is it legitimate social policy to punish thousands of
infants and children in order to discourage reproduction? Is it
legitimate social policy to discourage childbearing? Many criticize sex education in the schools because it means government
interference in people's personal lives. Isn't the family cap an
even greater governmental interference in the personal lives of
individuals and families? In addition, the family cap clearly may
lead to additional abortions. Since payments for abortions are
denied under Medicaid, what is the message to poor women?
Is the message that they should not be having sex at all or if
they do and become pregnant, they might have to resort to
solutions similar to those utilized by millions of women before
abortion was legalized—self-induced abortions?

One welfare recipient, a twenty-six-year-old woman who
has worked as a typist at Macy's and has been trained as a chef,
says the cost of child care is her major barrier to working. She
had her fourth child while receiving AFDC and spoke about
New Jersey's family cap:

They're telling us we can't have children, and I don't think
that's right. It wasn't planned, but I wasn't going to abort her.

Sixty-four dollars is not going to change my love for my child, and if I would have aborted her, it wouldn't have comforted my soul.

Another New Jersey mother of two felt that welfare workers had tried to pressure her to terminate her pregnancy: "They were telling me, 'Do you think you need to have another child?' They treat you like they own you. But you can't buy my kids. If I have to start stripping, that's what I'll do."

On November 1, 1993, Wisconsin obtained federal approval for its Work Not Welfare waiver proposal. The program, which went into effect in January 1995, and is being implemented in two pilot counties, contains the following features:

- A family seeking aid will embark on a four-year "benefit period."
- During the "benefit period," the family may be eligible for a total of up to twenty-four months of assistance. No more than twelve of the twenty-four months can be earned by participation in education and training; the remainder can be earned through work. The required hours of work will be determined by dividing the grant by the minimum wage; the total number of hours cannot exceed forty per week.
- Exemptions are limited—those entering the system while pregnant or with a baby under one year. If the mother has a subsequent baby, a six-month leave from participation in required activities will be permitted but the months will still count against the twenty-four-month limit.
- The subsequent child will not be covered by additional assistance.
- After a family has received twenty-four months of benefits,

they will be ineligible for cash assistance for three years unless they qualify for an exception.

While the Republican governor of Wisconsin, Tommy Thompson, and many others have touted the Wisconsin plan as a model for welfare "reform," the legislation has numerous severe deficiencies. First, Work Not Welfare offers no assurance of needed education and training services and, in fact, restricts individuals' access to such education and training. For example, how can a young woman who left high school before receiving her diploma finish her secondary school education and obtain appropriate skills to make a living for herself and her children in only twelve months? This limitation is a guarantee of failure. The only jobs available to many recipients will be low-wage, marginal employment that does not offer health benefits and is certain to keep the family well below the poverty line. These families may be off the welfare rolls, and the governor of Wisconsin may therefore proclaim this "experiment" a success, but these mothers and children will still in all likelihood be mired in poverty. Moreover, the plan disregards the fact that many families, because of low-wage jobs, lack of services, and fluctuating personal situations, need continued access to a safety net. Prohibiting them from receiving AFDC benefits for three years can, and I believe will, mean that many families in these two counties will suffer needlessly. It is clear that the Wisconsin plan does not in reality aim to help welfare recipients and their children out of poverty but rather is simply intended to reduce the numbers on the welfare rolls.

Michigan has also established a complex program that requires most welfare recipients to look for work and that establishes severe sanctions for those who do not cooperate. While individuals receive financial incentives for working, the vast majority are locked in low-wage jobs that keep them significantly below the poverty line.

In October 1995, Michigan's Governor John Engler proposed changes to this three-year-old program that would include insisting that women who receive benefits be working within six weeks of having a child or lose their benefits, that new welfare recipients who do not obtain jobs, either paid or unpaid, are likely to become ineligible in two months, and that recipients would be docked 10 percent of their benefits to reimburse landlords for damage to housing. These new regulations were proposed in anticipation of the passage of legislation transferring control of AFDC to the states. As Gerald H. Miller, director of the Michigan Department of Social Services, stated, "We want to be ready to go as soon as the legislation is passed in Washington. We want to be the first state. We want to be the model for the rest of the nation." But according to Sharon Parks, senior research associate at the Michigan League for Human Services, a research and advisory organization based in Lansing, the state capital, "From our standpoint, the speed with which they are moving is just appalling."

New restrictive regulations adopted by many states with the goal of reducing the welfare rolls and welfare costs in the cities often have unintended consequences in rural areas. The New York State legislature, for example, instituted regulations in 1995 that require able-bodied adult recipients to prove that they have contacted five employers each week while looking for work with no repeat employers in a month. This might not be so difficult for city dwellers who can simply walk down an urban block and find store after store, but for people who live in rural communities the rule could prove to be essentially impossible. According to the director of social services in Allegheny County near the Pennsylvania border, "That's an onerous requirement for some of our folks, because of a lack of job openings and the lack of means to travel." New York State's new rules also impose harsh penalties on welfare recipients who miss even one day of their public work, known as workfare. One unexcused absence can lead to a ninety-day suspension of benefits; four unexcused absences can cause expulsion from welfare entirely.

One welfare recipient, Sharon DeBargew, commented on the new regulations: "It stinks. What are us people in rural areas supposed to do, if you don't have a license, or you don't have a vehicle? The way I see it, the people who make the rules don't care. They have cars, they have jobs. They don't know what our situation is like."

In Allegheny County, for example, there is no public bus system, and most welfare recipients do not have and cannot afford to own cars. Finding five new potential employers can often be extremely difficult. One recipient, Susan Lewis, was forced to file and refile job applications along her town's four-block main street because these were the only businesses she could reach on foot. She described her predicament: "You get embarrassed because you're letting people know you're still not working, week after week."

While poverty is seen as largely an urban problem, a recent study commissioned by the New York State Senate found that rural areas have experienced a continuing decline in manufacturing jobs and are now left primarily with service jobs that are unlikely to provide health insurance or other benefits. These areas are now often characterized by lower per-capita income, higher rates of unemployment, and faster growth in the number of families living in poverty than many urban areas. Allegheny County, often thought to be far removed from the problems of New York City, has the third lowest per-capita income in the state and the fifth highest percentage of families living in poverty. Many recipients feel that legislators, in their zeal to control welfare in urban areas, have overlooked the impact of new legislation on the people who live in small towns in rural areas. As Susan Lewis says, "These nice little towns like Wellsville will see a lot of changes. You'll start seeing things here that you only expect to see in New York City."

Perhaps it is the Personal Responsibility Act that was a key component of the Republicans' Contract with America that most epitomizes this country's war on the poor. On March 24, 1995, the House of Representatives adopted legislation that would, in the words of *New York Times* reporter and social policy analyst Robert Pear, "undo six decades of social welfare policy. . . ." The central feature of the legislation is the replacement of AFDC by block grants totaling $15.4 billion a year. The states would be permitted to set their own eligibility criteria and benefit levels. People currently entitled to AFDC would not necessarily be entitled to assistance under block grants.

Other provisions of this legislation include the following:

- Federal money could not be used to provide cash assistance to unmarried women under the age of eighteen or to children born to mothers who are already receiving assistance;
- Adults would be expected to work after receiving aid for two years; and
- No family could receive cash assistance for more than five years.

Additional provisions include several restricting the highly successful and necessary food assistance programs such as food stamps, WIC, and the school breakfast and lunch programs.

Cash assistance, food stamps, Medicaid, Supplemental Security Income, and certain social services would be denied to people who are not U.S. citizens even though they are in the United States legally; alcoholism and drug addiction would no longer be classified as disabilities and alcoholics and addicts consequently would in general be denied cash benefits under SSI; and cash benefits would be ended for more than 360,000 children previously found to have physical or mental disabilities.

On September 19, 1995, the U.S. Senate also approved a bill fundamentally restructuring federal antipoverty policy and ending the government's six-decade policy guaranteeing assistance to families in need. Passing by a vote of 87 to 12, with only 11 Democrats in opposition, the bill included provisions that would put a five-year lifetime limit on welfare benefits, require 50 percent of recipients to be working by the year 2000, and place an array of federal antipoverty programs in the hands of the states. The Senate bill did not include the "family cap" provision denying additional benefits to women who bear children while on the welfare rolls that was part of the House bill. It also eliminated the provision refusing cash benefits to teenagers who have babies out of wedlock. During the debate on the Senate bill, Senator Edward M. Kennedy, Democrat of Massachusetts, stated, "After more than sixty years of maintaining a good-faith national commitment to protect all needy children, the Senate is on the brink of committing legislative child abuse."

Prior to passage of the Senate measure, a study of the impact of the bill by the Department of Health and Human Services found that the provisions, if signed into law, would push an additional 1.1 million children into poverty, increasing by almost 11 percent the number of children living below the poverty line. The study also found that the poorest fifth of the nation's families with children would face the largest cuts—an average of almost $800, or 6 percent of their total income. The report, dated September 14, 1995, was suppressed by the White House but leaked by an opponent of the legislation. The day after the report was discussed at a White House meeting, President Clinton indicated strong support for the measure. Senator Daniel Patrick Moynihan accused the White House of deliberately suppressing the study and stated, "Those involved will take this disgrace to their graves." Later he described the welfare legislation as "an obscene act of social regression" that "visits upon children the wrath of an electorate disillusioned with government and lost to principle."

As the U.S. House and Senate Conference Committee was working to iron out the differences between the two bills, Marian Wright Edelman, president of the Children's Defense Fund, described the welfare legislation as "an unbelievable budget massacre of the weakest." In an open letter to President Clinton she wrote:

We do not want to codify a policy of child abandonment. Franklin Delano Roosevelt correctly stated: "Better the occasional faults of a government that lives in a spirit of charity than the constant omissions of a government frozen in the ice of its own indifference."

The final legislation that emerged from the House and Senate Conference Committee and was adopted by the House of Representatives on December 21, 1995, and by the Senate on December 23, 1995, ended the federal guarantee of cash assistance to millions of poor children. Noting the timing of the vote, Senator Paul Simon, Democrat of Illinois, stated, "We in the United States Congress are going to celebrate Christmas by trashing poor people. What a record!"

Under the final bill, each state would receive a block grant to provide cash assistance to poor people and would have much more discretion than they have had over the past sixty years in setting eligibility standards and benefit levels. The bill would prohibit states from using federal money to increase benefits for women who have additional children while on welfare, but states could override this provision. The legislation would set a time limit of five years for cash assistance, but states could set stricter time limits if they wished. In addition, most adult recipients would be required to work after two years of benefits.

The legislation would also provide cash benefits to states that reduce births by unmarried women. It would sharply curtail federal benefits for immigrants who had not become citizens, would reduce the annual cost-of-living adjustment in food stamps, and would reduce or terminate cash payments for hundreds of thousands of children with disabilities. Commenting on the final bill, Senator Frank Lautenberg, Democrat of New Jersey, stated, "This piece of legislation represents the worst of Speaker Gingrich's agenda. It rips at the safety net, tears it to shreds."

On January 9, 1996, President Clinton vetoed this Draconian legislation, stating that it did "too little to move people from welfare to work" and that its cuts "would fall hardest on children."

Giving this much power and discretion to the states over aid to poor women and children has potentially far-reaching consequences. Many states have a long history of punitive policies toward the poor. States' use of relief policy to maintain a stable group of low-income workers who would have little choice but to accept the low wages and often intolerable working

conditions of local economic interests has been well documented. Frances Fox Piven and Richard A. Cloward have
demonstrated this meshing of welfare policies and local economic needs in their landmark work, *Regulating the Poor: The
Functions of Public Welfare.* As they state,

> . . . the structure of the American public welfare system meshes
> with and reinforces the work system, not least by excluding
> potential workers from aid. The "fit" of the welfare system in
> a stable but diverse economy is assured by varying the pattern
> of exclusion in accord with regional differences in labor re-
> quirements. Furthermore, harsh relief practices also maintain
> work norms by evoking the image of the shamed pauper for
> all, especially the able-bodied poor, to see and to shun. And
> so it is that if the justifications given for welfare restrictions
> are usually moral, the functions these restrictions serve are typ-
> ically economic. Those who exploit the cheap labor guaran-
> teed by these practices can take comfort not only in their
> godliness but in their profits as well.

Piven and Cloward also point out the frequently racist aspects of states' policies toward the poor. Decisions about who
are permitted on the relief rolls, how they are treated, and the
significant differences in amount of relief payments that are
based on the racial background of the majority of recipients
and the region of the country are well known. They report
that "Southern states especially have engaged in periodic campaigns to purge mothers and children from the rolls because of
'unsuitable homes' "; the vast majority of these "purged" families have been black.

We seem to be entering into yet another period of "states'
rights," a time in which the states will have the power to de-

termine who should receive aid, for how long, and under what conditions. During an earlier period in American history, "states' rights" was a euphemism for blatantly racist policies. Without federal regulations to hold them in check, are states once again embarking on policies that will favor local economic interests at the expense of the poor? With the current waiver system and with block grants in the offing, will states be free to discriminate at will against African Americans, Mexican Americans, never-married mothers, or whatever group is the target of hostility and denigration in their state? Are we opening the floodgates to overt discrimination against the poorest and most vulnerable in our society while claiming that these Draconian policies are "for their own good"?

Less than two weeks after cutting welfare and food assistance for the poor the House of Representatives approved a Republican plan of tax cuts that were, according to *The New York Times*, "the heftiest collection of tax breaks in 14 years" since the tax cuts in 1981, President Ronald Reagan's first year in office. The plan would reduce revenues by $189 billion over four years. In addition to a $500-a-child credit to families earning $200,000 or less, billions in tax breaks would go to corporations, investors, and retirees. Representative Joseph Moakley, Democrat of Massachusetts, summed up the Democratic denunciation of the bill when he declared that Republicans had "gutted school lunches, home heating assistance, and student loans. And for what reason? To pay for tax cuts for rich Americans. From the mouths of babes to the pockets of millionaires."

A fundamental requirement of the new welfare programs both at the state and federal levels, if these programs are to have any chance of success, is that the labor market include jobs for individuals with little education and training and that these jobs pay wages on which a family can live. The reality is that most welfare recipients, if they can find any employment, will have to take jobs such as "taking orders in restaurants, giving meals and baths to the old and the infirm, cleaning hotel rooms and offices, washing cars and pumping gas, running sewing machines, picking fruits and vegetables and patrolling as security guards." Many of these jobs pay little more than the minimum wage, $4.25 an hour (a yearly income of just over $8,000), well below the poverty line for a family of three. According to the U.S. Department of Labor, the lowest-paid 10 percent of full-time workers earn an average of $225 a week (approximately $10,800 a year), also below the poverty line for a family of three. And this is the average income for *full-time* workers. Most low-paid jobs are part-time or temporary. It is estimated that approximately 17 percent of the labor force works less than thirty hours a week. According to an economist at the Urban Institute, "It's very hard to find full-time permanent employment. Nobody hires that way anymore." And, again, many of these low-wage jobs, both full-time and part-time, do not include health benefits.

According to Katherine Newman, an anthropologist at Columbia University who has written extensively on downward mobility and has conducted a recent study on the low-wage labor market in Harlem, there are fourteen people competing for every new $4.25-an-hour fast-food restaurant job. Moreover, after looking for a year, 73 percent of them still don't have jobs. Newman states, "It's hopelessly unrealistic to expect that these welfare recipients will be absorbed into the low-wage labor market in these places where they live and would try to find work. . . . The market is already glutted with people who are better qualified than most welfare recipients."

Clearly the governors and legislators who are clamoring for

time limits for welfare recipients, insisting they take a job—any job so long as they are off the welfare rolls—know these data. They must be aware that they are consigning millions of people to lives well below the poverty line with little opportunity for advancement, little chance for a better life. In reality, the current wave of legislation is a way of punishing the poor for being poor, punishing mothers who are single—whether through separation, divorce, death, or having children outside of marriage—for being single, and punishing all those people who make us question the plausibility of the American Dream.

One of the great errors in equating "welfare" with assistance to the poor is that many other groups in the United States receive aid from the federal, state, or local government. Secretary of Labor Robert Reich has suggested that "federal aid to dependent corporations" is a major contributor to the federal budget crisis. The Cato Institute, a conservative, Washington-based think-tank, concurs and has analyzed what it terms "corporate welfare" in the United States. The Cato Institute report entitled "Ending Corporate Welfare As We Know It" states that the U.S. Congress funds more than 125 programs that subsidize private businesses and that these subsidies cost federal taxpayers approximately $85 billion a year. The institute claims that "every major cabinet department, including the Defense Department, has become a conduit for government funding of private industry." The following are some of the examples the Cato Institute documents:

- The Pentagon provides nearly $100 million a year to support the computer microchip industry;
- $1.4 billion is spent supporting the price of sugar with the thirty-three largest sugar farms each receiving more than $1 million;

- In 1994, the Forest Service spent $140 million building roads in national forests primarily for the benefit of logging companies;

- The U.S. Department of Agriculture spends $110 million a year supporting the cost of advertising American products abroad; in 1991 "American taxpayers spent $2.9 million advertising Pillsbury muffins and pies, $10 million promoting Sunkist oranges, $465,000 advertising McDonald's Chicken McNuggets, $1.2 million boosting the international sales of American Legend mink coats, and $2.5 million extolling the virtues of Dole pineapples, nuts, and prunes;" and

- In 1994, a House of Representatives investigation found that federal defense contractors were charging the Pentagon for millions of dollars in entertainment and recreation. Martin Marietta, for example, charged the Pentagon $263,000 for a Smokey Robinson concert, $20,000 for golf balls, and $7,500 for a 1993 office Christmas party.

According to Congress's Joint Committee on Taxation, corporate tax breaks in the 1995 fiscal year might reach 60 billion; Ralph Nader's group, Public Citizen, estimates corporate welfare as more than $167 billion. Conservative columnist Kevin Phillips claims that tax breaks to the wealthy and to corporations have "become the third-fastest-growing part of the federal budget" and will exceed $4 trillion over the next seven years." As Michael Wines of *The New York Times* states, ". . . the same Congress that believes welfare saps the spirit and dulls the will of people seems to have concluded that business cannot compete without it."

In 1994, for example, the U.S. Government paid farmers approximately $10 billion in grants. This subsidy does not only help the farmers; it helps all Americans by keeping the cost of food low. Americans spend an average of 12 percent of their budget on food, among the lowest in the world; thus, all Americans are receiving a form of welfare in the subsidizing of their food budget.

There are, of course, many other examples of "welfare" for the middle class and the affluent—a wide array of personal and professional tax deductions, veterans' benefits, Medicare, Unemployment Insurance, Workers' Compensation, and educational scholarships and loans, just to name a few. In a "conversation" among Mario Cuomo, former governor of New York; Ann Richards, former governor of Texas; and Lowell Weicker, three-term senator and then governor of Connecticut, the talk turned to middle-class "welfare." Lowell Weicker stated,

> What about everything that the middle class gets? What was the biggest part of our budget in the state of Connecticut? It was Medicaid driven by nursing homes for middle-income Connecticut, putting Mom and Dad at the poverty level just to get them in a nursing home—10 percent of the budget of Connecticut. You call that welfare? I think so.

Mario Cuomo responded by recounting speeches he made to middle-class residents of Long Island:

> You guys have one of the best university systems in the world. It doesn't cost you diddly—no tuition increase for my first seven years. You have one of the best highway systems in the world. Who uses it? You have the largest park system in the whole world, right here in New York State. That's all middle class. Who the hell do you think goes there? Not the black guys from my old neighborhood.

We have created a middle-class paradise and you're beating up on the poor people, because they're taking food off your table.

After Phil Gramm, Republican senator from Texas, announced his candidacy for the Republican presidential nomination, political columnist David Broder noted that Gramm's "life is a study in contradictions—most notably, his warnings about the corrupting influence of dependence on government." Broder stated that if the "government checks had stopped" when Gramm was growing up, "he would have been out of luck." Broder continued,

> Gramm was born in the base hospital at Fort Benning, Ga., where his father was living on a veterans' disability pension— an early entitlement program. He went to the University of Georgia, where his tuition and expenses were paid by the War Orphans Act, another entitlement. . . .
>
> His graduate work was paid for by yet another government program—a National Defense Education Act fellowship. . . .
>
> With his new PhD, Gramm headed to Texas A & M University, a state-supported school . . . he got on another government payroll as a member of Congress 16 years ago. . . .
>
> This year, he said on "Meet the Press," "I'd like to see everybody removed from welfare."

Broder ended his column by recalling that after Gramm switched from the Democratic to the Republican Party in the early 1980s, Broder had remarked, "In his new party, there's no telling how far a talent like Phil Gramm can go." The column continued, "Maybe he'll go all the way to the White

House. A presidential pension would certainly round out his life of warning against government handouts."

It is ironic that "welfare" has come to connote exactly the opposite of its traditional meaning. If welfare was once defined by Webster's Dictionary as "the state of faring or doing well," today it means living in poverty; if it once meant "good fortune, happiness, and well-being," today it means living at the margins of society, struggling to pay the rent and feed the children, enduring far more serious problems of fundamental health and well-being than those who are more affluent. And if "welfare" once meant "prosperity," today it means living with stigma and denigration.

The rhetoric against poor women, particularly against AFDC recipients, has become so relentless that it is affecting the fundamental self-image of the poor themselves. Carol Gagnon, formerly an upper-middle-class mother from suburban Massachusetts, talks about doing her grocery shopping "in the middle of the night" so that other shoppers will not yell at her when she uses food stamps. John Hochschild, a construction worker from Wisconsin whose family began receiving public assistance two years ago when his wife became too ill to care for their two children or work, said, "You start feeling like you're getting hit everywhere you turn, and it bites at you." Local welfare officials had recently pressured his wife, who is in the hospital in intensive care, to join a work program. A Florida woman said that she was so ashamed of receiving AFDC that she returned to the home of her father, who had physically abused her, rather than stay on welfare. She stated, "I was only on it a couple of months, but I felt like scum." When her father started abusing her again, she was forced to leave and return to the welfare rolls. Carol Gagnon summarizes what many of these recipients feel: "We already have very little self-esteem, so the last thing we need is to have the country turn around and point the finger at us and say we're the problem, but suddenly we're responsible for everything from the schools to the deficit. It's like ethnic cleansing. That's what it feels like."

The hopes of Maria Alvarez, whom we met earlier in this chapter, to complete her education and become a professional who can help others may well be torpedoed by so-called welfare reform. Many states are planning such stringent work requirements and time limits on aid that recipients will in all likelihood be locked into menial jobs—if they find jobs at all.

Maria is a living example of the inaccuracy of current stereotypes about welfare recipients and the harm that can be done by basing social policy on myths and false premises. In a recent speech, Maria described what her life is really like:

President Clinton addressed the nation recently and while doing so mentioned the words responsibility and opportunity. Well, I am testimony to what it is to be responsible yet my opportunities are rapidly diminishing. . . . Every morning I rise at 6 a.m. to prepare myself and my two children for the day. After walking my 12-year-old daughter to school, my two-year-old son and I take the train from Brooklyn to Manhattan where we attend school. Because I am active in advocacy work on welfare issues and am a member of the Board of Directors for my son's day-care center, I must oftentimes stay after my classes are finished. When my son and I go home to an already long day, my day is not over by a long shot. I straighten up what mess I may have left behind from the morning rush and I spend time with my daughter to check her homework.

Afterwards, I start to prepare dinner for my family all the

while trying to entertain an overactive two-year-old. After dinner, I clean the kitchen and prepare to do my homework. Many times my son has other plans for me so I must put off my work and give him the attention that he not only wants but deserves. By this time I must get the kids ready for bed but again my work still isn't done. If I am not doing what homework I couldn't do earlier, I am preparing myself for the morning to come and if I am lucky, I will get to bed by 11:00 p.m. to rise again at 6:00 a.m.

Maria feels that people need to be educated about the reality of life for welfare recipients: "People on welfare are not taking a ride on the backs of other people. I want to give people facts, replace lies with truth, break down those myths."

Maria had her first child during her older teenage years. Although she married before her daughter was born, Maria's life has been significantly affected by this early pregnancy. It precipitated her into an unhappy marriage and narrowed the choices she might have made. After much trial and error and considerable suffering, she seems to be embarked on a path that is both rewarding to her, to her children, and to others in the community. But many women do not emerge from similar experiences as active and empowered as Maria, feeling that they are having a real impact on others' lives. Let us examine the causes of teenage pregnancy and the impact early childbearing frequently has on young women.

Chapter 5

Teenage Mothers: Casualties of a Limited Future

> For a kid growing up now, in a town like Bergenfield [New Jersey], . . . the dreams of prior generations are lost. The suburban frontier no longer exists, there is no sure place to move to find a better life. Land is increasingly unavailable, unaffordable, or unusable. Home ownership is becoming unimaginable. The trend of remaining at home into adulthood drags on, making the dream of independent living seem impossible. You feel stuck in your hometown forever, like it or not.
>
> —DONNA GAINES
> *Teenage Wasteland*

WHEN CRYSTAL WATSON WAS FOURTEEN AND IN THE ninth grade, she became pregnant. Today she is a twenty-six-year-old African-American mother of two who works part-time and is a senior at Hunter College in New York City. She talks about her childhood:

I was born in New York City. I have an older brother and a younger sister. I lived with both of my parents until I was three but they were alcoholics and something must have happened because a great-aunt of mine took me and my sister to live with her. Actually we have two aunts and we lived with them 90 percent of the time when we were young. They were in their early fifties. One was married and one was a widow. One owned a store and the other helped her out. It was fine. They were the happiest years of my life.

When she was fourteen, her aunt was sick and Crystal was giving her "a really hard time" so she went to live with her mother. It was then that she realized that her mother had a serious drinking problem. She describes that period of time: "I had a lot of freedom. I went wherever I wanted; I did whatever I wanted."

At the age of thirteen, Crystal met an eighteen-year-old young man who, she feels, "gave me all the attention and love that I hadn't had." She describes her level of understanding about sex and reproduction at that time:

I knew what sex was but no one ever told me that once menstruation started you produced eggs and could get pregnant. I didn't know how sex led to pregnancy. No one spoke about sex, contraception, or menstruation. I never had that information. If I had had complete information, I would not have engaged in sex at that time.

When I got pregnant, I didn't tell anyone. But I put on a lot of weight and when I was four and a half months along, I felt the baby move and had to face reality. I had guessed but I was still getting my period a little bit. I didn't tell my mother. He told my mother. It was the only time she was understanding.

Abortion? I remember hearing stuff on TV about abortion. I remember reading about it. And someone gave me an anti-abortion pamphlet and I decided I was not going to do that.

My only notion was that I was not going on welfare. I would work in Burger King or McDonald's or pack bags in a supermarket but I was not going to go on welfare.

Teenage pregnancy is one of the central issues fueling the anger and outrage about welfare in the mid-1990s. Part of the larger issues of out-of-wedlock births and the prevalence of female-headed families, teen pregnancy is of special concern because of the physical, psychological, social, and economic consequences of early parenthood on young mothers and their babies. There is no question that becoming a mother before a girl or young woman has matured both physically and psychologically, before she has completed her education, before she has acquired the skills necessary to care for herself and another human being, particularly a totally dependent human being, can have serious consequences for all of the individuals involved—the mother, the baby, the families—and for the community as well.

Nonetheless, the shrill and punitive tone that is heard all too often around the problem of teen pregnancy does not serve to illuminate the issue. As with the stereotyping and stigmatizing of welfare recipients, views about teenage childbearing are frequently extraordinarily simplistic. It must be stressed that the causes of teens becoming pregnant are complex and multifaceted and often stem from ignorance about reproduction, from a profound lack of educational and economic opportunities, from social and psychological distress, and from sex roles that propel boys and girls, young men and young women, toward a premature, often imprudent expression of sexuality as a way of defining their masculinity, their femininity, and sometimes their very existence. This complexity and the multicausal nature of adolescent behavior have been largely overlooked in the current welfare debate and in the measures developed by the states and the federal government to curb teenage child-bearing. The elimination of cash assistance to unmarried mothers under the age of eighteen is, in reality, a punishment that will harm infants as well as young mothers rather than a rational preventive measure. The notion that the majority of teenagers who have children out of wedlock do so because of AFDC benefits was summed up by Representative E. Clay Shaw, Republican from Florida and chair of the House Ways and Means subcommittee responsible for welfare programs. He stated that denying cash benefits to families headed by teens would take away "the lure of the cash." Without the money, he continued, "the mothers are going to be more careful" and use contraception.

Virtually everyone who has worked closely with adolescents—both males and females—knows that their sexual behavior is neither so planned nor so straightforward. The factors that contribute to teens having sex and to their use or non-use of contraception include their level of knowledge and understanding about sex and reproduction; other alternatives in young people's lives; the boy's need to prove that he can do something, be someone, have some power in his world; the girl's desire to hold on to a boyfriend; and, of real importance, the impact of the millions of powerful messages sent and received constantly from the wider society—from advertising, the music industry, films, television, the fashion industry—about sex as a central route to intimacy, self-definition, and status.

As Michael Carrera, director of the Children's Aid Society National Adolescent Sexuality Training Center, has written:

> . . . adolescent males have heard loud and clear that their bodies must be competent to do something—not to feel

much, but to do much—and that the validation of their masculinity is derived principally from their bodies performing in ways in keeping with this stereotypical male social coding.

Similarly, adolescent females learn very early that "looks count." All of their natural biological changes during puberty are monitored and are interpreted through our culture's appearance-based ideals. Young women quickly learn to view their bodies cosmetically and to look to others for validation of their attractiveness.

When asked why they got pregnant, many young mothers echo the words of a sixteen-year-old Floridian who responded, "It just happened." Virtually all studies indicate that few unmarried teenagers become pregnant intentionally. Analysis of data by the Alan Guttmacher Institute indicates that 85 percent of teenage pregnancies are unintended. As Crystal's experience illustrates, part of the problem is that many teenagers do not really understand reproduction. According to one AFDC recipient from the Washington, D.C., area, parents frequently fail to talk to their children about reproduction and contraception:

> My mother told me "you better not get pregnant." She told me you better not. . . . I better not catch you. Well, you won't catch me. She never told me about protections or anything. If your mother would talk to you like your best friend and not your mother, then you could talk to her.

A poignant and revealing example of young girls' partial understanding of sex and reproduction came to my attention recently when an upper-middle-class eleven-year-old who attends a private school where she has been taught sex education indicated to her mother that she thought having sex *always* led either to pregnancy, AIDS, or to both consequences. Clearly, some facts about the dangers of unprotected sex were getting through to her—but just as clearly, not all of the facts. Many other myths abound.

In a study I did of young women's values and attitudes in the late 1980s, *On Her Own: Growing Up in the Shadow of the American Dream*, the widespread nature of these myths became clear. Young women and professionals who work with them recounted the misinformation that adolescents, particularly younger teenagers, receive. "You can't get pregnant the first time"; "You can't get pregnant if you don't enjoy it"; "You can't get pregnant standing up"; "You can't get pregnant if you drink ice water, because your reproductive system will be frozen"; and "Contraception, particularly the condom, significantly diminishes the man's pleasure" are myths that are passed from teen to teen, effectively sabotaging regular use of birth control among some young people.

Many young people also see themselves as invincible. Whether they are driving too fast or drinking and driving or using life-threatening drugs, teenagers frequently engage in risk-taking behavior. Compounding frequently death-defying acts, adolescents often engage in what some experts call "magical thinking." One professional who works with teen mothers observed, "Ninety percent never thought it would happen to them. They never, ever, ever thought they would get pregnant!"

In order to understand the nature of adolescent childbearing, it is necessary to examine the extent of teenage sexual activity. Contrary to public perception fueled by both politicians and the media, more than half of all teenagers, males as well as females, have not had sexual intercourse until they are seventeen. Actually, nearly 20 percent of adolescents have not had sex at all during their teenage years. Nevertheless, more teenagers are having sex today than in past decades. In the mid-1950s, just over 25 percent of women had had sexual intercourse by their eighteenth birthday; by the early 1990s, more than half of females and almost three-quarters of males had had intercourse by the age of eighteen.

Moreover, as a result of later ages of marriage, most teenagers having sex are unmarried. This change is particularly striking among white women. The likelihood that a white teenager would have sexual intercourse before marriage more than doubled between the late 1950s and the late 1980s.

Furthermore, among young women who have had sex during their teenage years, a significant percentage have not done so voluntarily. Studies indicate that 74 percent of girls who had intercourse before age fourteen and 60 percent of those who had sex before age fifteen report having had sex involuntarily. Some were sexually abused as younger children, some were physically forced to have sex as teenagers, and others have been pressured by their peers. As Dr. Helen Rodriguez-Trias, a California pediatrician and former president of the American Public Health Association, has stated, "There is real concern about how much young women have to say about their sexuality. In teen women's lives there is often an element of coercion and pressure . . . an element of violence."

According to a study conducted in Seattle, 62 percent of pregnant and parenting teens were prior victims of sexual abuse. University of Washington co-author Debra Boyer reports that victims of sexual abuse (which she defines as "contact molestation, rape or attempted rape") frequently begin having voluntary sex at a younger age than teens who are not abused, are more likely to use drugs and alcohol, and are far less likely to use contraceptives. Boyer states that these young women often talk about "leaving their bodies." She continues, "These young women have stopped feeling. They are not making decisions about sexuality. They have become very passive. They feel tainted and spoiled."

Despite the myths about reproduction and contraception, contraceptive use has increased significantly in recent years. Studies indicate that among fifteen- to nineteen-year-old women, condom use at first intercourse rose from 23 percent to 48 percent between 1982 and 1988. Nonetheless, many young women are sexually active for a period of time—some for as long as one year—before they obtain medical contraceptive services. One explanation of this pattern was given by a New Orleans–based professional who works with young people on the issues of contraception and unplanned pregnancy. According to her, many young women do not think of themselves as sexually active. She says, "If you ask them 'Do you have sex?' the answer is yes. If you ask them 'Are you sexually active?' the answer often is no." Many young women see themselves as passive participants in occasional sex rather than as active participants who need to plan for the consequences. In general, "higher income" teenagers (defined by a Guttmacher Institute study as 200 percent or more of the federal poverty line) are much more likely to use contraceptives than "lower income" young women (defined as 100 to 199 percent of the poverty line or "poor" (those below or at the poverty line).

But while contraceptive use has risen significantly, it is not as simple for teenagers as politicians would have us believe. Many young women are too uncomfortable to seek medical help in order to obtain contraception; others are too embarrassed to purchase condoms or even to discuss the issue with their partners. Many are concerned about the pill ("It will make me sick." "It will make me fat."); and condoms, even in this era of AIDS and other sexually transmitted diseases, are often strongly resisted by men. There are, moreover, other barriers to using birth control. The message is out there among many teenagers that if a girl takes the pill or carries condoms, then she is planning for sex and is therefore a "slut." According to many young women, "Only bad girls plan for sex." Being overcome by desire, being persuaded by a male friend, or succumbing to sex at the last minute is acceptable; protecting oneself from sexually transmitted diseases and from pregnancy can label a young woman as "that kind of a girl."

Many teens are afraid to use contraceptives because their parents might discover them. Elena Webb, a Los Angeles single mother, had such an experience. When she was a teenager, she felt she could not ask for advice from her parents when her boyfriend asked her to have sex. Webb talks about her experience: "In our house, they thought that not talking about something meant not doing it. I felt when I became sexually active that I couldn't tell them." Webb went to a nearby Planned Parenthood office and obtained oral contraceptives. She hid them in a shoebox in her closet. She says, "I was responsible enough to know to take it every day." But when her mother found the pills, "I lied and said that I wasn't having sex." Within one month, she was pregnant. But Webb was more fortunate than most teens in her situation; her parents helped her raise her son while she attended college and she is now studying for her master's degree in social work. She talks about the predicament in which many teens find themselves: "I needed someone to tell me that it is normal to be curious about sex but that you don't have to act on it. . . . If you are a teen and you are thinking about sex, you're considered bad, you're wrong. But kids need to know it's normal to think about sex."

Despite significant increases in the numbers of young people using contraception, approximately one million adolescent girls and young women become pregnant each year. It is important to note that nearly two-thirds of these pregnancies occur among eighteen- to nineteen-year-olds and that their rate is only slightly lower than that of twenty- to twenty-four-year-olds. Among the one million pregnancies, half end in birth, approximately one-third end in induced abortion, and the remainder end in miscarriage.

Since more adolescents are having intercourse, the pregnancy rate among all teenage women has risen 23 percent over the past two decades but among sexually experienced teenagers ages fifteen to nineteen the pregnancy rate has actually declined 19 percent. This means that sexually active teenagers are using contraceptives more effectively than they have in previous decades.

In general, teenagers from more affluent families are more likely than those from poorer families to terminate their pregnancies. According to the Guttmacher Institute, "Nearly three-quarters of higher income teenagers who accidentally become pregnant have abortions, compared with fewer than half of those from poor or low income families." Similarly, pregnant adolescents whose parents have more education are more likely than those with less well-educated parents to terminate the pregnancy and those "with a stronger orientation toward the future" are more likely to choose abortion.

As Judith S. Musick, author of *Young, Poor and Pregnant* and founder of the Ounce of Prevention Fund for pregnant and parenting teenagers in Chicago, has stated, "Middle-class girls get pregnant, they just don't have the baby. They say, 'If I have

this kid I won't be able to go to college or do this or that.'
They not only have the desire to do something else, they have
the means. And they have the family to support them."

My research corroborates these findings. Young women
with educational and/or career plans either managed to avoid
pregnancy or, if they did become pregnant, often made the
decision to have an abortion. As one high school student stated,
"They can't get pregnant; they have too much to lose." Those
who had few dreams for the future, are burdened by dilemmas
of day-to-day living, and feel hopeless about their lives, those
with personal or family problems, and those so mired in poverty and a lack of options that they cannot imagine another
way of life are the girls and young women who often become
teen mothers.

For teens who discover that they are unintentionally pregnant, the choices are difficult at best and often wrenching.
Many young women speak of their reluctance to have an
abortion—some for religious reasons, some because their families would strongly disapprove, and some because of their own
personal distaste for abortion. For young women who choose
to terminate their pregnancy, the decision is often not easy to
implement. First, the cost can be prohibitive. In 1993, for example, the average cost for a first-trimester outpatient abortion
was $296. The cost varied state by state with the average charge
in several states above $350.

Abortions after the first trimester cost considerably more
than those within the first twelve weeks. This can be a particular problem for pregnant teens since many may not realize
they are pregnant until after the first three months, many are
fearful of telling a parent or anyone else in a position of authority, and many attempt to deny their condition even to
themselves. They therefore may find themselves at the begin-

ning of the second trimester when the cost for an outpatient non-hospital abortion—$593 on average at sixteen weeks of gestation—has increased substantially and often well beyond the means of a teenager.

Women who live in non-metropolitan areas must often travel considerable distances because of the shortage of providers. The cost of the abortion plus the cost of the travel may well place abortion beyond the reach of many young women. In addition, since the passage and implementation of the Hyde Amendment in 1978 limiting federal funding of abortions to procedures needed to save a woman's life, Medicaid pays for very few abortions for poor women. In 1992, in fact, the federal government paid for abortions for just 267 women!

The recent climate of opposition to abortion has clearly had an impact on young women's attitudes toward terminating their pregnancies. Many speak of their negative feelings about abortion even when they recognize that they are not ready— emotionally, economically, socially, or in any way—to care for a child. As Crystal stated, "I remember hearing stuff on TV about abortion. I remember reading about it. And someone gave me an anti-abortion pamphlet and I decided I was not going to do that." She made that fateful decision at age fourteen with the substantial help of the anti-abortion groups. These young women are literally caught between two impossibly difficult choices at a time in their lives when they are often ill-equipped to make such a momentous decision.

While it is clear that teenage pregnancy often contributes to the young mother and her child or children living in poverty —due to factors such as her lack of education, her lack of occupational skills, her caretaking responsibilities, and the lack of support services in the community, particularly the lack of accessible, affordable child care—what is less frequently mentioned is the fact that the young women who give birth during their teenage years are far more likely than other teenagers to come from economically disadvantaged families. Although 38 percent of all teenage females are from poor or low-income families, 83 percent of teenage mothers are from such families. In other words, while approximately 25 percent of the young women who become mothers when they are teenagers are poor in their twenties and thirties, many of them, an estimated 16 percent, would have been poor even if they had not given birth. Their initial disadvantage is a significant factor in both their early childbearing and in their later poverty.

Not only is teenage childbearing concentrated among young women who are poor and disadvantaged in multiple ways—nearly 60 percent of teenagers who become mothers are living in poverty at the time—but at every age young black and Hispanic women are more likely to give birth than white women. One in four black women and one in seven white women are already mothers by the age of nineteen, yet the black-to-white birthrate is closing for unmarried teens. In 1970, the birthrate for unmarried black teens was ten times higher than for whites; by 1990 it was just four times higher.

The racial and ethnic background of pregnant and parenting teens varies, of course, in different parts of the country. In California, for example, a disproportionately high number of Hispanic teens are giving birth. In 1993, this group accounted for 60 percent of all births to adolescents in that state. Several factors seem to contribute to this disturbing statistic:

1) Poverty—Hispanics are more likely to be poor than any other ethnic group in California and, as we have seen, poor teens are far more likely to give birth than those who are more affluent;

2) Education—Hispanic students are more likely to drop out of school, another factor that frequently precedes teen pregnancy;

3) Religion—Seventy percent of the Hispanic population in California is Catholic and while Catholic teachings prohibit sex before marriage, they also strongly condemn contraception and abortion; those adolescents who do have sex are far less likely to use contraception or obtain an abortion than other teenagers; and

4) Culture—the majority of Hispanic teens in California originally come from countries in which early childbearing is not frowned upon as it is in the United States; this factor combined with high levels of poverty and dropping out of school may lead these teens to see little reason not to become parents.

According to Alicia Thomas, executive director of the East Valley Community Health Center which serves many Hispanic adolescents, "Many of the teens come from families where teen motherhood is very natural. Their mothers may have been teens when they had them; their grandmothers too." As another observer has noted, "A fifteen-year-old from Mexico is not looking around at five or six colleges and wondering whether to be a computer engineer or a physician. These women feel they have fewer options open to them. This is something they know they can do: Make a baby and have respect in the community that they are a woman now."

While millions of young women see few educational and occupational options in their lives, the relentless message of the media is that sex—looking sexy, acting provocatively, having sex—is the way to get a man and hold on to him. From the daytime soaps to prime-time sitcoms, from the omnipresent TV talk shows that focus on the bizarre and the salacious, from frankly provocative models such as Claudia Schiffer to the childlike yet erotic Kate Moss, the use of overt sexuality is portrayed as central to a woman's success, essential to her very being. As a divorced twenty-five-year-old mother of two from Southern California observed,

> Sex is everywhere, but it is sex without repercussions. People have great sex on TV and they don't get pregnant. People have great sex in books, in movies; friends talk about great sex. But no one talks about reality issues such as birth control and pregnancy.

The fashions of the mid-1990s tell us the messages with which young women are constantly being bombarded: the immense popularity of the Wonderbra, the return of stiletto heels, dresses that resemble underwear, the frequency of sadomasochistic images in fashion layouts, and the constant emphasis on women presenting themselves as sexual objects. Perhaps John Berger in his revealing and insightful book *Ways of Seeing* best captures the culture's relentless insistence on perceiving women as objects:

> A woman must continually watch herself. She is almost continually accompanied by her own image of herself. . . .
> She has to survey everything she is and everything she does because how she appears to others, and ultimately how she appears to men, is of crucial importance for what is normally thought of as the success of her life.

For women with limited options—for the poor, the disadvantaged, the inadequately educated, the disheartened and depressed, for those with few hopes and dreams—being noticed by a boy/man, being singled out for attention, being touched, hugged, or loved—can be everything. We must recognize that young women are systematically taught that the road to that attention and affection is sex. As a fifteen-year-old New Yorker stated, many girls are "insecure" and "do it with anybody" because they "need somebody to love them." Most girls she knows start having sex largely because the guys are pressuring them. "At sixteen or seventeen," she states, "that's all the guys want from the girls. Then the girls have sex; the guys dump them and never talk to them again."

Except for the issues of determining paternity and requiring child support, the role of men in producing single-parent families has been virtually ignored in the demagoguery around welfare. The role of males in forcing or persuading young women to have sex, in refusing to use condoms, in discouraging women from using other kinds of birth control, and in walking away from their responsibilities once their partners become pregnant has barely been addressed by politicians and many social policy experts. Yet studies indicate that the males who impregnate teenagers are themselves frequently over the age of twenty. California birth statistics show that men over twenty father 2.5 times more babies by high school girls than do younger boys, and that adult males are responsible for four times more births among junior high school girls than are junior high school boys. National statistics indicate the same pattern. A 1991 study by the National Center for Health Statistics of over 300,000 teenage mothers found that 67 percent were impregnated by men over twenty and that men over twenty-five cause more than 400 teen pregnancies every day!

Where is the outcry against these men? Where are the sanctions? Where are the governors and members of Congress with their scathing rhetoric? If an adult male has sex with a teenager, is this not statutory rape?

Certainly, the worsening economic situation of males with

less than a college education contributes to the transitory nature of relationships between young people. A young man without steady employment, earning wages insufficient to help support a family, with few if any prospects of future earning power is unlikely to make an emotional and economic commitment to a woman or to children for he will, in all likelihood, be unable to fulfill those commitments. And of course the economic situation of African-American men and other men of color is significantly more bleak than that of white men.

While the overall U.S. unemployment rate has declined in recent years, the rate for blacks and Hispanic people is considerably higher than for whites. In 1993, for example, the civilian unemployment rate for blacks was more than twice that of whites (14 and 6 percent respectively) while the rate for Hispanic workers was nearly 12 percent. As William Julius Wilson has pointed out, "The extraordinary rise in male joblessness" is "perhaps the most important factor in the rise of black female-headed families." He goes on to state that "the decline in the incidence of intact marriages among blacks is associated with the declining economic status of black men" and that "black women nationally, especially young black women, are facing a shrinking pool of 'marriageable' (i.e., employed) black men."

What are the implications for young women who give birth during their teenage years? Seventy percent of teenage mothers complete high school but they are significantly less likely than women who give birth during their twenties to go on to college. Young women who give birth before age nineteen have lower future incomes than women who give birth in their twenties. In the mid-1980s, for example, teenage mothers' median income was less than half the income of women who gave birth at age twenty-five and older.

While being a teenage mother makes young women extraordinarily vulnerable to becoming welfare recipients, according to a U.S. Government Accounting Office report, "the dramatic growth in never-married women receiving AFDC has not been due to a dramatic increase in teenage mothers receiving AFDC." Data indicate that among never-married women who give birth as teenagers, those receiving AFDC increased from 11 percent in 1976 to 22 percent in 1992. However, among those who did not give birth as teenagers, the increase was even greater—from 9 percent in 1976 to approximately 26 percent in 1992. Current teenage mothers comprise only 13 percent of all recipients but current and former teenage mothers make up approximately 42 percent of all single mothers receiving AFDC. Women who originally gave birth as teenagers are less likely, as a group, to have high school diplomas, more likely to have larger families, and more likely never to be married. Although they work in the same proportions as other women who receive AFDC, they earn less and are more likely to have total family incomes below 50 percent of the poverty line. In addition, many of the characteristics of teenage mothers are associated with longer stays on AFDC. Therefore, it is clear that women who bear their first child during their teenage years should be specially targeted for help in completing their education, in job training, and with first-rate child care.

Children of teenage mothers are also more likely than children of older mothers to have special problems—to be born at low birth weight, to be born prematurely, to have health problems, and to be hospitalized during childhood. These problems in the children of young mothers have often been associated with the teenagers' low economic status, educational disadvantage, poor nutrition, and lack of prenatal care. Recent studies, however, indicate that even white, middle-class teens who receive good health care are almost twice as likely as older women to deliver premature babies.

Teenage pregnancy is, in great part, the result of conflicting values and mixed messages about sexuality, an inadequate and unequal educational system, jobs that do not pay a living wage or offer any hope of upward mobility, and an inequality that leaves millions of young women (and young men) outside the perimeter of middle-class America. These complex factors combine to set up young women for becoming single mothers before they are really ready.

We tell them their looks are all-important. We tell them that sex is the road to intimacy and getting and holding a man. But we give them mixed signals about protecting themselves from disease and conception and we surely give them mixed signals (or negative ones) about abortion. We tell young women they are responsible for their lives but teach them a certain passivity in their relationships with men. We provide some sex education, but is it enough to clarify the myths and confusions about a topic fraught with mystery, silence, guilt, and danger? We do not really give young women permission to be in charge of their bodies and we surely don't teach young men that young women have the right to be in charge of their own bodies.

While so many young people—males and females—see sexual activity as a symbolic step into adulthood and as a substitute for other, more elusive ways of achieving status, millions of teenagers attend grossly inferior schools that leave them totally unprepared to function effectively in the twenty-first century. Often only too aware of the inadequacy of their knowledge and skills and the shortage of jobs that can lend some meaning to life or, at the very least, lead to middle-class status, they see few opportunities for the future.

Donna Gaines, author of *Teenage Wasteland: Suburbia's*

Dead End Kids, describes the plight of young people in late-twentieth-century America in which the American Dream seems dead except for the highly skilled, highly trained, fortunate few:

Stuck without hope, dreaming of jobs that no longer exist, with the myths of better days further convincing them of their individual fate as "losers," kids today are earning almost one-third less, in constant dollars, than comparable groups in 1973. For white kids, the drop in income is almost 25 percent; for black kids, it's 44 percent. The scars of race discrimination run deep, and minority youth feel hopeless because they get the message that this nation does not value its nonwhite citizens.

White kids have scars too, but with no attending socio-economic explanation, they personalize their plights. They are "losers" because they are shit as people. They are failures because they are worthless. Either way, it hurts. . . .

In nonaffluent white suburbia . . . [Y]ou're middle-class, you think. You believe that this country works for you. You do what you are told. It doesn't work, even though you're sure you made all the right moves. So who's fault is it? Yours. You have shit for brains and you'll never be anybody. This feeling becomes part of you.

Some politicians, social-policy analysts, and conservative leaders today are promoting the denial of cash assistance to mothers under the age of eighteen and insisting that teen mothers remain at home or live in some as yet undeveloped group setting. Again, we see certain elements in American society trying to turn back the clock to the 1950s when white, single, pregnant girls were frequently sent to maternity homes because they offered secrecy, protection, and an opportunity in the words of Rickie Solinger, author of *Wake Up Little Susie: Single Pregnancy and Race Before* Roe *v.* Wade, to "find a repaired or reconstructed identity. . . ."

Or, as Alice McDermott in her novel *That Night* describes the fate of pregnant girls in 1960s suburbia:

Unwed mothers at that time, at the time Sheryl joined their ranks, were a specific group; they fell somewhere between criminals and patients and, like criminals and patients, they were prescribed an exact and fortifying treatment: They were made to disappear.

Some of the young pregnant girls today have been assaulted and sexually abused in their own homes. Are we saying that we as a society will insist they remain in those homes or, as their only alternative, they must move to a group home in which they know no one? Rather than punishing young women who become pregnant, we must more effectively educate young men and young women about the dangers of unprotected sex. We must educate high school students more effectively so that they will have the skills to perceive and plan for a life beyond today and tomorrow. We must provide jobs for young people so that they can feel as though they have a stake in American society, so that they will have the confidence in their futures that will enable them to make commitments to one another and to the next generation. And we must work to sensitize young (and not so young) men about the needs and rights of young women and their responsibilities as fathers.

Let us return to Crystal Watson, who had her first child at age fourteen. How did she survive? How did she manage to become educated, work to support her family, and avoid remaining in poverty? She talks about how she managed after her son was born:

I stayed out of school for two weeks and then went back. My mother and aunt took care of my son and I stayed in school and graduated from junior high school and high school on time. At that time my mother was receiving AFDC and the baby was added to her budget. I got a part-time job at a community center; during my sophomore year in high school I worked in the kitchen helping to prepare the snack for the kids in the after-school program.

Crystal describes how she happened to get involved with a teen pregnancy prevention program:

One day I was in the center with my sister and two cousins [female] and we were asked if we were interested in being part of a pregnancy prevention program. The program offered sex education, help with homework, sports, help in expressing our feelings and, if you completed the program, guaranteed admission to Hunter [College]. There's not much for girls to do so the program was a breath of fresh air. The first five years the staff remained the same and we were all like a little family.

When Crystal finished high school she worked for several years at health facilities. For the past year and a half she has worked with girls ages nine to thirteen in the same community pregnancy prevention program that she herself was part of as a teenager. She helps the girls understand issues such as puberty, hygiene, boys, crime, and drugs. Before she began working there, she volunteered with young people at the same center. She feels they are drawn to her.

Several years ago she enrolled at Hunter College. At first she went part-time and, after being uncertain about her major for a time, she settled on physical education. She currently plans to go on for a master's degree in public health or in sports medicine. She would really like to obtain a certificate in athletic training so she could work in colleges or hospitals, do rehabilitation with athletes or even be a personal trainer.

In her early twenties, Crystal became pregnant with her second son, Bobby. His father and she had been together for three years at that time. (Her older son's father has been incarcerated for many years; they never see him.) He sees both boys "really often—about every other day" and, while she characterizes their relationship as having its "ups and downs," she feels they will get married one day, when it's the "right time." She talks about the timing and the kind of wedding she would like:

> It's not the right time now because I have to graduate and then I have to apply to graduate schools. I don't have the time to plan a wedding right now. I want a big wedding. I think I've earned the right to a nice wedding—with a wedding gown and bridesmaids—and a nice honeymoon. I've worked hard enough. People who have overcome extreme barriers deserve a reward and this is the reward I want. And I wouldn't think of marrying anyone but Bobby's father.

Crystal talks about her sons, their education, and the ways she balances parenting, school, and work:

> Both of my kids go to Catholic school. They're really intelligent kids. My older son is a nice kid, very verbal. You can really talk to him. My younger son is mischievous.
>
> Their school is near Bobby's father's mother's house. She is

really like a second mother to them. She's really been there for them. She's at home if the kids want to go there after school. Three days a week they go to an after-school program; the other days they go to their grandmother's.

We're all up at 5:45 in the morning and out of the house by 6:45. We take the bus and I drop them off at school where they have a breakfast program. I have to be at Hunter for an 8:10 a.m. class. At the end of the day either I pick them up or they may stay overnight at their grandmother's. I'm very glad the kids are in Catholic school. If they weren't, they'd get lost in the [public school] system. The tuition? We split it—Bobby's father and I.

Crystal is the only one of her siblings to go beyond high school. She talks about some of the factors involved in her level of achievement:

I've always had more desire, will power, drive. I've always been like that. I had the drive to do more and get more. Even in school if I got "S's" or "G's" ["Satisfactories" or "Goods"], I wanted "E's" ["Excellents"]. I've always been like that. And as my life progressed I met people who have encouraged me or have been there to support me. I've had both support and opportunity.

Despite having a child at an early age, Crystal has clearly put it all together. The stereotypes about teenage mothers don't work for her as they don't work for millions of other women. A highly intelligent, highly motivated, and extremely personable young woman, Crystal has had numerous supports along the way. The anti-teen-pregnancy program in which she participated and in which she continues to work has been key in her development. Her guaranteed admission to college was an important opportunity. Her immediate family—despite their problems—enabled her to stay in school after her first child was born; her current extended family (Bobby's father and grandmother) help her balance all of her responsibilities today. Crystal has had steady, stable personal relationships, family support, the benefits of first-rate community programs, and educational opportunities. If she hadn't had any one of these, she might not be where she is today.

But, as we know all too well, millions of mothers and their children are not so fortunate. Crystal's children are decently housed, well nourished, and are attending a good school. They go to an after-school program and have a loving grandmother. Perhaps most important, on a day-to-day basis they see their mother working, studying, achieving, succeeding. They have a sense of what is possible. What of children who are not so fortunate? What of the millions of children who grow up in this rich society hungry, poor, undereducated, and surrounded by violence? What are their hopes and dreams? Can they afford to dream?

Chapter 6

Poor Children:
The Walking Wounded

Every Day in America

15	children die from guns
95	babies die before their first birthday
564	babies are born to women who had late or no prenatal care
788	babies are born at low birth weight
1,340	teenagers give birth
2,217	teenagers drop out of school each school day
2,350	children are in adult jails
2,699	infants are born into poverty
8,189	children are reported abused or neglected
100,000	children are homeless
135,000	children bring guns to school
1,200,000	latchkey children come home to a house in which there is a gun

—CHILDREN'S DEFENSE FUND

OF ALL THE SEGMENTS OF THE POPULATION WHO ARE poor, children are the poorest and the most vulnerable to the pernicious effects of poverty. Every day millions of poor children suffer from the physical, social, and emotional repercussions of living in poverty in one of the richest countries in the world.

Perhaps the most vivid image of the paradox of poor children living among plenty can be seen in our nation's capital.

According to sociologists Walda Katz-Fishman and Jerome Scott, Washington, D.C., is "a city with two faces." It is a city of "the middle and upper classes," part of the metropolitan region that is home to a white population that is highly educated and highly paid, an area that also has an African-American population that is "more affluent and better educated" than any other metropolitan region in the country. At the same time, in 1993, the District of Columbia, home to a declining population of approximately 570,000, had a poverty rate of 26.4 percent. More than one Washingtonian out of every four officially lives in poverty. Between 1985 and 1993 the median income fell from $31,152 to $27,304 and Washington lost over 130,000 jobs.

In 1993, in this city of stark contrasts nearly one-third (29.5 percent) of the children, the vast majority of whom are children of color, lived below the poverty line. The annual death rate for children one to fourteen years of age was 55.4 per 100,000; the national death rate for that age group is 30.7 per 100,000 persons, nearly half the rate for D.C. The capital of arrest rates among young people ages ten to seventeen, Washington is also the place where teenagers ages fifteen to nineteen are "most likely to meet a violent death." It is perhaps symbolic of America's indifference to the well-being of children that young people living in such misery should be tolerated in the shadow of the White House and the Houses of Congress.

Despite improvements in the U.S. economy during the 1990s, the U.S. child poverty rate has continued to rise. In 1993, the child poverty rate was higher than in any year since 1964. Data on child poverty were discussed in chapter 3 but they are important enough to mention again:

•In 1993, 22.7 percent of all children under eighteen in the United States, 15.7 million children, officially lived in poverty;

- Very young children are most likely to be poor; 27 percent of children under three lived in poverty in the same year;
- Minority children are disproportionately poor—more than 46 percent of all black children and 41 percent of all Hispanic children lived in poverty in 1993 compared to 14 percent of all non-Hispanic white children;
- Two-thirds of all poor children (61 percent) lived in families in which someone worked; nearly one in four (23 percent) lived in families in which parents worked full-time, year round; and
- Children of mother-only families are far more likely to live in poverty, 54 percent, than children in married, two-parent families (12 percent).

As shocking as these statistics are, they cannot really communicate the true cost, the human toll for the nearly 16 million children who are living in absolute poverty. It is well known and indisputable that poor children are likely to live in decrepit housing, in dangerous neighborhoods, are at significant risk for becoming homeless, may well suffer from inadequate or poor nutrition, have reduced access to quality child care, are likely to attend inferior, dispiriting, often unsafe schools, and have reduced access to adequate health care. What is less well known are the devastating effects of poverty on the day-to-day health and well-being and even the life expectancy of poor children. According to *Wasting America's Future: The Children's Defense Fund Report on the Costs of Child Poverty*,

Poverty wears down . . . [children's] reliance and emotional reserves; saps their spirits and sense of self; crushes their hopes; devalues their potential and aspirations; and subjects them over time to physical, mental, and emotional assault, injury, and indignity.

And as the report states, *"Poverty even kills."* (Emphasis in the original.) Compared to other children, low-income children are

- Two times more likely than other children to die from birth defects;
- Three times more likely to die from all causes combined;
- Four times more likely to die from fires;
- Five times more likely to die from infectious diseases and parasites; and
- Six times more likely to die from other diseases.

In addition, poor children are two or more times as likely as other children to suffer from problems such as significant physical or mental disabilities, severe asthma, iron deficiency, and fatal accidental injuries. These problems are not limited to any specific group of children, to children of any one race or children from female-headed families, but are characteristic of poor children from all backgrounds.

According to Barbara Starfield, M.D., director of health policy studies at Johns Hopkins University, "Low-income children are twice to three times more likely to be of low birth weight, to have delayed immunizations, to get bacterial meningitis, to be lead poisoned, and, at least until recent years, to contract rheumatic fever."

One of the reasons for the continuing rise in the number of children living in poverty is the sharply declining economic status of young families with children, particularly those headed by parents under the age of thirty. Because of the loss of manufacturing jobs, the increase in low-wage service and retail jobs, the dropping value of the minimum wage and the increasing number of young single-parent families, during the last two decades the median income of young families with children fell 34 percent after adjusting for inflation. By 1992, 42 percent of the children in young families were officially living in poverty, more than double the percentage twenty years earlier.

In examining the impact of poverty on children's well-being, what we are often really discussing are life chances. The negative consequences of living in poverty can be so severe that many young people are unable to recuperate from the damage done at an early age. The health of children is rooted in great part, of course, in the parents' overall health and in the care of the mother during pregnancy. In 1992, 77.7 percent of all mothers received early prenatal care, beginning within the first three months of pregnancy. But if we look at differences by race, we see that 80.8 percent of white women received early prenatal care compared to only 63.9 percent of black women. Children's chances of survival past the first year of life are directly connected to their economic status and racial background. In 1992, the infant mortality rate for black babies (16.8 per 1,000 live births) was more than twice the rate for white babies (6.9). The District of Columbia had far and away the highest overall rate—19.6 for all races and 22.0 for black infants. The highest infant mortality rate for black babies in the United States in 1992 was in Michigan: 22.1 infant deaths per 1,000 live births.

Low birth weight is another measure of the well-being of infants and children. Conventionally defined as less than 5.5 pounds at birth, low birth weight afflicted 7.1 percent of all babies in 1992. Again, the data for black and white infants are extremely disturbing: the percentage of black babies born at low birth weight (13.3 percent) was over twice that of white babies (5.8 percent).

If an infant survives into the second year of life, the next measure of well-being is protection against preventable childhood diseases. Far too many children—poor and nonpoor; urban, suburban, and rural; and children from all racial backgrounds—are inadequately immunized. In 1993, among children ages nineteen months to thirty-five months, nearly one-third (29.5 percent) of nonpoor children and 41.3 percent of poor children were inadequately immunized. Inadequate immunization affects children from all racial backgrounds. Nearly one-third of white children (31.6 percent), 38.2 percent of black children, and 41.6 percent of children from other racial backgrounds were inadequately protected. If we look at rates by geographic location, we see that 37.9 percent of urban children, 34 percent of rural children, and 28.6 percent of children living in suburban areas are underimmunized.

But of course children's health problems do not end with childhood immunizations. Clearly poor children are at significant risk of hunger and poor nutrition. If inadequate income, whether due to low wages or a meager welfare check or a combination of both, must be split between rent and food, food is often shortchanged because the consequences of not paying the rent may well be eviction and subsequent homelessness. That families are forced to survive on cheap but relatively filling foods such as rice, beans, and mashed potatoes has been well documented in recent years. A study conducted at eleven sites in different parts of the country by the Community Childhood Hunger Identification Project of the Food Research and Action Center (FRAC) between 1992 and 1994 indicates that approximately four million low-income children under age twelve are hungry during some part of the previous twelve months. An additional 9.6 million low-income children under age twelve are at risk of hunger (their families experience "chronic insecurity" about whether there will be sufficient food) during some part of one or more months over the past year. The researchers point out that for many low-income families, hunger is cyclical. At certain times each month—for example, at the end of the month or when food stamps run out—or at certain times during the year—for example, during months when children do not have any meals from school food programs—families' lack of resources will limit their ability to provide enough food for all family members. The study also found that in the vast majority (97 percent) of "hungry households" adults report that they cut the size of their meals or skip them entirely to enable children to eat. It is important to note that at least one person is working in 60 percent of "hungry households" and in almost half of these households at least one person is working full-time.

As the report of the FRAC study notes, "hungry children are more likely to have health problems than their non-hungry peers":

> Children from hungry families are more than three times as likely as children from non-hungry families to experience unwanted loss of weight and to have frequent headaches as children from non-hungry families. Hungry children are four times as likely to suffer from fatigue and to have difficulty concentrating.
>
> Children from hungry families are significantly more likely to be anemic, to have asthma, allergies, and diarrhea, and to have frequent colds, ear infections, and other infections as children from non-hungry families.

The recent rise in the number of children receiving food stamps reflects the economic conditions of millions of American families and their increasing difficulty in making ends meet. Between 1989 and 1993 the number of children receiving food stamps increased by 51 percent. During the summer of 1993, a record level of 14.2 million children received benefits. Contrary to popular perception, most of the children receiving benefits were white (42 percent); 35 percent were African-American, 17 percent Latino, 3 percent Asian, and 1 percent Native American. According to the U.S. Department of Agriculture, the average size of a household receiving food stamps was 2.6 persons.

By 1994, a study done by the U.S. Conference of Mayors, *Status Report on Hunger and Homelessness in America's Cities: 1994*, indicated that requests for emergency food assistance in the thirty surveyed cities increased by an average of 14 percent in just one year. More than half of the cities reported that facilities providing emergency food assistance could not keep up with the food assistance demand and that public resources for food assistance had decreased by 4 percent during the year. In 1993, Second Harvest, the largest network of private hunger relief agencies, served 26 million individuals, 43 percent of whom were children. More than 10 percent of the families served stated that their children had missed meals in the previous month because of the family's lack of money and food. Moreover, representatives of Second Harvest reported that nearly one-third of the families who used their services had at least one employed worker.

Many other programs—the Special Supplemental Food Program for Women, Infants, and Children (WIC), free and reduced-price school breakfasts and lunches, and the Summer Food Service Program, for example, provide children with nourishment. In 1993, 13.5 million children benefitted from school lunch programs, 4.7 million benefitted from school breakfast programs, and 2.1 million children benefitted from the Summer Food Service Program. But during the same year there were 8.9 million poor children of school age; therefore, millions of poor children failed to receive nutritional assistance from these programs.

Many of these nutrition programs have been threatened with cuts by the Republican-controlled Congress. As we have seen in chapter 4, the Personal Responsibility Act adopted by the House of Representatives included several provisions dealing with food assistance. Despite the often desperate need for food assistance on the part of millions of children and their families, Congress has attempted to curtail significantly the very food programs that have proved so successful in recent years. If these politicians have their way, there may literally be no free lunch for millions of children!

One of the most devastating and heartbreaking aspects of poverty over the past two decades has been the increasing prevalence of homelessness in the United States. According to the U.S. Department of Housing and Urban Development (HUD), since the mid-1970s homelessness has increased faster among families with children than among any other group. The 1994 report of the U.S. Conference of Mayors found that children account for approximately 39 percent of the homeless population and that requests for emergency shelter increased in all but three of the cities surveyed by that group.

Poor children and their families experience numerous severe housing problems: overcrowded conditions; inadequate heating; cockroach and rodent infestation; and dangerous, often life-threatening, structural problems. But homelessness has to be one of the most devastating experiences for a child. It means literally that one has been "put outdoors." Whether actually living on the street or in a shelter teeming with strangers where a human being is often treated as no more than a number and where one must constantly be on guard against theft, drugs, violence, and even rape, homelessness demonstrates with great clarity to children and adults alike how little control they have over their lives and how extraneous and expendable they are to mainstream society.

Families become homeless for a variety of reasons. For many, unemployment or illness can lead to eviction; many people then move in temporarily with family or friends but rents are so high in many urban and suburban areas that homeless families often have great difficulty finding other housing. When they are forced to leave their substitute housing because of overcrowding, stress, or increased conflict, the next step is the street or a shelter.

In 1992 in New York City, for example, 5,200 families were homeless with close to 1,000 new families entering the system each month. Comparing homeless families in 1992 with those in 1987, we find that homeless families in New York City in the early 1990s were considerably younger than five years before (56 percent of the adults were under age twenty-five compared to 27 percent in 1987), the average age of head-of-household was twenty-two, and virtually all of the families were headed by women (97 percent). The average number of children per family was two and their average age was three. In fact, 78 percent of the homeless children were under the age of six. Between 1987 and 1992, there was a sharp and alarming increase in substance abuse among heads-of-households (from 23 percent to 71 percent) and 43 percent of the mothers had suffered from domestic violence.

But statistics, it has been said, are "people with the tears washed off." The story of Maritza Jimenez illustrates many of the severe and interlocking problems faced by poor women and their children in the United States today.

Maritza Jimenez is a mother of four children who lives in the Bronx. Once homeless, she currently works as a community organizer and welfare activist and is a much-sought-after public speaker on the issues of women, poverty, and welfare. She talks about her life and what circumstances led to her becoming homeless:

> I was born and raised in the South Bronx. Both of my parents were from a small town in Puerto Rico, a town so small that it only had nine streets. I was the oldest of six children. My father was a laborer and my mother was at home.
>
> My father used to drink. He was a good provider but he believed children should be seen and not heard. He would hit us and my mother would get in the way while trying to protect her kids. He would beat her to a pulp. I wanted to protect my mother but I was afraid I would get hurt. My brothers and sisters didn't get hit as much. It all mostly fell on me.

Maritza graduated from junior high school and went on to high school but left after one month. She says, "It so overwhelmed me, I never went back. Junior high school was small; I knew the teachers. High school was so big I was frightened. I went to a counselor but she didn't have time to see me."

Maritza worked for a while and then stayed home to help her mother take care of the younger kids. When she was seventeen, the family moved to Puerto Rico. Her father was in and out of the home. She remembers one time when her father beat her because she and her sisters were fighting over a shirt. She recalls that he once beat her so severely that "I didn't feel the punches. I didn't feel the blows." She was so badly hurt that a male friend of hers took her to the hospital, where they took X rays of her skull. Although she decided not to press charges against her father, she was too frightened to return to her home, so she went to stay at her friend's home with his mother. As Maritza recalls, "One thing led to another," and she became pregnant.

She then spent several years in and out of an abusive relationship with this man. He drank, would leave and not return for days, and often she and their two children went hungry. She states, "I didn't know about birth control; sex was never talked about at home. I didn't even know about immunizations for the children."

Maritza returned to New York when she was pregnant with her third child. She worked as a cashier at a movie house, returned home to cook dinner, and went back for the second shift. Life was so difficult that she decided to return to Puerto Rico. She found out as she was ready to leave that she was pregnant with her fourth child. She remained in Puerto Rico until the baby was ten months old. She describes this period of her life:

> There was no welfare; there were no jobs. We had as many as four days at a time without food. The father of the kids was asking me to go back to New York. The third time he asked he sent the tickets and we went. We had suffered so much—morally and spiritually. We had experienced so much hunger.
>
> One month after we returned to New York, he started drinking again. He had a minimum-wage job but it wasn't enough to support us so I applied for supplementary welfare. They put him on the case too because he was the "Head of

Household." They used to mail the checks to the house but the checks were in his name and he was drinking up the money. He wasn't paying the rent and we got a dispossess notice. I went to welfare to get them to put the checks in my name but they said he would have to go to the welfare office in order to take his name off the case but of course he wasn't going to do that.

The day we received our eviction notice I went across the street to the church to ask for help. The priest told me to go back home and wait. Fifteen to twenty minutes later a patrol car drove up. The policeman said, "O.K., get the kids ready; we're going to the precinct. The worker is going to come pick up the kids." I thought they were going to take us to a convent or a shelter. Instead they took the kids away in the patrol car and told me to wait. Then they took me to Montefiore Hospital to the psychiatric ward. They just left me there. After a half-hour I just left. I was going from place to place crying.

Maritza really couldn't believe what was happening to her. Her children were placed in foster care and she had no place to go. She started staying in friends' houses but soon "came to the realization" that she "had no friends." They would insist she take care of their children or clean house for them in exchange for a place to sleep. She was homeless for two and a half years. She describes the experience:

Sometimes I slept at my brother's house; sometimes I slept at my mother's house. Sometimes I had no place to sleep. I was so upset sometimes I had to drink beer in order to sleep at all.

Maritza started to work with the foster care workers to get her children back. She now describes her plight as a Catch-22 situation: "I couldn't get the kids without an apartment. I couldn't get an apartment without welfare. I couldn't get welfare without the kids."

Finally someone sent her to a vocational program in the Bronx that taught basic office skills and had a women's residence. While she was part of the program, she was sent to "an affluent area" to help a "disabled Caucasian woman" get ready for bed each night. She describes her duties:

> I had to wash her legs and thighs and feet. Once I just broke down and cried. I've never been proud; I've always been a humble person but I felt humiliated. Then I remembered Jesus when he cleaned his disciples' feet and at that point I accepted my situation. The woman offered me gifts in appreciation for my help but I said, "No, thank you." To me it was important to let her know I was not going to take advantage of her.

After that, Maritza was sent to a law office for a job interview. She had no clothes for such an interview and was frightened, but she says, "I wanted the kids back. I wanted to get out of the cycle." She assuaged her anxiety by thinking, " 'They don't know who I am, like I don't know who they are.' I looked confident and got the job at $200 a week. It was a godsend!"

Eventually, Maritza found an apartment and finally got her children back. Today she balances a complex life of work, caring for her two youngest children and two grandchildren; she has obtained her high school equivalency and is currently considering going back to school to get a college degree.

Until she found a job and broke out of the cycle of poverty,

Maritza's story is, unfortunately, all too typical. She had her first child at a young age. As a young woman she was uninformed about sex and ignorant of birth control. Although extremely intelligent, she did not complete high school when she was young and therefore held low-paying jobs. She has suffered from domestic violence at the hands of both her father and the father of her children. She and her children have experienced considerable periods of hunger and despair. And while she was eventually helped by the social welfare system to get on her feet and to reunite her family, she had to cope with sudden and totally unexpected separation from her children and work through the complex and often convoluted maze of AFDC and foster care.

Maritza managed to survive her extended bout of homelessness through the kindness of friends and family and by living on the streets of New York City, but hundreds of thousands of homeless individuals and families must resort to shelters for survival.

While Maritza's children suffered the trauma of separation from their mother during her period of homelessness, spending those years in foster care, thousands of children must endure the often devastating experience of living in a shelter or hotel for the homeless. Jonathan Kozol, in his moving book *Rachel and Her Children: Homeless Families in America*, describes his reactions when he first visited the Hotel Martinique in New York City, where homeless families were housed during the 1980s:

> It is difficult to do full justice to the sense of hopelessness one feels on entering the building. It is a haunting experience and leaves an imprint on one's memory that is not easily erased by time. . . .

Some of the children in the Martinique talk about their experiences and feelings while living there:

TWELVE-YEAR-OLD ANGIE: Ever since August we been livin' here. The room is either very hot or freezin' cold . . . We used to live with my aunt but then it got too crowded there so we moved out. We went to welfare and they sent us to the shelter. . . .

There's one thing I ask: a home to be in with my mother. That was my only wish for Christmas. But it could not be. . . .

SIX-YEAR-OLD RAISIN: Mr. Rat came in my baby sister's crib and bit her. Nobody felt sorry for my sister. Then I couldn't go to sleep. I started crying. . . .

ANGIE: School is bad for me. I feel ashamed. . . . My teacher do not treat us all the same. They know which children live in the hotel. . . . Last week a drug addict tried to stab me. With an ice pick. Tried to stab my mother too.

RAISIN: People fight in here and I don't like it. Why do they do it? 'Cause they're sad. . . .

I was in this lady room. She be cryin' because her baby died. . . . He was unconscious and he died. (Soft voice) Tomorrow is my birthday.

Many states report that between 15 and 30 percent of children who are placed in foster care have been removed from their families primarily because of housing problems. Once they are enmeshed in the often-chaotic foster care system it is extraordinarily difficult to get out of it. Fueled by the crack-cocaine epidemic, the massive problems of poverty, homelessness, child abuse, and neglect as well as other problems, the number of children receiving federal subsidies for foster care skyrocketed from 262,000 in 1982 to 480,000 in 1994. While child welfare experts call for a permanent home for every child—be it with their biological parents, relatives, or in an adoptive home—thousands of children languish in foster care without the system providing meaningful help to their parents to facilitate family reunification, without helping the children cope with the traumas they must bear, and without adequate permanency planning. Tragically, children often remain in this limbo far beyond the age when they can successfully be re-united with their parents or are considered "adoptable." Child welfare agencies, on the whole, are grossly understaffed, the workers greatly overworked, the turnover of staff, many of whom are untrained, so rapid that the result often is continued neglect, both institutional and societal, of these often desper-ately unhappy children.

In this Kafkaesque context, the suggestion by Newt Gingrich that children of the poor be placed into orphanages seems al-most a macabre joke. It is certainly the next logical—or illogical—step in the heartless treatment of poor children and their families. As Richard Wexler, author of *Wounded In-nocents: The Real Victims of the War Against Child Abuse*, has noted:

> The orphanage movement is based on the premise that the same governments that have given us the prison system and the juvenile justice system, and dotted the landscape with hid-eous warehouses for the mentally ill and the retarded, will somehow come up with loving, humane institutions for chil-dren, most of them black and almost all of them poor. But institutions for the poor are almost always poor institutions.

The willingness to revert to the Dickensian warehousing of children, long known to be harmful, particularly to young children, is based on a stereotypic view of poor parents—that they are so abusive, so immoral, so addicted to drugs and/or alcohol, so mired in their personal pathology that any alternative, even orphanages, would be an improvement for their children. But tales of the horror of many such institutions have long been widely known. One former resident of an orphanage recalls his experience:

> One day my brother and I were living a quiet . . . existence. . . . The next day we were put into an orphanage. Donald was five; I was seven. . . . It was my first . . . encounter with mindless fear. As they tried to lead my brother away, he held on to my arm . . . and let out a terrible yowl. . . . My poor brother, like many children who undergo this kind of emotional uprooting, wet the bed. Their treatment was to beat him every morning for months. The orphanage may have been purgatory for me, but it was hell for Donald.

During most of the twentieth century, it has been clear to professionals concerned with the well-being of children that institutional care is undesirable for children. There is a fundamental difference between orphanages and small group homes or residential institutions for children with special physical and/or psychiatric needs. After World War II, noted psychiatrist John Bowlby studied the effects on children of institutionalization, separation, and maternal deprivation. He published the results of his research in a monograph, *Maternal Care and Mental Health*, in which he stated that children need an intimate, caring, and continuous relationship with their mothers or with a permanent mother substitute. He found that children who have never had the opportunity to form a bond with a mother figure, those who suffer from long-term deprivation of the maternal relationship, and those who have been cared for by a series of maternal figures suffer from long-term negative effects. Psychiatrist René Spitz also studied institutionalized children and came to similar conclusions—that the loss of a maternal figure and the lack of a single substitute caregiver may well lead to severe depression in infants and problems in their personality development. Research on the effects of institutional care on older children indicates that they are likely to suffer from behavioral problems and have more social and emotional problems during adolescence and adulthood. Recent studies also indicate that child abuse may occur twice as often in institutional settings as in families.

What is so disturbing about the current rhetoric and policy changes is that both are likely to lead to larger numbers of children being warehoused in large institutions. The rhetoric —that economically impoverished parents are by definition bad or grossly inadequate parents—if repeated often enough, will make separating children from their parents and even institutionalizing them more acceptable in the eyes of politicians, policy makers, and the public. Moreover, severely restricting social welfare programs, refusing aid to certain categories of mothers and children, and forcing parents off AFDC whether or not they have found employment is likely to result in additional parents becoming economically unable to care for their children. This will therefore necessitate the children's removal to alternative care; to some extent this has become an example of the self-fulfilling prophecy. Impoverished parents, particularly welfare recipients, are seen and portrayed as irresponsible, sometimes as morally depraved, as people who do not play by the society's rules, and therefore are unfit and unable to care for their children. Given this premise, many feel that society must attempt to resocialize these parents by punishing "bad" behavior and rewarding "good." As part of this policy, federal, state, and local governments have for some time been lowering the amount of money and other benefits poor parents receive and in some cases refusing to provide benefits altogether. Refusing parents aid without regard to whether they have alternative income may well lead to their becoming unable to care for their children and thus the prophecy comes true.

Not only is removing children from their families, except when they are in dire need of alternate care, detrimental to their well-being, but it is also far more costly than maintaining them in their own homes. In 1993, for example, the median AFDC benefit for a family of three was $367 per month; the average cost of foster care for two children was $655 plus state and local supplements, almost twice the cost of AFDC. The average cost of residential care for young people which must include education, health care, the availability of psychiatric services, and leisure activities was $36,500 in 1993, eight times the cost of the average AFDC grant. Clearly, removing children from their homes and placing them in large institutions except in extreme situations makes little sense from an emotional or a financial perspective.

The violence that children experience in shelters for the homeless is a reflection and concentration of the violence children experience in the wider society on a daily basis. In 1992, 5,379 children and adolescents were killed by guns—one every 98 minutes. Nearly two-thirds (63 percent) died as a result of gun homicides; 26 percent as a result of gun suicide; and 9 percent as a result of accidents involving guns. According to a study by the Centers for Disease Control and Prevention (CDC) released in 1994, the murder rate for males ages fifteen to nineteen more than doubled between 1985 and 1991. In 1985 there were 13 homicides per 100,000 boys; by 1991 the number had increased to nearly 33 per 100,000. For black males in this age group the increase was even greater. In 1985, 46 black teenage boys were killed per 100,000; by 1991 the homicide rate nearly tripled, to 124 per 100,000. According to the CDC study, 97 percent of this shocking increase was due to guns. As the Children's Defense Fund report *The State of America's Children Yearbook 1995* states,

> The victims of gun violence are not limited to those children who die, however. They also include many thousands of children who are physically injured and hundreds of thousands of children scarred emotionally by exposure to violence in their homes, neighborhoods, and schools.

These homicides were due to young people killing one another as well as their being gunned down by adults. According to data released by the Federal Bureau of Investigation, the number of juveniles arrested for murder increased 168 percent between 1984 and 1993. Young people report that guns are extraordinarily easy to obtain. In January 1995, the National Institute of Justice released the results of a survey that found that 40 percent of students surveyed in ten inner-city high schools reported that they had a male relative who carries a gun. The same study showed that one in every three males surveyed in these schools had been stabbed, shot at, or injured in some other way with a weapon at school or in going to or from school. Handguns, specifically, are used in approximately 70 percent of all adolescent suicides in which guns are used and they account for 50 to 60 percent of all accidental deaths due to firearms among young people.

One observer has described the omnipresence of violence in the inner cities:

> For more than twenty years the children of the ghetto have witnessed violent death as an almost routine occurrence. They have seen it on their streets, in their schools, in their families, and on TV. They have lived with constant fear. Many have come to believe that they will not live to see twenty-five. . . .
>
> These young people have been raised in the glare of cease-less media violence and incitement to every depravity of act and spirit. Movies may feature scores of killings in two hours' time, vying to show methods ever more horrific; many are quickly imitated on the street.

As poor children are far more likely to become enmeshed in the foster care system, so are they more likely to become enmeshed in the juvenile justice system. According to the Criminal Justice Institute, as of January 1, 1994, more than 100,000 juveniles were incarcerated—some in institutions maintained exclusively for young people and some in institutions maintained for adults.

Sara Mosle, a third-grade teacher in the Washington Heights section of New York City, describes her students as living under "virtual house arrest." Their parents won't let them out to play on dangerous streets. One of her students wrote in her daily journal, "I did not get to play with the snow none of the days. . . ." She wrote that instead of playing outdoors she had "played with the snow on the window."

The teacher herself reports that "Last year, I had to duck behind a dumpster as I was walking a student home because gunfire erupted across the street." She continues,

Last fall, a thirteen-year-old boy who had attended my school the previous year was shot to death in his apartment doorway by drug dealers testing their new guns. (His father had been murdered a year earlier for testifying as a witness to a crime.) One girl in my class this year explained how a man had been burned to death right outside her apartment door. She kept repeating how it had all happened "really close."

Mosle points out that as politicians at every level of government are cutting programs for young people, her students "desperately need and want a place to go," a place to talk and interact with one another, a place to do the work of children, to play.

The differences between rich and poor are perhaps most significant, most visible, and most poignant in the lives of children. While Mosle's students live in constant danger and don't even have opportunities to play, the children of the affluent often seem to have everything. During the 1994 holiday season, I received a photocopied letter that graphically illustrates the chasm in the life chances between rich and poor in the land of "equal opportunity":

Much of our lives is organized around the many activities of Robert, now 10 years old and a 6th grader. . . . He's doing well on trumpet and piano. . . . [H]is soccer team completed five playoff rounds undefeated and won the City . . . Championship on Robert's shootout goal. . . . [H]e was rookie of the year at shortstop in Little League baseball, took tennis lessons from a pro, learned to ski . . . and in August (!) learned to ice skate. . . . In the summer, he participated in . . . [a] program for capable & talent[ed] youths . . . with challenging readings in philosophy and anthropology. . . . Best of all, he's a loving and thoughtful young fellow.

The contrast between Mosle's students living under "virtual house arrest" and Robert's trumpet and piano lessons, soccer, baseball, tennis, skiing, and skating, not to speak of his participation in a summer program for talented youth, is truly heartbreaking. How can poor students hope to compete—for college, for jobs, for positions in today's world? How can we as a society talk about admission to higher education or hiring for a job on the basis of "merit"? How can we possibly determine "merit" when such enormous gaps exist in the opportunities and life experience of the candidates?

Robert is not only learning an incredible variety of skills, many of which he will be able to use in various social and professional situations later in life. He is not only exploring his own interests in order to determine his special abilities and desires. Perhaps most important, he is being given the opportunity to work hard at a variety of exciting activities, to excel at some and do less well at others, to receive instruction, support, and feedback from many different adults, and to feel the real sense of accomplishment and confidence that is so crucial for success in this complex world. He is, at the age of ten, exploring his incredibly diverse environment and in so doing has the opportunity to discover where he fits in.

Aren't less fortunate children entitled to *some* of these experiences and opportunities? Aren't they entitled to discover what *they* love to do, what *their* special skills are, and, above all, aren't they entitled to have the feeling that the wider society cares? How can we possibly measure the loss suffered by them and by the rest of us because they never have the chance to explore and develop *their* special talents, *their* special way of making a contribution?

Chapter 7 suggests several steps the United States might take in order to truly reform America's social and economic systems—steps that would help millions of families out of poverty and enable millions of children to live decent lives, to contribute to the larger society, and to move closer to fulfilling their promise.

Chapter 7

A Return to Caring

We have come to a clear realization . . . that true individual freedom cannot exist without economic security.
. . . We have accepted . . . a second Bill of Rights under
which a new basis of security and prosperity can be established for all—regardless of station, race, or creed.
  Among these are:

The right to a useful and remunerative job . . .
The right to earn enough to provide adequate food
  and clothing . . .
The right of every family to a decent home;
The right to adequate medical care and the opportunity
  to achieve and enjoy good health;
The right to adequate protection from the economic
  fears of old age, sickness, accident, and
  unemployment;
The right to a good education.

—PRESIDENT FRANKLIN D. ROOSEVELT
annual message to Congress, 1944

OVER THE PAST SEVERAL YEARS, BUT PARTICULARLY SINCE
the 1994 congressional election, we have witnessed the systematic stereotyping, stigmatizing, and demonizing of the poor,
particularly of poor women. They have been pictured as the

embodiment of the characteristics Americans revile—laziness, willful dependence on government, wanton sexuality, and imprudent, excessive reproduction. They are frequently described as transmitters of negative values or, even worse, of no values at all; their family structure and child rearing have been blamed for fostering violence, crime, school failure, out-of-wedlock births, and, above all, for passing their poverty on to the next generation. In the eagerness of many in positions of power to deny the structural causes of poverty and the other ills that beset American society, politicians and policy makers have revived the "culture of poverty" analysis and laid the responsibility for poor people's problems and many of the problems of the wider society at the feet of the most impoverished and powerless among us. "They" don't want to work, it is said. "They" want something for nothing. "They" are like animals who have been given too much, conditioned to be dependent, and consequently can no longer make it on their own. "They" have too much sex, have too many babies, and all too often care for them miserably. "They" breed violent children who, when they reach adolescence, will rape, pillage, murder, and burn.

"They" as a group have been portrayed as the "underclass," a group with multiple, severe problems, increasingly considered impossible to reach, a breed apart from mainstream Americans. The image of the underclass has expanded to include virtually all of the poor, particularly single mothers and welfare recipients, and is envisioned by many to consist largely of African Americans. And it is the race factor, the stereotype that most poor people are black, that holds the entire image together. This mythology is in part embedded in our history. Large elements within the United States have since colonial times despised and feared the poor and have particularly despised and feared African Americans. A critical consequence of dividing people into "them" and "us" is that it clouds our perceptions of the reality that millions of people face daily and therefore propels society toward solutions that will harm rather than help those in need. I believe these divisions and misperceptions will ultimately harm us all.

It is much easier to oversimplify, to claim despised groups are evil or unworthy, label them as the cause of our severe economic and social problems, and banish them metaphorically to the edge of town, so far out that they can no longer see, feel, or touch mainstream America or the American Dream, than it is to examine closely exactly who those individuals and families are across the country who must scrimp and yet barely survive, who are hungry and homeless, who are working but earn too little to pay the rent.

The poor are not a homogeneous group. They include families whose earnings dip below the poverty line for a relatively brief period of time as well as long-term, multiproblem families; they include those who live in enclaves within urban America and the less visible but nonetheless often abject poor of rural America. But what is irrefutable is that women and children are indeed last in America. The single largest group of impoverished Americans are children; the majority of adults living in poverty are women. Mother-only families are at particular risk of poverty as are families with parents under the age of thirty. It is essential to recognize that because the circumstances of the impoverished—women and children as well as men—are so varied, the solutions must be varied as well. Just as one brush cannot depict all the faces of poverty, so one policy cannot begin to solve the problems of poverty in America.

In contrast to the widespread images of the poor, many people have a Norman Rockwell image of the nonpoor living good, God-fearing, hardworking lives in Middle America—lives like those epitomized in the Frank Capra film *It's a Wonderful Life*—but in reality the nonpoor are enormously varied as well. Many of the problems that afflict those at or below the poverty line afflict other Americans as well. Increasing numbers of nonpoor families are headed by single parents—the vast majority by the mother. The nonpoor have high rates of divorce. Sexual relationships outside of marriage are increasingly the norm and many nonpoor women become pregnant. And nonpoor unmarried women are deciding to have and keep their babies with far greater frequency than in previous eras. Millions of working-class, middle-class, and affluent Americans engage in a wide range of violent and self-destructive behaviors including wife battering, child abuse, excessive drinking, drug addiction, and criminal behavior.

The nonpoor obviously include a wide economic spectrum as well. *Forbes* magazine counted seventy billionaires in 1995, topped by Warren Buffett, the duPont family, and Bill Gates, each of whom was estimated to be worth over $10 billion. As was detailed in chapter 1, the "super-rich," the richest half of one percent of the population, own nearly one-third of all U.S. household wealth; the richest 20 percent of the population, a group *Newsweek* cleverly and aptly designated the "overclass," own an incredible 84.6 percent of total U.S. wealth. A recent comprehensive international study commissioned by the Paris-based Organization for Economic Cooperation and Development found that during the 1980s the gap between rich and poor was greater in the United States than in fifteen other industrialized countries.

While some earn incredibly high incomes, have vast wealth, and live in luxury, millions of middle-class and working-class Americans have looked on helplessly as their companies have downsized, laying off hundreds, often thousands of workers. A significant percentage of these workers never regain their previous standard of living; many are forced to work extra jobs and to ask for help from family, friends, community resources, and the government in ways they never anticipated. Financial insecurity has become a fact of life for significant segments of the middle and working classes. Just as the poor are heterogeneous and therefore require complex, multifaceted social and economic policies, so are the nonpoor an enormously diverse group. Clearly, policies that help the super-rich may well not improve—and in fact may actively damage—the lives of the working and middle classes.

In devising social policy, therefore, we must recognize that levels of financial insecurity characterize significant segments of the American population, that very few families are able to fully purchase in the marketplace the services they need, and that dependence—on family, community institutions, and/or government programs—is widespread. In other words, dividing the population of the United States into "us" and "them" is neither accurate nor useful in evaluating existing social programs or in devising new ones.

Furthermore, dichotomous, stereotypic thinking makes it far more difficult for groups in society to feel empathetic toward one another, to see their commonalities rather than simply their differences. The labeling of one group, be they witches in Puritan America or Jews in Nazi Germany, as the enemy within, the source of all of our troubles and problems, serves to isolate that group, to demonize them, to make them less than human, beyond our empathy. It has been suggested, in fact, that we in the United States are in the midst of a "retreat from caring."

One of the central factors in this "retreat from caring" may be the enormous power of the media in shaping our feelings and our views. The relentless focus on violent crime in the local news ("If it bleeds, it leads") and in dramatic television programming as well as in films leaves millions of Americans suspicious and fearful even if they live in relatively low-crime areas. The constant repetition of a point of view by the media often makes it so in the minds of many readers and listeners. That poverty is caused by individuals' behavior, specifically by single motherhood, rather than by economic recession, inadequate education, a shortage of jobs, wages that are inadequate to lift families out of poverty, and a profound shortage of social supports, becomes conventional wisdom when repeated over and over by the evening news, the Sunday morning "talking heads," the daily newspapers, and by the influential weekly news magazines. When politicians on the floor of Congress, local officials, and social scientists are all reported by the mainstream media as condemning the welfare system, vowing to "end welfare as we know it," and implying that decent jobs are available if only welfare recipients would lift a finger to work, this view becomes the prevailing point of view.

A recent program of *Meet the Press* is illustrative of the emphasis on "values" and the need for individual change rather than on the structural problems that plague the United States and their impact on individual behavior and family life. The overall topic on Sunday morning, July 23, 1995, was "race in America." The guests were Bill Bradley, Democratic senator from New Jersey; William Bennett, former secretary of education; Kweisi Mfume, Democratic congressman from Maryland and former chair of the Congressional Black Caucus; and J. C. Watts, the first Southern black Republican elected to Congress since Reconstruction. Leading the discussion was the host, Tim Russert, and joining him was Gwen Ifill of NBC News.

The program started with a discussion of affirmative action, discrimination, and separatism, and finally moved to issues concerning single-parent families, particularly out-of-wedlock births. In the response following Russert's question "What do we do to stop single-parent families and have people get married before having children?" the answers ranged from "strengthen[ing] the family," "strengthen[ing] educational institutions," encourage people to take pride in the community, teach individuals about the work ethic, and teach people that "life is sacred," and that "respect is due your elders." Senator Bradley stated, "Values aren't a part of the game; they are the whole game." Representative Watts spoke about teaching the Ten Commandments, teaching "responsibility." It wasn't until the last five minutes of the discussion that Senator Bradley said,

> I don't think that we should end this discussion without at least considering the economic facts of life. I mean, *the problem in this country as it affects race, but a lot of other things, is inadequate economic growth, unfairly shared*. And until we confront that, we are simply going to be talking about dealing with some of the issues around the edge. Now, the work ethic—a lot of other important value demonstrations are, I think, a step toward improving the quality of economic activity, but *there's no way to separate somebody's earning power from their prospects for life*. If you were an African-American cotton picker in the South in the 1940s, the cotton-picking machine displaced you. You went to Chicago, you worked in an automobile plant, automation displaced you. In the 1970s, you start to work for the government and cuts in the eighties displaced you. [Emphasis added.]

His statement was immediately followed by Tim Russert emphasizing the theme of that morning's program, indeed the theme of virtually all media coverage of these issues: "But lack of jobs is no substitute for lack of values." He was underlining the central message of our day—that these serious social issues are "their problem" rather than society's problem and are due to individual deficiencies, due to a "lack of values," rather than to problems such as inequality, economic insecurity, and joblessness.

This separating of problems into "theirs" as opposed to "ours" is facilitated by the fact that we are living at a time when there is among Americans a weaker sense of solidarity, of uniting for the social good, than perhaps at any time in recent history. As Hugh Heclo points out, events such as the Great Depression and the two World Wars fostered a sense of unity among Americans, a sense that people were experiencing cataclysmic events together and that, in order to survive, they needed to endure "shared sacrifices for the common good."

Institutions such as trade unions, political parties, and defined, stable neighborhoods that foster a sense of solidarity have been weakened during the second half of the twentieth century and replaced by institutions that encourage separateness and passivity—television and other mass media, consumerism, and spectator sports, for example.

Not only does the organization of our daily lives—the likelihood that we will not spend the better part of our lives in one place of employment working beside the same people, the likelihood that we will not spend the better part of our lives in one neighborhood living next to the same people, the fact that over the past decade and a half the United States has experienced a massive surge of immigration that is literally redefining what it means to be American, and the continuing de facto segregation of our schools and neighborhoods by both race and class—encourage feelings of separateness and fragmentation but the wretchedness of much of *fin de siècle* America encourages us to withdraw our feelings, to become morally insensitive to the horrors around us. How else can we cope emotionally with the homeless lying on our streets, the beggars plaintively telling us they are hungry as we rush to a lunch appointment, and the murder or rape in the next block if not by withdrawing emotionally, walking a little faster, pulling our coats around us more tightly? Particularly when many of us feel helpless, impotent in making real societal change, the common reaction is to withdraw and live our own lives as best we can or perhaps to lash out in anger at "those people" who make us so sad, so uncomfortable, so afraid. But perhaps, as we move into the twenty-first century, we are faced with dangers that can bring us together rather than separate us one from another—the dangers that come from increasing inequality, extreme individualism, escalating fear and hatred against marginalized groups of all kinds, and above all, the danger that comes from the profound sense of despair and alienation felt by people from every stratum of society but perhaps most of all by the young and the dispossessed.

In all of the discussion over the past decade about welfare policy, the problems of female-headed families, dependency, and poverty in the United States, it is striking how rarely policy makers examine these issues in cross-national perspective. The diatribes on the floor of the House of Representatives and the Senate, the reports and analyses in the press and on television deal almost exclusively with the American scene as though it was unique, divorced from the rest of the world, as though it shared few similarities with other Western industrialized countries, and as though we have virtually nothing to learn from other societies. This perception is extraordinarily misleading. What becomes apparent when we examine the experience of other comparable nations is that the issues the United States is facing are issues that are of central concern in virtually all of the Western European countries and that these societies have a great deal to teach us about solutions.

Perhaps the "most dramatic change in family structure experienced throughout the advanced industrialized West over the last 20 to 30 years," according to Sheila Kamerman, professor at the Columbia School of Social Work and author of numerous works on social policy and cross-cultural comparisons, has been the "growth in lone-parent, female-headed families as a proportion of all families with children." Whether due to divorce, out-of-wedlock births, or widowhood, single mothers constitute a large group—and an important "at-risk" group for poverty—in virtually all industrialized societies.

While the United States has the highest marriage rate of the twelve countries examined in a major cross-national study, *Poverty, Inequality and the Future of Social Policy: Western States in the New World Order,* it also has the highest divorce rate. Although they have recently leveled off, divorce rates had risen significantly in virtually all of the Western European countries; this phenomenon clearly contributes significantly to the increasing number and percentage of families headed by women in these nations.

Another factor in the growth of mother-only families has been the dramatic increase over the past thirty years of female participation in the paid labor force both in the United States as well as in the highly industrialized Western world. Between 1960 and 1990, labor force participation in the United States by married women with children under eighteen more than doubled; during the same years the rates of working wives with children under six more than tripled. While single mothers were 50 percent more likely than married women to be in the paid labor force in 1970, by 1990 the rates were virtually identical.

During the same period, the transformation of the United

States and many countries of Western Europe from manufacturing to service societies has resulted in far less demand
for low-skilled labor. Today, many countries in South Asia
have a larger percentage of their workforce in manufacturing than do the older Western industrial countries. This redistribution of jobs worldwide and the movement of unskilled
jobs out of the center cities have excluded large enclaves of
workers from the "dynamic sectors of the emerging world
system of production." According to Stanley Aronowitz and
William DiFazio in their book *The Jobless Future: Sci-Tech and
the Dogma of Work*, "Technological change and competition in
the world market guarantee that increasing numbers of workers
will be displaced and that these workers will tend to be rehired
in jobs that do not pay comparable wages and salaries." As
noted in chapter 1, these global economic shifts have already
taken their toll on the wages of American workers, particularly on the wages of younger workers, male workers, and
minority workers. Persistent unemployment and underemploy-
ment have also plagued workers in many advanced countries
with younger workers and members of minority groups again
hardest hit.

Thus, many factors—the declining wages and economic opportunities of men, the increasing need for women to take on
a wage-earning role and their increasing economic opportunities, the high divorce rate, and the low fertility rate that enables women to spend an increasing proportion of their lives
in the paid labor force—have had a profound effect on the rise
of solo parenthood in Western industrialized societies. The im-
permanence of marriage, the fact that millions of men cannot
provide economic security and, in many cases, flee from familial responsibilities, and the greater sense of independence
experienced by women have also contributed to the weakening

of the traditional two-parent family and the growth of the lone-parent, especially the mother-only, family. The female-headed family is then at considerable risk of poverty. Because women's wages are often inadequate to provide the bare necessities families require, because of a profound scarcity of adequate, affordable social supports such as health care, child care, and after-school care, and because fathers all too often fail to provide support for their children, millions of families hover just above the poverty line or plummet below it. It is urgent that we recognize that these demographic and economic shifts are not due to individual weakness or moral laxity, that they are not due to a preference for "idleness" or "a lack of values" but rather that they stem from worldwide changes that often have greatest impact on the poorest and most vulnerable among us.

In a disturbing and illuminating article, University of California/Berkeley sociologist Troy Duster demonstrates the impact the "great economic and social transformation of Western industrialized societies" over the past quarter-century has had on African-American young people in the United States. Duster suggests that young black Americans may be the proverbial "canary in the coal mine"—the harbinger of future massive economic dislocation for millions of other young workers. Duster explains his analogy:

Working in a coal mine can be very dangerous. Not only are there cave-ins and explosions, but there are noxious fumes. However, the levels of toxicity in these fumes are not noticeable to humans until it is too late. The canary is a delicate bird with a small lung capacity. Someone conjured the bright idea to take a canary down into the coal mine so that, at levels of toxicity far lower than those that would be fatal to humans, the canary would succumb—a warning signal to the coal miners.

As Duster and others have pointed out, in the United States approximately one-third of those who complete high school fail to find stable employment by the age of thirty. While unemployment among all high school dropouts was high in the early 1990s, unemployment among African-American dropouts was over 70 percent. In addition, while approximately 14 percent (one in seven Americans) was persistently poor, 40 percent (one in 2.5) of African Americans were persistently poor. Duster suggests that this phenomenon is due in large part to the transformation of the American economy from manufacturing to service. During earlier decades of this century, black workers, including young people, moved from farm work to factory work with far greater success than they are now able to move from factory work into the service sector. According to Duster, this has happened because of three factors: active discrimination on the part of retail employers, a "lack of fit" between mainstream white culture and inner-city black culture, and the expectations of employers in the service economy. Experiments sending out pairs of matched job applicants, black and white, indicate substantial discrimination in hiring. For workers employed in the manufacturing sector, productivity is a crucial consideration, but in hiring workers for the service sector, employers' perceptions of the way in which employees will relate to the customer and the general public becomes an overriding concern. In these settings, Duster states, ". . . mature female workers replace younger male workers, immigrant workers replace native-born racial and ethnic minorities, and suburban workers replace workers from the more ethnic urban cores."

As the unemployment rate of black youths has skyrocketed over the past three decades, so has their incarceration rate. As they have been increasingly excluded from entry-level service jobs, African-American young men have turned to the underground economy. In addition, many studies indicate that drug laws are selectively enforced, that black youths are far more likely to be arrested than are white youths, and that mandatory minimum sentencing in drug cases has dramatically increased the lengths of time African Americans serve in prison. According to Duster, in 1933 blacks were incarcerated approximately three times as often as whites; in 1950, that rate increased to approximately four times; by 1960, the rate was five times; in 1970, six times; and by 1989, the black incarceration rate was seven times that of whites. Andrew Hacker, author of *Two Nations: Black and White, Separate, Hostile, Unequal*, points out that in the mid-1980s, blacks comprised over 45 percent of the prison population. In the late 1980s, there were more black males in prison or jail than there were attending college or university full-time.

When we examine the high rates of mother-only families in the African-American community, we must recognize the impact of these factors—factors that are largely beyond the control of individuals. While individuals surely make decisions about their lives, these decisions are made within a specific social, economic, and psychological context. The sixteen-year-old young woman growing up in the suburbs, attending first-rate schools, hoping to study at Yale or Amherst, and considering a career in medicine or law clearly has a very different framework for personal decision-making than the poor or near-poor teenager living in an inner-city neighborhood in Detroit or Los Angeles, attending crowded, dilapidated schools, surrounded by violence, with few opportunities for jobs that offer the possibility of any significant future social mobility. Equally important in terms of teenage or mother-only childbearing, these two young women will meet men with very different life options, life options that will determine to a great extent the way they see their future, their family connections and commitments. Until we dramatically alter the structural conditions under which millions of Americans live, we cannot expect that they will make different personal decisions.

Rapidly rising rates of out-of-wedlock births in the United States have fueled the debate about whether social programs, particularly AFDC, are an incentive to the growth of female-headed families, about the negative effects of teenage pregnancy and childbearing, and about the nature of "family values" in America. But as we note that out-of-wedlock births as a percentage of all births in the United States increased fourfold between 1960 and 1986, we must recognize that such births increased fivefold in Denmark, Norway, and the Netherlands, and more than quadrupled in Sweden. In Finland, Canada, and the United Kingdom, there was nearly a fourfold increase. While these demographic shifts may be similar to those in the United States, what is clearly different are the ways these societies have chosen to deal with these changes.

Studies of seven Western industrialized countries (Canada, France, the former West Germany, the Netherlands, Sweden, the United States, and the United Kingdom) indicate that in the late 1970s and mid-1980s the United States consistently had the highest poverty rates, followed by Canada and the United Kingdom. While all of these countries were experiencing high unemployment rates and economic dislocation during this period, and five of the seven countries experienced an increase in poverty rates (only in France and the Netherlands did the poverty rate remain the same), the societies varied dramatically in the effectiveness of government policies in lifting families out of poverty. Among the seven countries studied, the United States was the only country in which tax policies and shifts of income and services from the affluent to the less well off had virtually no effect on the poverty rate. In Canada, approximately one in every five poor families and in the United Kingdom nearly one out of every two poor families were lifted out of poverty. In the Netherlands, over 60 percent were lifted out of poverty leaving a poverty rate of less than 8 percent despite extremely difficult market conditions; in France, over half and in Sweden over 43 percent were lifted out of poverty, leaving a national poverty rate of less than 9 percent. These data clearly indicate that generous welfare benefits do not lead to higher rates of poverty. On the contrary, countries with far more generous benefits have significantly lower poverty rates than does the United States, which has both the lowest level of benefits and the highest rates of poverty.

What are the policies that lift families out of poverty in these European countries? First, all the countries provide a children's or family allowance—universal cash benefits based on the number of children in a family and provided regardless of the family's income. In most of these countries, the amount of money is not large but represents a commitment on the part of the society to the well-being of all of its children. And in families living on the edge of poverty or in poverty, the children's allowance can make a real difference when other sources of income are running dry.

A second element of the family policy in place in all European countries—and virtually all other industrialized societies as well—is some form of national health insurance or national health service which assures all families and individuals access to health care. Third, most of these countries provide universal, low-cost, or free preschool care to all or almost all children from the age of two or three. Fourth, many industrialized countries provide special benefits for divorced families, guaranteeing a minimum amount of child support if the noncustodial parent fails to pay the required amount.

The question for the United States today is what social and economic policies will most effectively help families in our extremely affluent society to live decent lives without the specter of poverty hovering over them. Should a family policy stress universal benefits? Should policies be targeted for specific at-risk groups or should we move toward a combination of the two approaches? Many other countries use a complex combination of tax policy, employment policy, universal social policy, and specific programs targeted to the most vulnerable. Sweden, for example, has focused on employment policies and universal benefits which combine to produce extremely low rates of poverty. The Netherlands has low rates of poverty for women because it has developed a generous social policy that provides a relatively high income floor for all citizens. Poverty rates are low for Dutch women because poverty rates are low for all Dutch citizens.

In thinking through an appropriate U.S. family policy for the twenty-first century, we must recognize that most mothers today, particularly single mothers, are caught in a difficult and often painful role conflict that is exacerbated by the unwillingness of American society to recognize and respond to the real needs of families. As Lydia Morris, author of *Dangerous Classes: The Underclass and Social Citizenship*, has pointed out,

> Recent developments in the conceptualization of citizenship
> have increasingly placed at least as much emphasis on obliga-
> tions as on rights, the prime obligation being work as a means
> to independence. This places women in an ambiguous posi-

tion: either they earn their "public" citizenship rights by their own paid employment, or they perform their "private" family obligations and remain dependent. This conflict can only be resolved by a redistribution of the "private" obligations of unpaid labour, or by some acknowledgement of the "public" service such labour performs, or by increasing state involvement in the "private" obligation to care for children.

This is exactly where the United States stands today. Women are still expected to care for the home and particularly for the children but they are increasingly expected to participate in the paid labor market. As we have noted, in most two-parent families women's income has helped keep the family afloat as men's wages have declined over the past two decades. But while virtually all of the Western European countries have developed a panoply of social supports for families, American society has not seen fit to redistribute the private obligations of women on a significant scale either to men or to the public sector. What "welfare reform" really means is that women are being forced to take on both roles full-time without either adequate salaries or adequate help in providing for their children. Many mothers must provide care and love and food and clothing and values and discipline while holding down a full-time job and earning wages either below or close to the poverty line. They are increasingly expected to do all this both without the help of a man, since many of the men are nowhere to be found, and without the help of the society.

As Lester Thurow, professor of economics at the Massachusetts Institute of Technology, has written,

> Whether it is fathering a family without being willing to be a father, whether it is divorce and being unwilling to pay alimony or child support, or whether it is being an immigrant

from the third world and after a time failing to send payments to the family back home, men all around the world are opting out.

In addition, policies recently adopted by state and federal levels of government in the United States mean that the society is opting out as well. What we are asking of women is virtually impossible. It would be exceedingly difficult under the best of circumstances—with family supports, a living wage, and adequate benefits. Yet, poor women often have none of these.

In *Women and Children Last*, I called for a universal family policy—one that would simultaneously reach all Americans and target the most vulnerable among us with special programs. It may seem quixotic at best and foolhardy at worst to propose a universal family policy at a time when conservatism is in the ascendancy, when government programs are viewed with widespread pessimism and even cynicism, and when the United States has incurred a massive deficit. Nonetheless, we need nothing short of this today.

A universal family policy should include, I believe, children's allowances. As in many European countries, every family, regardless of income, should receive a flat amount per child under the age of eighteen. This transfer would indicate that we all have a stake in the well-being of every child; it would help families when funds are particularly low, but would not be a large enough amount to provide an incentive for having additional children. We might want to consider the amount taxable for affluent families, but the principle of universalism is important nevertheless.

America's families must have comprehensive, affordable health care whether through a system of national health insurance or a national health service. All of our families need prenatal care, well-baby care, immunizations, access to contraception and abortion services, and health care for all family members including the elderly. Despite the fiasco of proposals for "health care reform" during the first two years of the Clinton Administration, a universal health care system must be a priority for America's families.

We should consider instituting paid, parental leave for all parents at the time of the birth or adoption of a baby. If such leave is unpaid, as it is now for millions of workers, only the affluent or members of two-parent families can afford to take it. Sweden currently offers a twelve-month leave of which one month must be taken by the father. We, too, should consider ways of encouraging fathers to participate more fully in child rearing from the time of the birth of the baby and even, when possible, during pregnancy. Everyone will gain—fathers, mothers who desperately need to share child rearing responsibilities, and the children; sharing parenting more fully may well give the family unit a greater sense of cohesion.

First-rate, accessible, affordable child care must also be a priority. With the vast majority of women, including mothers of preschoolers, currently participating in the paid labor force, public, private, and nonprofit institutions must work together to establish a variety of child-care options, including after-school care, with priority going to working parents, to parents who are students, to single parents, and to parents with special needs. The urgency of after-school care is clear; an estimated 2 million children under the age of thirteen have no adult supervision either before or after school. Moreover, if these are truly creative environments in which children can explore, socialize with one another and with their caregivers, and be nourished physically, emotionally, and intellectually, the entire society will benefit in the long run.

With at least 1 million Americans, including a growing number of children and working adults, homeless at some time each year, the United States must rethink its housing policy. As Peter Dreier, Distinguished Professor of Politics at Occidental College, and John Atlas, attorney and president of the National Housing Institute, note, "Among Western democracies, the U.S. relies most heavily on private market forces to house its population." They point out that while the United States provides more than $100 billion a year to housing subsidies, by far the largest amount, $64 billion, goes to mortgage interest and property tax reduction for home owners while $13 billion goes to tax breaks for wealthy investors in rental housing and mortgage revenue bonds. They further point out that only 4.1 million low-income households receive aid while twice as many, 9.7 million households, are eligible but do not receive any help. Dreier and Atlas call for a policy that would spend the same money we are spending now but would target that money for those most in need.

And, of course, our grossly unequal system of education must be reformed. If we really believe in fairness, in equality of opportunity, we must consider how to restructure a system that provides every opportunity imaginable for the privileged while other young people are left to grow up virtually ignored and illiterate, discarded as disposable in a society dominated by the need for technology and sophisticated expertise. Until these children are educated for life in the twenty-first century, they will live at the margins of society and we will all, in the long run, be the losers.

A central component to any family policy must be a coherent employment policy. Decent jobs—for men and for women—that pay an income above the poverty line are essential to lift families out of poverty, to strengthen the American family, to keep young people out of the underground economy, thus reducing crime, and, perhaps most important, to give people some hope of improving their lives. Several aspects of the family policy proposed above, particularly a universal health care system and greatly expanded child care and after-school care, would result in the creation of millions of additional jobs providing needed services.

The private sector must be stimulated to create jobs rather than lay people off in order to increase their companies' profits. Direct creation of jobs by the public sector will be essential as well. During the 1930s, in the midst of the Great Depression, public works programs built much-needed hospitals, bridges, roads, stadiums, and parks; today, during a period that some have called a "silent depression," we should do no less. Our public buildings, particularly our schools, hospitals, and public housing, our bridges and tunnels, and our parks and playgrounds are sadly—and sometimes dangerously—in need of repair, renovation and—dare we suggest it—beautification. Government at all levels could create millions of jobs at decent wages, thereby putting the unemployed and the underemployed to work rebuilding our society's infrastructure.

But in order for such a work program to help lift people out of poverty, we must raise the minimum wage. As some politicians are fond of saying, people who "play by the rules" should not be mired in poverty. If we examine the minimum wage as a percentage of the poverty line over the past thirty-five years, we see that in the early 1960s, full-time, year-round minimum-wage earnings provided an income equal to the poverty line for a family of three. By 1969, full-time minimum-wage earnings provided 120 percent of the poverty line. But by 1994, full-time work at the minimum wage provided only 75 percent of the poverty line. Millions of minimum-wage workers are women; therefore, children in mother-only families in which the wage earner is paid $4.25 an hour, the current minimum wage, are by definition living in poverty. Simply raising the minimum wage to a level where a family of four would live at or above the poverty line would lift millions out of poverty and would, I believe, strengthen all families.

One way to create additional jobs and to strengthen families would be the reduction of the work week. A thirty-hour work week would "share the work" and would be particularly valuable to parents of young children, single parents, and workers who have responsibilities caring for infirm or aged family members. Clearly, such a shortened work week must be available with little or no reduction in pay. Furthermore, rather than hiring new workers, many companies are relying on and in some cases requiring their workers to put in massive amounts of overtime. Despite worker fatigue and the dangers that come with exhausted women and men working extra hours, frequently under hazardous conditions, workers are often pressured to work long hours of overtime because it is more cost effective for companies than hiring additional people. Such practices should be sharply curtailed in order to protect health and safety, in order to give employees time to be with their families, and in order to provide jobs to additional workers.

If Americans doubt that the lives and well-being of the working- and middle-classes are intertwined with the lives and well-being of the poor and near-poor, we only need consider what severe cutbacks in human services have meant and will mean for those who provide those services. As the federal, state, and local governments have cut funds for education, teachers are being laid off. As funds are diminished for preschool care, early childhood educators will find themselves out of work. As food programs, health care services, and job training are defunded, the poor will surely be harmed and harmed severely, but those who provide these services will be harmed as well. Social work, health care, and education have traditionally provided avenues for the poor and the working class to move into the middle class. If these opportunities are cut back still further, what jobs will be available to these workers, the vast majority of whom are women? Will they too be forced to flip hamburgers for the minimum wage, with no benefits, and no career path?

When we move to the exceedingly difficult question of what should be done with the welfare system, I must reiterate that while AFDC surely needs to be reformed, the key question we should be asking is how do we as an extremely affluent society dramatically diminish the number of people living in poverty? We know the pernicious effects of poverty—the social, psychological, physical, and intellectual effects of deprivation, of marginalization, of hopelessness. The question we must ask is how should American society help individuals and families out of their impoverished state, and, subsumed under that broader question is the narrower one, how should we truly reform the welfare system?

If we examine the broader and far more important question first, we see that virtually all of these proposed policies would help diminish the number of Americans living in poverty—as they do in Western European countries. Paid parental leave; children's allowances; a comprehensive health care system; accessible, affordable child care and after-school care; a more equitable education system; decent housing at an affordable cost; and a far more effective child support system would go a long way toward helping families, particularly women and children, climb out of poverty or, even better, avoid the poverty trap in the first place. An employment policy raising the minimum wage, creating new jobs, and shortening the work week will also sharply lower the number of people living in poverty. But there will still be a significant number who will not be helped sufficiently by these measures and for them we will need a completely reformed welfare system.

For those who remain in need, the United States should, I believe, maintain a welfare system mandated and controlled by the federal government. This would mitigate against abuse of the system by the states—abuses that in the past have stemmed from racism and other forms of discrimination, from the power of local economic interests, and from the intense pressure of local political considerations. Second, such a welfare system must provide a cash benefit equivalent to the poverty line. In the United States, a society in which the top 20 percent of families owns nearly 85 percent of the wealth and yet boasts of a fundamental belief in equality of opportunity, poor families should be provided no less. Third, training programs leading to real jobs paying wages at least equal to the poverty line must be available for those recipients who can and wish to participate. Payment of an extra stipend for the training period would provide additional incentive and the provision of child care is, of course, essential. Health care must also be assured either under Medicaid or through some comprehensive universal system since most jobs that AFDC recipients might qualify for do not include health benefits. Fourth, welfare recipients who work part-time or full-time but earn less than the poverty line should be permitted to keep their wages and receive a certain percentage of their benefits. Mothers who work in the paid labor force should not be punished; rather, they should be rewarded. Therefore, financial incentives for recipients who work must be developed. And finally, we should stop harassing and humiliating the poorest among us. Virtually all studies indicate that the incidence of welfare fraud is low and the cost to the system through fraud by individual recipients is almost negligible. The recent practice of fingerprinting recipients, for example, only serves to communicate to them and to the rest of the community that they are regarded as no better than criminals. If we truly wish to bring poor Americans into the mainstream, we must treat them with civility and respect.

Many have suggested that the United States should move toward some system of guaranteed annual income. One mechanism might be a "refundable tax credit." Journalist and author Holly Sklar details one version:

> Those with incomes below the basic human needs line would get a cash grant to make up the difference, payable in regular installments, whether they are in the paid workforce or not. . . . For people with incomes above the line, the tax credit would ensure they do not fall below it after taxes; it would serve as a greatly enhanced version of the personal and dependent deductions now in existence.

Such a "refundable tax credit" or guaranteed annual income might well take the place of many of the financial functions of the current welfare system. In any case, such an option should be evaluated and included in any national discussion about poverty and the need to reform our current economic system.

Concerning the "hot button" issues of teenage pregnancy and the dramatic increase in out-of-wedlock childbearing, it is clear that if we seriously wanted to encourage teenagers to postpone childbearing rather than simply punish them afterward, we would enact measures that would enable them and their families to move out of poverty; improve the education available to disadvantaged young people; educate boys and girls and continue to educate young women and young men about reproduction, sexually transmitted diseases, and contraception; and make contraception easily accessible. We must also ensure young people—both males and females—the opportunity for meaningful work and a place in society.

These measures will help to lower the number of teenage pregnancies but the key to encouraging two-parent families, I believe, is an employment policy that will guarantee decently paying jobs for all who wish to work and a support system that will enable parents to play their roles as both caregivers and as members of the labor force. As Lester Thurow has stated, "The traditional family is being destroyed not by misguided social welfare programs . . . but by a modern economic system that is not congruent with 'family values.' "

The work of Harvey Brenner and other social scientists indicates the negative effects that unemployment has on the individual worker and on the entire family's health and well-being. These researchers have found that male unemployment, for example, is associated with alcoholism, insomnia, anxiety, and higher levels of psychiatric symptoms. The longer the period of unemployment, the greater the stress on the family and on family cohesion. In a study of the unemployed in Hartford, Paula Rayman and Ramsey Liem found three times as much marital separation among the unemployed group as among the control group. In his novel *The Mayor of Casterbridge*, Thomas Hardy observed, ". . . being out of work, he was, as a consequence, out of temper with the world, and society, and his nearest kin."

Urban anthropologist Elliot Liebow, in *Tally's Corner*, his memorable study of sporadically employed and unemployed menial laborers in Washington, D.C., found that when the men could not fulfill their role as breadwinners, their ties to their families became progressively weakened. As Liebow states,

> The way in which the man makes a living and the kind of living he makes have important consequences for how the man sees himself and is seen by others; and these, in turn, importantly shape his relationships with family members, lovers, friends and neighbors.

Liebow continues by discussing the impact of menial, low-wage employment on men and on their family relationships:

> The longer he works, the longer he is unable to live on what he makes. He has little vested interest in such a job and learns to treat it with the same contempt held for it by the employer and society at large. From his point of view, the job is expendable; from the employer's point of view, he is. . . .
>
> He carries this failure home where his family life is undergoing a parallel deterioration. . . .
>
> Sometimes he sits down and cries at the humiliation of it all. Sometimes he strikes out at her or the children with his fists, perhaps to lay hollow claim to being a man of the house in the one way left open to him, or perhaps simply to inflict pain on this woman who bears witness to his failure as a husband and father and therefore as a man.

But these measures, a comprehensive family policy including a jobs-creation policy, will not be sufficient to help the poorest among us, the most disheartened, those with severe drug and alcohol abuse problems, those who have not worked for years, those without confidence and without hope. A comprehensive family policy and even the creation of jobs at livable wages will not solve the problems of devastated neighborhoods plagued with crime and hopelessness. For those inner-city areas and those desperately poor rural areas, we should consider a domestic Marshall Plan. As the United States launched a comprehensive effort fifty years ago to rehabilitate the countries of Europe that had been devastated by the Second World War, so should the society launch an all-out mobilization to rehabilitate our poorest neighborhoods. Demonstration projects could be developed in a few small areas to evaluate what works and what doesn't, and then with joint funding and leadership from the federal and local levels of government as well as support from foundations and voluntary organizations, people could be employed cleaning up the parks and the schools, repairing housing and hospitals; local leadership could work at the grass-roots level to help the population prioritize their needs and participate in the effort. American society must indicate in a variety of ways that all of our people are important and deserve a chance.

This must not be a paternalistic effort. It may bog down in the myriad problems of democracy and some would attempt to take advantage of the effort for personal gain, but it is worth the effort. Before American society gives up on its poor and forces all of us for the foreseeable future to live in a mean-spirited, violence-ridden society divided by class, race, and, to some degree, gender, a new effort is worth trying.

Critics will say that the United States does not have the money for a comprehensive family policy, for decent housing and education and health care for all, for a Marshall Plan for its poor. To them I say we cannot afford not to enact these measures. Moreover, we are spending the money now in other ways. We are spending it on jails and prisons; we are spending it on treating tuberculosis and lead poisoning. We are spending it on low-birth-weight babies and learning disabilities. We are spending it on the effects of addiction and violence, on a largely bankrupt welfare system, on an inadequate foster care system, and on shelters for the homeless. We are spending it on wasted human potential.

Finally, there is strong evidence that these policies save money in the long run. This is perhaps clearest in issues involving health status: adequate, early, comprehensive prenatal care is surely cheaper—and of course more humane—than dealing with the often severe complications of low-birth-weight babies; immunizations are clearly more cost-efficient than treating the consequences of preventable childhood diseases; and routing out lead-based paint in housing and schools is less costly both in dollars and in preserving human potential than permitting children to suffer from lead poisoning. In virtually all other areas prevention is cheaper than dealing with the consequences of severe, preventable individual, family, and societal problems. Keeping families together is far cheaper than foster care and vastly less expensive than any form of institutionalization. First-rate education costs the society less than maintaining families who cannot adequately support themselves. An entire panoply of human services is less costly—in every sense—than drug and alcohol programs and markedly less costly than incarceration. It is thus in the society's best interest—in human terms as well as financial terms—to help individuals and families function effectively.

We are spending vast sums of money today trying to separate "them" from "us"—through private schools and private hospitals, through neighborhoods with private roads and car services, through doormen guarding our apartment buildings and security guards patrolling our streets. Those who want to balance the budget now say they do not want to leave the burden of an enormous deficit on the next generation, but that is exactly what we will do if we leave them the burden of healing a broken society. What we pay now to assure that the vast majority of Americans have a real chance, have a real stake in this country, is negligible compared to what the cost of "containment" of the poor will be in thirty years. Although our political system encourages us to think in terms of two, four, or perhaps six years, we must think in terms of generations. Can we afford to let this generation slip by without adequate food, shelter, or medical care, without marketable skills, without hope?

The United States has resources to finance a humane family policy. One source is to shift federal spending from the grotesquely bloated military budget to productive purposes. Analyst after analyst has noted that the United States, a country with 6 percent of the world's population, spends annually on arms over 40 percent of the world's total annual arms expenditures, an amount greater than the total arms expenditure of the next highest ten nations combined. These analysts have estimated that all U.S. security needs could be met by less than half the current expenditures, thus saving $150 billion annually, more than $1 trillion over the next seven years. Some of this money could be invested in our decaying infrastructure, thus providing productive jobs for those released from the work of producing instruments of death and relieving what economist John Kenneth Galbraith has called our "public squalor" amidst "private opulence." Some could be invested in the family policy suggested here, both meeting urgent needs and providing urgently needed jobs. Overall more than two million jobs could be created, more than enough to offset the jobs lost by ending unneeded and dangerous military programs.

As noted in chapter 1, the 1980s and 1990s have seen a vast

concentration of wealth among the richest in the society. We must, I believe, move toward a more equitable, progressive tax policy. At present the United States has one of the lowest rates of taxation in the industrialized world. The enormous concentration of wealth—and hence power—in the hands of a very few is neither healthy nor wise for a democratic society. As Kevin Phillips has suggested:

> Taxes on the really rich—as opposed to taxes on the not-quite-rich—must rise to a more equitable level. Leading economic powers at their zenith or past it have been notorious for concentrated wealth, just like the United States of the 1990s. Gaps between the rich and the middle class invariably widen, as do gaps between the rich and the poor. . . . The richest 100,000 families—million-dollar-a-year folks or close to it—are the group that, by historical yardsticks, has too much money and influence in a declining great economic power. . . . Equity and sensibility both lie in trying to raise some serious additional revenue—perhaps $30 billion to $40 billion a year—from the top one tenth of one percent so that their payments are fairer before it becomes necessary to raise some further money from the ordinary Americans. No shared-sacrifice theme can resonate nationally while the truly rich remain so much better off than they were in 1980.

A direct tax on wealth is one way to narrow the gap. Many European countries including Denmark, the Netherlands, Sweden, Switzerland, and Germany have a tax on wealth. Edward Wolff, professor of economics at New York University and author of *Top Heavy: A Study of Increasing Inequality of Wealth in America*, estimates that "a very modest tax on wealth" that would exempt the first $100,000 in assets could raise as much as $50 billion in tax revenues and "have minimal impact on the tax bills of 90 percent of American families."

It must be recognized, however, that little of this agenda will be possible unless a larger percentage of the American electorate—particularly the poor, the near-poor, members of minority groups, and the young—participate in the political process. Currently, only about 50 percent of eligible voters participate in national elections and a significantly lower percentage participate in off-year elections. Less than 40 percent of eligible voters voted in the crucial 1994 congressional elections that gave the Republican Party control of both houses of Congress. In order to increase their political participation, voters must feel they have a real choice in the policies advocated by those running for office; they must feel that their votes really count, and that they have some way to influence the ideology of the political parties and of the candidates themselves.

The first task before us if we want greater involvement by a broad range of voters is to enact serious campaign finance reform. So long as large corporations and special interest groups such as the National Rifle Association, the tobacco growers, the American Medical Association, and the for-profit health care industry provide candidates with millions of dollars, politicians will be indebted to these interests and are likely to reflect their priorities. Only when we strictly limit such contributions and the amounts that can be spent on election campaigns can we hope to attract candidates who are not in thrall to the richest and most powerful among us and can we advance toward an equitable democratic political process.

But as we work on campaign finance reform, on registering increasing numbers of eligible voters, and on increasing participation in the political process, we must also, in the words of long-time political and peace activist Jerome Grossman, "build a movement" for economic justice. We must work across class lines, across racial barriers, and across gender differences to abolish poverty in our affluent society and to give every child the opportunity to lead a decent, productive, and fulfilling life. We must look back to the civil rights movement of some thirty years ago and recognize that the only way to make fundamental change in the United States is for individuals and groups who share a vision of fairness and equality of opportunity to unite. Large numbers of people must lock arms and state clearly that we will no longer tolerate the misery that poverty inflicts amidst our "pastures of plenty," to use the imagery of Woody Guthrie. We have the resources; we must mobilize the will.

Over three decades ago, Michael Harrington ended his powerful exposé of poverty in America, *The Other America*, with the following words: "The means are at hand to fulfill the age-old dream: poverty can now be abolished. . . . How long shall we look the other way while our fellow human beings suffer? How long?"

Abandoning the Poor

The relentless stereotyping, stigmatizing, and demonizing of the poor, particularly poor women, during the early to mid-1990s culminated in the passage of the Personal Responsibility and Work Opportunity Reconciliation Act. This legislation was signed into law by President Bill Clinton on August 22, 1996. Peter Edelman, a Clinton appointee to the Department of Health and Human Services, who resigned in protest over the new welfare law, aptly termed the signing of the legislation "the worst thing Bill Clinton has done." Euphemistically known as "welfare reform," the Act ended the sixty-one-year-old Federal guarantee of aid to poor children. The legislation was based on several underlying assumptions: that reliance on welfare benefits creates debilitating dependency; that this dependency prevents poor people from seeking work and committing themselves to the labor market; that jobs are indeed available for those who wish to work; and, ultimately, that only through work outside of the home can the poor become responsible, upright citizens worthy of respect. These views, only recently considered harsh and punitive positions of the extreme right, have become mainstream ideas over the past two decades. Because poverty is seen as the result of personal failings rather than as a consequence of the structure of the U.S. economy, because the belief in the efficacy of work has been a central value in this country since colonial times, and because of the increasing conviction on the part of legislators, policy makers, and large segments of the American public that millions of poor people are lazy, irresponsible, and in a multitude of ways morally deficient, this landmark legislation mandated some form of work for the vast majority of poor people and instituted a variety of limits and sanctions to force poor families to modify their behavior in ways legislators deemed essential.

The central provision of the legislation converted Aid to Families with Dependent Children (AFDC), emergency assistance, and work programs into block grants with funding to be controlled by the states. The legislation provides that states receive a fixed level of money for income support and work programs based on what they spent on these programs in 1994, regardless of the level of need in the state. Under the new state-controlled program, Temporary Assistance for Needy Families (TANF), assistance will no longer be guaranteed even if children are very poor, even if their family meets all of their state's eligibility requirements and their parents are prepared to meet all work requirements. A state could, for example, run out of block grant funds and place such children and their families on waiting lists.

In addition, the legislation established a five-year lifetime limit on receiving benefits but permits individual states to set even shorter time limits. Millions of children will be adversely affected by the Federal five-year time limit and the even shorter time limits adopted by many states. States will be permitted to exempt 20 percent of their caseload from the time limit provision but it must be noted that when the welfare legislation was passed, approximately half of all AFDC recipients had received benefits for more than five years.

As part of the ideology that poor people should work outside their home in order to receive benefits, the legislation established stringent requirements on the states to place an increasing proportion of recipients in work activities. By 1999, for example, 35 percent of a state's caseload must be participating in work activities. If, however, a state's caseload fell by 15 percent between 1995 and 1998, then its work requirement for 1999 would be reduced by 15 percent—from 35 percent to 20 percent. This provision gives states incentive for reducing caseloads by rendering families ineligible for aid whether or not they need and qualify for assistance. Moreover, while states are required to place recipients into work situations, funding for job programs falls far short of what is necessary. The Congressional Budget Office has estimated that the funds fall $12 billion short of what will be needed over the first six years of TANF to meet the work requirements.

The Personal Responsibility and Work Opportunity Reconciliation Act of 1996 also cut food stamp benefits significantly. The two major groups affected by this reduction were able-bodied adults without dependents and legal immigrants. Benefits to many disabled children receiving Supplemental Security Income (SSI) were reduced and aid for legal immigrants was slashed as well. Under the welfare law, noncitizens, including many who had worked in the United States and paid taxes for up to ten years, lost Supplemental Security Income (benefits for the aged and disabled poor), Medicaid, and Federal food stamps.

Describing the impact of the 1996 welfare legislation on legal immigrants, George Soros stated,

The welfare reform law broke the long-standing agreement between future citizens and their adopted homeland. Legal immigrants share the same responsibilities as citizens. They pay taxes. They serve in the military.

The United States has always embraced legal immigrants, who enrich our culture and work hard to make our nation stronger. But just like anyone else, immigrants can sometimes fall on hard times.

In August 1997, the Balanced Budget Act passed by Congress and signed by President Clinton gave tax cuts to wealthier Americans but also returned Supplemental Security Income (SSI) and Medicaid benefits to legal immigrants who resided in the United States as of August 22, 1996. Those arriving after that date continue to be excluded. The balanced budget legislation also provided additional funds for job-hunting assistance and training, and restored benefits for some disabled children. One of the most significant provisions of this legislation was the expansion of Medicaid to half of the nation's ten million uninsured children. Moreover, as of this writing, the U.S. Senate has voted to restore food stamps to legal immigrants and refugees who were living in the United States on August 22, 1996; the House of Representatives still must vote on this provision.

In an attempt to understand the impact of the sea change in providing aid for poor women and children, let us examine welfare legislation in one state. On August 20, 1997, the New York State Welfare Reform Act of 1997 was signed into law by Governor George Pataki. The Act established two new programs to replace AFDC: Family Assistance (FA) and Safety Net Assistance (SNA). The FA program is funded by the Federal TANF block grant as well as state and local money while the SNA program is only funded by state and local dollars. These new programs, which took effect in November, 1997, provide five years of assistance through FA followed by additional assistance to families who remain financially needy through the SNA program. The Act also established a new Food Assistance Program to provide nutritional aid to legal immigrants who are elderly, are children under the age of eighteen, or are disabled adults, as well as a Child Care Block Grant which incorporates all Federal and state funding for child care.

Under the Family Assistance program, families with children under eighteen (or under nineteen if the child is a full-time student) will continue to receive benefits at the same level as before the passage of the New York State legislation. A family of three in New York City, for example, received a maximum grant of $577 per month including a maximum monthly shelter allowance of $286. This amounts to only 57 percent of the Federal poverty line for a family of three. Needy families will receive these benefits for a maximum of five years; the clock began ticking on December 2, 1996. FA provides hardship exemptions beyond the five-year limit for individuals with mental and physical impairments, including those caused by domestic violence, and for households in which an adult is receiving SSI. New York's Safety Net Assistance program provides cash and non-cash assistance for impoverished individuals, childless couples, and families, such as those who exceed the time limits, who are ineligible for assistance through the FA program. In addition, New York State will provide varying degrees of benefits to legal immigrants who resided in the United States prior to August 22, 1996. Illegal immigrants continue to be ineligible for public assistance but their children, if born in the United States, continue to be eligible. While the New York State legislation does provide some long-term protection for some residents in extreme need, the vast majority of the impoverished will be forced to survive within the structure of the new stringent regulations.

The Act attempts to modify the behavior of recipients in a

variety of ways. It establishes sanctions in the form of reduced benefits or benefits limited to direct payments to the landlord and utility company if recipients fail to meet the requirements in one of many ways. The major new requirement is that recipients must work in exchange for benefits, and are guaranteed child care for children over twelve weeks of age and under age thirteen. By 1998, 30 percent of the employable adults in single-parent families must participate for at least twenty hours per week in "subsidized or unsubsidized public or private sector employment, work experience program (WEP), on-the-job training, job search or job readiness for up to six weeks, community service, vocational educational training for a one year maximum period of time, or in job skills training directly related to employment." By the year 2002 and after, that percentage rises to 50. There are several exemptions to the work requirement—adults who are disabled or over the age of sixty; teen parents who are in high school; and parents who are unable to obtain child care for children under thirteen—but many people will be forced into some form of work experience whether or not it fits in with their family's needs or provides a way out of poverty.

Yet another effort to separate the "worthy" poor from those deemed "unworthy" is the mandating of universal drug and alcohol screening as a new component of determining eligibility and recertification for benefits. Recipients who test positive will be referred to treatment programs; failure to particiate in available programs will result in the recipient becoming ineligible for public assistance although benefits will still be provided for the children. The Act does not, however, address the critical issue of the shortage of treatment slots.

Like many other states, New York has instituted a Learnfare program intended to promote school attendance of elementary school children whose families receive public assistance. Parents are sanctioned by losing some of their benefits if their elementary school children have five or more unexcused absences in a three-month period. Learnfare is being implemented gradually and will be in place statewide in the school year 1999–2000.

New York State policy dealing with teen parents is yet another effort to modify the behavior of poor people. Under most circumstances, unmarried pregnant and parenting teens cannot receive Family Assistance for themselves or their children unless they live with parents, other adult relatives, or in another adult-supervised living arrangement. Parenting teens must also be enrolled in a high school, GED, or training program by the time their child is twelve weeks old.

Yet another widespread policy that attempts to control the behavior—in this case, the reproductive behavior—of poor women is the family cap. This provision, not adopted by New York State but in use in New Jersey and in some twenty other states, eliminates additional benefits for children who are conceived while the mother is receiving welfare. In other words, the grant is not increased to meet the nutritional and other essential needs of the newborn. The mother and the existing children must therefore share their food, their clothing, their bed, and other requirements for daily existence with their sibling. Clearly, this provision is meant to remove any incentive to have additional children while receiving benefits and indeed to penalize both the mother and the other children for such behavior. Studies to determine the impact of the family cap on reproductive behavior are underway. One such study in New Jersey seems to indicate that the family cap has contributed to an increase in abortions among welfare recipients since the policy was enacted in 1992.

The New York State legislation has been severely criticized by many analysts. According to the Citizens' Committee for Children of New York, the Act will mean increased poverty for many families, particularly those being sanctioned because of an adult's or child's behavior. Almost 30,000 families have been sanctioned, for example, for non-cooperation or non-participation in New York's workfare program, the Work Experience Program (WEP), which itself has come under increasing criticism. As this chapter is being written, for example, New York City has just started requiring physically and mentally disabled recipients to participate in workfare in order to receive their welfare checks. The mothers who had been classified by city doctors as unemployable because they suffer from seizures, severe arthritis, mental illness, or other ailments will be required to work twenty hours a week in jobs supposedly tailored to suit their specific disabilities. Only those women who qualify for Federal disability benefits will be exempt. Critics suggest that this policy clearly conflicts with the state law that exempts the disabled from participating in mandatory work activities. According to one Legal Aid Society attorney, "This is mind-boggling. . . . This means hundreds more people are going to be sicker and risk death."

Perhaps the key complaint against the workfare program is that participants are denied the basic rights that other workers usually have. Workfare participants, for example, do not receive a paycheck, are not entitled to Social Security or Unemployment Compensation, do not earn promotion, pension, or vacation time, and do not accrue seniority. Moreover, while many of the participants work in jobs for the Parks Department or the Sanitation Department, they are often not provided appropriate equipment such as gloves and outerwear.

In July 1997 a case was filed in New York State court by

nine WEP workers alleging that the City was violating state law by assigning welfare recipients to workfare without providing adequate health and safety protection and that, moreover, the City was endangering the safety, health, and lives of these WEP workers. Several of the plaintiffs described their experiences with WEP. One woman, Anastacio Serrano, gave the following testimony:

> On June 18th . . . , we came across two dead cats and two dead dogs. . . . They had been dumped by the side of the road. Because I had no gloves, I had to pick them up with my bare hands. The animals had been run over by automobiles and were oozing blood and entrails. When I picked up the animals to throw them into the garbage truck, the guts splattered on my shoes and pants. My co-worker vomited and the supervisor in the van said nothing.

Another plaintiff, Tamika Capers, explained that workers assigned to the Department of Transportation

> have no access to a toilet either in the parking lot or out on the highway. If we need to urinate or move our bowels, we have to squat behind a tree or bush or ask one of our co-workers to hold up a plastic bag to shield us from the passing cars.

On August 18, 1997, a New York state court judge ordered the New York City Human Resources Administration to stop assigning WEP workers to street cleaning work until they are provided with access to drinking water, washing facilities, toilets, protective equipment, protection from traffic, and training. The City has appealed this order.

Yet another serious criticism is that the New York State legislation dramatically increased the need for child care but has not sufficiently increased the funding for such services. The shortage of child care—particularly adequate, licensed child care—is a critical problem throughout the United States. Child care is, of course, one of the most crucial factors that will determine whether poor women will be able to move from welfare to work. Since millions of women will be required over the next few years to move into work-related activities when their children are only twelve weeks old, there will be substantial need for infant care as well as care for older, pre-school children. Moreover, after-school care is also a necessity since working hours extend far beyond the school day.

In an effort to estimate the amount of child care necessary for the anticipated increase in working mothers, the U.S. General Accounting Office studied the current and future availability of child care in four sites—two urban and two rural. The selected urban areas were Baltimore City, Maryland and Chicago, Illinois; the rural areas were Benton and Linn counties in Oregon. The greatest shortages were of infant care and after-school care. The study found, for example, that prior to the implementation of the new welfare regulations, the supply of known child care in Chicago would meet just 16 percent of the demand for infant care. By 1997, when Federal law required that 25 percent of the welfare population be engaged in work-related activities, the existing supply of infant care would only meet 14 percent of the demand; by the year 2002, when the legislation calls for 50 percent participation, the current supply of infant care would only meet 12 percent of the demand.

Parents moving into jobs with non-standard hours will have even greater difficulty finding child care for all ages. Lack of transportation is yet another critical barrier in obtaining child care. Many communities, particularly rural and suburban areas, lack the public transportation to enable parents to bring their children to child care providers and then to get to work themselves. And, of course, transportation from school at the end of the day to after-school facilities is often nonexistent.

For many parents, alternatives to worrying about latchkey children are virtually nonexistent. One woman quoted in *Making Ends Meet: How Single Mothers Survive Welfare and Low-Wage Work*, a study of the economic realities of low-income women by sociologist Kathryn Edin and anthropologist Laura Lein, describes the poignant reality for millions of families.

> I am ashamed to say it, but I have a latchkey child. When he comes home from school, he locks himself in the house and waits for me to come home. In the summertime, he can go outside, but only if he calls me to check in every hour. I had to get him a little watch with a timer so that he would remember to check in with me. If I don't get that call, I leave work to go find him.

Child care has been termed a "perpetual emergency" nationwide for low-income working parents. They are "the forgotten class," earning too little to afford the options of professional women—hiring an *au pair* or a nanny or working part-time rather than full time—but too much to qualify for government programs. Others qualify for aid but have low priority compared to recipients who must leave the welfare rolls. Florida, for example, added over $100 million to its child care budget during 1997, yet most of that money is targeted to welfare recipients moving to work while thousands of children in low-income families in which a parent is already working remain on waiting lists.

The United States clearly needs to make a serious and significant commitment to child care—both for the well-being of children and to enable parents to move into the workforce. In January 1998, President Clinton announced a major child care initiative; its passage and implementation are uncertain, however, since the funding for this initiative is dependent on the passage of controversial anti-smoking legislation that will financially penalize the tobacco industry. Legislation has also been introduced in the U.S. House of Representatives and the Senate to increase Federal child care funding and to give tax breaks both to parents and to businesses that provide child care. The numbers of children cared for must not, however, be the only concern. The United States must assure that children, particularly infants, receive first-rate care from trained providers in licensed centers and family day care sites.

A recent study conducted by the New York-based research group, the Families and Work Institute, found that children fare better in day care when teacher-to-child ratios are lowered. Based on data collected at 150 child-care centers in Florida in 1992, 1994, and 1996, before and after the state lowered its teacher-to-child ratios, the study reported that when teachers are responsible for fewer children, the children are less likely to have behavior problems, spend more time in learning activities, are more proficient in language, and are more securely attached to their teachers. Lower ratios also had a direct effect on the teachers: the amount of threatening, yelling, scolding, or hitting was reduced by more than half. In 1992, Florida law began to require one adult for every four infants, for every six one-year-olds, and for every eleven two-year-olds. Groups such as the National Association for the Education of Young

Children and the National Academy of Science have developed even higher standards; they recommend that there should be at least one adult providing care for every four children under the age of two and for every six two-year-olds.

Some centers, particularly for-profit chains, are hiring welfare recipients to care for young children. A recent survey by the Center for the Child Care Work Force, a non-profit research and advocacy group, found that twice as many for-profit chains, the fastest growing segment of the day-care industry, were hiring welfare recipients as the non-profit centers were hiring. According to Deborah Phillips, an author of the study, "For-profit child care has a history of going after low-wage workers. They used to go after grandparents, and now they're going to welfare recipients. They are hired primarily as the lowest-paid assistants at centers with the lowest wages." Phillips goes on to point out that these workers rarely receive any training. In fact, according to the Bureau of Labor Statistics, the median hourly wage of child care workers is $6.12, less than that of a parking lot attendant ($6.38) or an animal caretaker ($6.90)!

These are clearly crucial issues for the well-being of children. Nationwide, 29 percent of young children are cared for in child care centers and an additional 21 percent are in family day care. Thus, 50 percent of the young children in the United States are being cared for by child care providers other than family members. Much of this care, especially in family day care settings, is unsupervised and unlicensed. We must develop national guidelines for staffing, training, salaries, and appropriate teacher-child ratios particularly at a time when U.S. social policy is forcing millions of mothers of very young children into the labor force.

Another critical consequence of the 1996 welfare legislation has been increased hunger and demand for emergency food. In Idaho, the number of people on welfare has fallen sharply but "the lines of soup kitchens are stretching into the streets." Community agencies have seen the demand for free food and meals rise significantly. In New York City the need for emergency food by able-bodied legal immigrants between the ages of eighteen and fifty-nine has surged. In Brooklyn, a forty-two-year-old mother of four from Trinidad spends her rent money on food; in the Bronx, a forty-year-old woman from Peru travels on the subway from food pantry to food pantry begging for groceries. She says, "I'll keep looking. My children have to eat." The complexity of recent legislation, moreover, has caused hundreds of the poorest of New York City's immigrants to lose food stamps or see them sharply reduced due to error. These people, many of whom are citizens, were mistakenly ruled ineligible by local welfare workers. According to one observer, "I have never seen so much confusion."

Recent welfare legislation has been described by some analysts as "devolution"—that is, the Federal government passing the responsibility for dealing with the poor to the states. Local management of programs dealing with the poor are, of course, not new. Prior to the New Deal, programs to aid the poor were primarily developed, funded, and administered by local governments and by charitable organizations. Even as early as the Colonial Poor Laws of the 1600s, authority was vested in the lowest level of government—the town in the north and the parish in the south—for the regulation and provision of aid to the poor. It was not until the establishment of programs created to combat the high unemployment and widespread poverty of the Great Depression of the 1930s that the Federal government took a more active role in planning and financing services for the poor. According to a report sponsored by The

Nelson A. Rockefeller Institute of Government entitled "The Newest New Federalism for Welfare: Where Are We Now and Where Are We Headed?," several states are currently moving even further and practicing "second-order devolution,"—assigning more responsibilities to local governments. For example, California, Iowa, Maryland, Michigan, North Carolina, and Texas have all assigned services such as job-finding and job placement to local areas. Those areas, in turn, have contracted out some of these services to both non-profit and for-profit groups. A central question is whether local governments can actually manage these responsibilities which could become overwhelming, particularly during an economic downturn. Will they have the financial and administrative resources? Will they provide assistance and services to the neediest among us, many of whom are despised and denigrated by the larger society, with fairness and compassion?

Since the passage of the Personal Responsibility and Work Opportunity Reconciliation Act of 1996, the welfare rolls have declined dramatically. In 1994 the number of welfare recipients—the vast majority of whom are women and children— peaked at more than 14 million. By May 1998, 8.9 million people were receiving cash assistance, a drop of more than 3.3 million since the welfare legislation was signed nearly two years earlier.

What are the causes of this dramatic decline? The low national unemployment rate is clearly a factor but not the entire explanation. The recent strict work requirements in place virtually all over the country are another factor. Minnesota and Wisconsin, for example, have had the same relatively low level of unemployment over the past four years but the welfare rolls have fallen three times as fast in Wisconsin where Governor Tommy Thompson initiated a stringent work program and all but eliminated cash aid. It is particularly startling that the numbers of recipients have also dropped significantly in the Mississippi Delta where the unemployment rate is very high. Declining welfare benefits and the harsh anti-welfare rhetoric of the mid-1990s are also important factors. One observer has suggested that the anti-welfare rhetoric "scolded away" many recipients. A more apt analysis might be that it has shamed and hounded them away.

But while some politicians are claiming that the drop in the welfare rolls means the recent policy is a success, it is important to point out that significant numbers of people leaving the rolls do not have jobs. In fact, many studies indicate that there is a severe mismatch between people looking for jobs and the jobs that are available. This incompatibility is particularly troublesome for poor, relatively unskilled people who have a higher rate of unemployment than other workers. Some states have conducted surveys to find out how many people who have left the welfare rolls actually have jobs. In Massachusetts, only 50 percent of the former recipients said they had jobs; in New Mexico, 54 percent; in Idaho, 52 percent.

A study of former welfare recipients in New York City found that among people who came off the welfare rolls from July 1996 through March 1997, only 29 percent found full-time or part-time work during the first several months. What is particularly disturbing is that for the purposes of the study, anyone who earned as little as $100 or more in three months after leaving welfare was counted as employed. Among the New York City adults without children who left Home Relief, only 20 percent were found to have jobs; statewide the average was approximately 23 percent. These numbers are alarming because they come at a time when the economy is relatively good. As one observer stated, "The true test will be when the economy takes an inevitable downturn and the people who remain on the caseload are less skilled and harder to serve. It's troubling."

The Maryland Department of Human Services and the University of Maryland School of Social Work are jointly conducting research on the 2,000-plus families who left welfare either voluntarily or involuntarily during the first year (October 1996–September 1997) of Maryland's welfare program, the Family Investment Program. The families will be tracked for two years but preliminary findings indicate several characteristics common to those who left public assistance: these families have few children; the children, for the most part, are school-aged; the mother has received assistance for a relatively brief period of time; and perhaps most important, in the words of the report, "the large majority of adults in existing cases have a demonstrated attachment to the labor force."

This report from Maryland reflects conditions in many parts of the country: those recipients with higher levels of education, recent job experience, and with fewer and somewhat older children are most likely to find work while those with more severe problems such as homelessness, illiteracy, addiction, and mental illness will have far more difficulty finding and keeping emloyment. Many recipients have no choice but to take entry-level jobs with low wages. Moreover, both job loss and part-time work are frequent. Thus, while the drop in the welfare rolls has been dramatic, many of those leaving remain in poverty.

Moreover, millions of women in the labor force earn wages significantly below the poverty line. In *Making Ends Meet*, Edin and Lein document and analyze the realities of daily life for poor mothers—both those who are, in their terms, "welfare-reliant" and "wage-reliant." Stressing the similarities rather

than the differences between these groups, Edin and Lein analyze the amount of money each takes in, their expenses, and
their survival strategies for closing the gap between income and
outgo. The vast majority of women in both groups received
too little money to meet their monthly expenses. For mothers
on welfare, AFDC and food stamps covered only 60 percent
of their expenses; for mothers who worked in the labor market,
wages covered only 63 percent of their expenses.

Many poor women recognize the unfortunate reality that
going from welfare to work generally does not make them
better off economically and, in fact, often makes them worse
off. One woman with more than ten years of work experience
said, "There were many days where I got my paycheck and I
just looked at it and cried. It was not enough to pay my rent.
. . . It was never enough that I could go buy groceries." The
only jobs open to the majority of poor women pay only five
or six dollars an hour and provide few, if any, benefits and
virtually no job security. Moreover, work outside the home
involves significantly higher expenses for clothing, transportation, and incidentals; working mothers may also lose part or all
of a housing subsidy and eventually are likely to lose both
health care and child care benefits.

While the mere drop in the number of recipients has been
taken by some to signify that so-called "welfare reform" is a
success, millions of Americans continue to live in poverty. In
1996, the overall poverty rate in the United States was 13.7
percent. This means that approximately 36.5 million people
lived below the poverty line which, in 1996, was set at $12,516
for a family of three and $16,036 for a family of four. Among
non-Hispanic whites, 8.6 percent were officially poor; among
blacks, 28.4 percent; and among Hispanics, 29.4 percent lived
below the poverty line. This was the second year Hispanics
had a higher poverty rate than blacks. While these rates are

lower than those during the recession of the early 1990s, they are as high or higher than the rates in 1989, before the recession began. African Americans are the only group whose poverty rate has declined since the late 1980s. Their rate of poverty, 28.4 percent, was the lowest level recorded since the Census Bureau began collecting these data in 1959. The rates for blacks and Hispanics, however, remain more than three times higher than that of whites.

In 1996 one out of every five children in the United States officially lived in poverty. Among non-Hispanic white children, the poverty rate was 11.1 percent. Poverty rates for black and Hispanic children were over three times that of white children—39.9 percent and 40.3 percent, respectively. Moreover, the number of "extremely poor" children, those who live below half of the poverty line, increased from 6 million in 1995 to 6.3 million in 1996. Yet another disturbing phenomenon is the dramatic rise in the percentage of poor children living in families in which someone worked, from 61 percent in 1993 to 69 percent in 1996.

Perhaps of greatest concern are the number of children under the age of six who continue to live in poverty. While the number has declined by almost 14 percent sice 1993, 5.5 million children were officially poor in 1996—a figure higher than in any year from 1975 to 1990. Children under six have the highest rate of poverty, 23 percent, of any group. In 1996, 43 percent of children under six, ten million young children, lived in poverty or near-poverty (185 percent of the poverty line). Moreover, nearly half of all poor children, 47 percent, lived in extreme poverty (below 50 percent of the Federal poverty line).

Poverty rates vary significantly for young children of different races and ethnic groups. In 1996, the poverty rate for young non-Hispanic white children was 13 percent, for non-Hispanic black children under six, 44 percent, and for Hispanic children, 42 percent. With all poor children, young children living in mother-only families are five times more likely to be poor than are children in two-parent families.

It is noteworthy that these poverty rates existed and the legislation ending the guarantee of Federal benefits to poor children was passed at a time of skyrocketing income inequality in the United States. From the late 1970s to the mid-1990s, the average income of the poorest families with children, the bottom 20 percent, fell more than 20 percent after adjustment for inflation. In contrast, the average income of the most affluent, the top 20 percent, increased nearly 30 percent. Despite a long period of economic growth, many lower- and middle-income families have faced stagnant or declining incomes; only the top two-fifths of families have seen their incomes rise since the mid-1980s.

In 1996, for example, the lowest fifth of all households received only 3.7 percent of the total national income, one of the lowest figures on record, while the highest 20 percent, the only quintile whose share increased, received nearly three-quarters, 72.3 percent, of the total national income. Moreover, Internal Revenue Service data indicates that between 1980 and 1995 the pay of senior executives of companies rose even faster than corporate revenues and profits. In 1995, total tax-deductible executive pay, before inflation, rose 182 percent while corporate revenues rose 129.5 percent and taxable profits rose 127 percent. But these statistics understate the magnitude of executive pay because many executives defer part of their salary, bonus, and especially their stock option profits until after they retire. Experts say that the total runs into the tens of billions—and perhaps even into the hundreds of billions—of dollars.

If we examine income levels in individual states, the gap between rich and poor becomes even clearer. The incomes of the poorest fifth of families with children fell more than 30 percent over the past twenty years in Arizona, Connecticut, Kentucky, Louisiana, Michigan, New York, Ohio, Oklahoma, West Virginia, and Wyoming. Several of these states—Connecticut, Kentucky, Louisiana, New York, and West Virginia—were among the ten states where income inequality between the top and bottom was the greatest from 1994 to 1996. If we examine the income of the poorest fifth and the richest fifth of families with children in New York State, for example, we find that between the late 1970s (1978–80) and the mid-1990s (1994–96), the income for the bottom 20 percent declined 36 percent while the income for the top 20 percent rose 46 percent. The only other state with a more dramatic shift is Connecticut, where the income of the bottom fifth of families with children declined 36 percent while that of the top fifth increased 53 percent. Ironically, Connecticut, which has the widest gap between rich and poor in the nation, has enacted the harshest lifetime time limits for welfare recipients in the nation; after twenty-one months, the majority of families will lose all cash benefits. Some have termed these extremely short time limits part of a "race to the bottom," the adoption of extremely harsh policies by some states in order to avoid being a magnet for poor people from surrounding states. Thus, as the gap between rich and poor widens dramatically, aid to those in the lowest income group is being drastically curtailed.

One of the beliefs about social policy that influenced the development of the 1996 welfare legislation was that anti-poverty programs, including AFDC, have been a failure. The success of several Western European countries in lifting families out of poverty was described in Chapter 7. Policies such as a child or family allowance, universal health insurance, low-cost or free preschool care, and special child support policies prevent millions of European families from falling into poverty or lift them out of it. What do the data about government benefit policies in the United States indicate about their success or failure? According to a study published by the Center on Budget and Policy Priorities, "The Safety Net Delivers: The Effects of Government Benefit Programs in Reducing Poverty," "federal and state anti-poverty programs have lifted millions of children and disabled and elderly prople out of poverty. Many of those who remained poor were significantly less poor than they would have been without government assistance." Safety net programs lowered the number of people living below the poverty line by nearly 50 percent. The impact of government programs on children's poverty is equally impressive. Between 1983 and 1995 Federal expenditures for children doubled and the number of children lifted out of poverty also doubled. As the authors of the study state, "The Census data . . . show that the stronger the safety net is, the more people it lifts out of poverty. When the safety net is weakened, it lifts fewer people out of poverty and poverty rates increase."

One of the central theses of this book is that a relentless campaign to stereotype, stigmatize, and demonize poor women, particularly poor, single mothers was conducted in order to pave the way for the passage of harsh, restrictive new legislation. "Welfare mothers" were repeatedly portrayed as lazy, dependent, and unwilling to work; they were also often portrayed as promiscuous and even as unfit mothers. It is particularly ironic that the success of the recent welfare legislation will in part depend on the rehabilitation of the reputation of mothers receiving public assistance.

Since the passage of the Personal Responsibility and Work Opportunity Reconciliation Act of 1996, many politicians,

Republicans and Democrats alike, as well as business leaders, have made gestures toward diminishing the stigma of receiving welfare benefits. An advertising campaign sponsored by the non-profit Welfare to Work Partnership, for example, has attempted to persuade employers to hire recipients by transforming the image of poor women. One print advertisement attempts to "present the stereotype and smash it at the same time." The stereotype, "Welfare mothers are irresponsible," is rewritten to read, "Welfare mothers make responsible employees." The idea hamered home in the mid-1990s, "Welfare is a program that creates dependence" is rewritten to read, "Welfare to work is a program that creates independence." Can the attitudes of the American public in general and business leaders and employers in particular be shifted so fundamentally and in a relatively short period of time? And if not, what will the negative attitudes toward the poor mean for their chances of obtaining jobs once their benefits cease?

Such a dramatic shift is, I believe, highly unlikely. The hostile campaign against the poor fed into far too many entrenched prejudices and stereotypes about issues that are highly volatile in American society, particularly those involving race, class, and gender, to be erased by some clever, well-placed advertising campaigns or exhortations by political leaders. Individual recipients may well be given a chance, especially those who do not trigger all of the harshest stereotypes. Some have already been given such a chance by a variety of companies, many of which were able to provide extensive training and support services. Early reports indicate that retention rates have been relatively high, but these former recipients may be the easiest to place and to train. Others have and will continue to obtain employment in those industries and regions of the country that need low-income workers, but millions of recipients and former recipients will be forced to search for jobs while simultaneously struggling to counteract deep-seated suspicions, fear, biases, and often outright hostility toward the poor—attitudes that were mercilessly and systematically encouraged just a short time ago by our national and local leaders.

It is especially disturbing that while poor women with children as young as three months are being forced to leave their infants to take jobs outside of the home or to participate in training or make-work programs, middle class and upper-middle class women who leave their children—even school-aged children—to participate in the labor market are increasingly looked upon with suspicion or in some instances with outright hostility. Leaving one's children with a nanny or an *au pair* or bringing them to day care is all-too-often seen as an abrogation of maternal responsibilities, a betrayal of "family values," while poor women who remain outside the labor market are villified, their fundamental moral worth questioned, even their ability to raise their children debated in state legislatures and in the U.S. Congress.

In her recent book, *A Mother's Place: Taking the Debate About Working Mothers Beyond Guilt and Blame*, Susan Chira, a *New York Times* reporter and editor, describes the "new conventional wisdom" for middle-class and upper-middle-class women: "When mothers forsake their rightful place at home, children are the victims." She continues, "The good mother who sacrifices, the selfish mother who works, the evils of day care, the obsessions with men's and women's different natures, the public laments by mothers torn from the arms of their children by jobs, the breast-beating over the state of children —these are the themes of the chorus bewailing a lost paradise, the days when mothers stayed at home."

Headlines blare the evils of mothers working, articles recount the stories of female executives forsaking their high-level jobs for full-time motherhood, and radio talk shows bitterly criticize the mother of a baby allegedly killed by his *au pair* for working part-time as an ophthamologist. As Chira states, this mother, and by implication all working mothers, was found guilty— guilty "of careerism, of callousness, of hiring someone to do a job only a mother should do." Why should poor women be driven out of their homes to work in menial jobs that pay poverty wages while middle- and upper-middle-class working women are driven by the relentless questioning about the quality of their mothering to guilt, self-blame, and in some instances back to the home? Moreover, while affluent women are often berated for working and poor women for not working outside the home, working-class and middle-class mothers who do not have the options to remain at home or even to work part-time are encouraged by the politics of division to resent both those who are poorer and those who are richer than they.

Recent studies indicate, furthermore, that politicians and policy makers may be overestimating how much mothers of young children in the general population work for pay. Recent data indicate that only 30 percent of married mothers with children under the age of six worked full-time, year-round in 1997. If married mothers with young children have relatively low rates of full-time participation in the labor force, why are impoverished women being forced to enter the labor force and leave their children for full-time, year-round work? Why is the government intruding to this extent into the lives of poor women when adequate, alternate care-giving frequently does not exist?

What is to be done now that welfare policy is in the hands of the states and the thrust all over the country is to dramatically lower the number of recipients, to force remaining recipients into the workforce, or at very least to work for their benefits? There are several directions advocates for the poor can take during this difficult time. First, we must continue to insist that the central problem faced by the poor is not welfare; it is poverty. If families are forced off of the welfare rolls and remain in poverty, what will they have gained? What will American society have gained? If parents are forced to work for meager wages and their income remains below the poverty line, they and their children will still face all of the deleterious effects of being impoverished in a very rich society. We must therefore redefine the problem—the United States must find ways of helping families out of poverty, not simply off the welfare rolls.

Second, advocates for the poor must fight at the state level to obtain as many essential benefits as possible for those in need. From food stamps to child care, from educational opportunities and job training to health care for the uninsured, we must pressure state legislatures for decent living conditions for the poor and near-poor. The struggle today is largely at the state level where legislators and local officials are often both accessible to organized lobbying and vulnerable to public opinion.

Third, unless the United States mobilizes to provide far greater access to first-rate child care and universal access to health care as well as extensive job training and possibly the creation of public sector jobs, we will not be able to truly reform our welfare system. So-called welfare reform must not force mothers to neglect the well-being of their children in order to fulfill the work mandate of the state. Moreover, parents cannot be expected to leave the welfare rolls and take jobs that will mean forfeiting their families' access to health care. We as a society must not insist that families make such cruel choices.

Fourth, we must both raise the minimum wage and expand the Earned Income Tax Credit so that all families with members who work will earn an income above the poverty line. The Earned Income Tax Credit, established in 1975 and expanded several times since, benefits low- and moderate-income working people, primarily those with children. In 1996, the EITC lifted 4.6 million people, including 2.4 million children, out of poverty. If participation in the workforce is the key standard by which we choose to judge the moral worth of adults in American society, then we must at very least reward workers with a livable income. With the ever-widening gap between rich and poor, this is not only the most sensible policy but the moral one as well.

Finally, advocates for impoverished children and adults must consider the tactics of social protest. Massive letter writing, e-mail, fax, and telephone campaigns, lobbying state capitols en masse, demonstrations, and marches are not merely nostalgic reminders of the civil rights and anti-war movements of the 1960s but are effective and valuable ways of encouraging the poor to demand their rights, of mobilizing their supporters, of giving heart to individuals who are all too often discouraged at the pace of social reform, and of attempting to dramatically shift public opinion.

Developing an effective and humane safety net as well as guaranteeing basic living conditions for all people in the United States will require the efforts of generations of activists. But one day the United States can truly become a society in which all children grow and flourish, in which parents work and nurture, in which citizens and non-citizens, affluent and less affluent, whites and people of color, old and young, find meaningful roles and make significant contributions to the social, economic, and political life of the community.

Notes

Introduction

Page

xii *of April 14, 1912:* Walter Lord, *A Night to Remember* (New York: Bantam, 1956), 1.

xii on board that night: Ibid., 34.

xiii 70 percent, drowned: Ibid., 82–83.

xiii to 38.1 million: "Census Bureau Releases Information on Income, Poverty, and Health Insurance Coverage in 1994," United States Department of Commerce News, October 5, 1995, 1–8.

xiii–xiv fell into poverty: *Despite Economic Recovery, Poverty and Income Trends Are Disappointing in 1993,* (Washington, D.C.: Center on Budget and Policy Priorities, October 1994).

xiv to 6 million: *Young Children in Poverty: A Statistical Update,* (New York: National Center for Children in Poverty, 1994).

xiv of white children: *Despite Economic Recovery.*

xiv share ever received: Ibid.

xv family of three: *The State of America's Children Yearbook 1995* (Washington, D.C.: Children's Defense Fund, 1995).

xv ages fifteen to nineteen: Ibid., 125.

Chapter 1

1 ". . . ours as well": Elaine Pagels, *The Origin of Satan* (New York: Random House, 1995), xix.

3 ". . . can identify themselves": Charles Murray, *Losing Ground: American Social Policy 1950–1980* (New York: Basic, 1984), 234.

3 ". . . to untie it": Ibid., 227–28.

4 ". . . as we know it": Jason DeParle, "The Clinton Welfare Bill: A Long, Stormy Journey," *New York Times*, July 15, 1994.

4 ". . . on the streets": Robert Pear, "Moynihan Promises Something Different on Welfare," *New York Times*, May 14, 1995.

5 ". . . of every American": Jason DeParle, "Welfare Plan Seeks Limit on Benefits," *New York Times*, May 12, 1994.

5 ". . . danger he represents. . . .": Erving Goffman, *Stigma: Notes on the Management of Spoiled Identity* (Englewood Cliffs, N.J.: Prentice–Hall, 1963), 5.

6 ". . . to alternative families?": Michael Wines, " 'Not My Job.' 'Not Our Job.' So Whose Job Is It?": *New York Times*, April 9, 1995.

7 ". . . system of dependency": Robert Pear, "House Backs Bill Undoing Decades of Welfare Policy," *New York Times*, March 25, 1995.

7 ". . . provide for themselves. . . .": Ibid.

8 ". . . capacity for empathy": Richard Goldstein, "The Age of Rage," *Village Voice*, May 16, 1995.

8 ". . . promised to protect": *Contract with the American Family* (Nashville, Tenn.: Moorings, 1995), 142.

10 envisaged as "nonhuman": Pagels, *Origin of Satan*, xviii.

10 ". . . *within* the community": Ibid. 34.

10 ". . . and beyond redemption": Ibid., 184.

11 ". . . our metaphysical condition": Toni Morrison, *The Bluest Eye* (New York: Pocket, 1974), 18.

12 pregnancies are unintended: *Sex and America's Teenagers* (New York: Alan Guttmacher Institute, 1994), 42.

12 welfare is two: "Overview of AFDC Program: Fiscal Year 1993," U.S. Department of Health and Human Services, June 1994, 2.

12 inadequate poverty line: *Living at the Bottom: An Analysis of*

1994 AFDC Benefit Levels, (New York: Center on Social Welfare Policy and Law, June 1994), 8.

12 so to work: *Problems with the Proposed WORK Program*, (New York: Center on Social Welfare Policy and Law, July 1994), 1.

12 comprised 38.9 percent: "Overview of the AFDC Program," 23.

13 from 16.8 percent to 20 percent: *Despite Economic Recovery, Poverty and Income Trends Are Disappointing in 1993*, (Washington, D.C.: Center on Budget and Policy Priorities, October 1994), 7.

13 ". . . $17 million a year": Kevin Phillips, *Arrogant Capital: Washington, Wall Street, and the Frustration of American Politics* (Boston: Little, Brown, 1994), 206–7.

14 of all Americans (15.4 percent): Edward N. Wolff, "Trends in Household Wealth in the United States, 1962–83 and 1983–98," *Review of Income and Wealth* (Series 40, No. 2), June 1994: 143–74.

14 ". . . in the '80s": Edward N. Wolff, "How the Pie Is Sliced: America's Growing Concentration of Wealth," *The American Prospect*, Summer 1995, 58–64.

15 13 percent for females: Barry Bluestone, "The Inequality Express," *The American Prospect*, Winter 1994, 81–93.

15 profits have soared: Bob Herbert, "Firing Their Customers," *New York Times*, December 29, 1995.

15 Taiwan and Australia: Keith Bradsher, "Skilled Workers Watch Their Jobs Migrate Overseas," *New York Times*, August 28, 1995.

16 "federal regulatory apparatus": Thomas Byrne Edsall and Mary D. Edsall, *Chain Reaction: The Impact of Race, Rights, and Taxes on American Politics* (New York: W. W. Norton, 1991), 13.

17 ". . . the larger society": Ibid., 4.

17 ". . . to conservative assault": Ibid., 158.

19 "on something now": Chandler Davidson, *Race and Class in Texas Politics* (Princeton, N.J.: Princeton University Press, 1990), 222–23.

20 ". . . what I am": Ruth Sidel, *On Her Own: Growing Up in*

the Shadow of the American Dream (New York: Penguin, 1991), 43.

20 ". . . depend on anyone": Ibid., 27.

20 ". . . make it, have money": Ibid., 18.

20 ". . . all work out": Ibid., 25.

22 ". . . the ready scapegoat": Howard Winant, "The New International Dynamics of Race," *Poverty and Race*, (Washington, D.C.: Poverty and Race Research Action Council, July/August 1995), 1–4.

22 ". . . and social stability": Mimi Abramovitz, *Regulating the Lives of Women: Social Welfare Policy from Colonial Times to the Present* (Boston: South End Press, 1988), 53.

22 ". . . the social order": Ibid., 52.

22 ". . . subordinate to men": Ibid., 53.

22 ". . . and mother laws": Ibid., 77.

23 ". . . in our culture": Martha Albertson Fineman, *The Neutered Mother, the Sexual Family and Other Twentieth Century Tragedies* (New York: Routledge, 1995), 103.

23 "pathological" or "deviant": Ibid., 68.

23 "with deviant motherhood": Ibid., 101.

23 ". . . to its attention": Kai T. Erikson, *Wayward Puritans: A Study in the Sociology of Deviance* (New York: Macmillan, 1966), 5–7.

24 ". . . he 'really' is": Ibid., 7.

24 "own group identity": Pagels, *Origin of Satan*, xix.

24 "symbolize their difference": William Scott Green, quoted in Pagels, Ibid., xix.

25 ". . . than existed before": Erikson, *Wayward Puritans*, 4.

27 ". . . society conceives itself": Philip Jenkins, *Intimate Enemies: Moral Panics in Contemporary Great Britain* (New York: Aldine de Gruyter, 1992), 6–7.

27 ". . . anxiety and crisis": Ibid., 7.

27 ". . . of a society": Erich Goode and Nachman Ben-Yehuda, *Moral Panics: The Social Construction of Deviance* (Cambridge, Mass.: Blackwell, 1994), 32.

28 ". . . and with heterosexuality": Winant, *Poverty and Race*.

28 of its iniquities: *Encyclopaedia Britannica Micropaedia*, Volume VIII, 1974, 945.

29 ". . . harmful to society . . .": Goode and Ben-Yehuda,
Moral Panics, 28–29.

30 ". . . difficult to challenge": Leith Mullings, "Images,
Ideology and Women of Color," in *Women of Color in U.S.
Society*, Maxine Baca Zinn and Bonnie Thornton Dill, eds.
(Philadelphia: Temple University Press, 1994), 265–89.

30 ". . . emasculating matriarch": Ibid.

31 "their own victimization": Patricia Hill Collins, *Black
Feminist Thought: Consciousness, and the Politics of Empowerment*
(Boston: Unwin Hyman, 1990), 74.

Chapter 2

Page

33 ". . . what was chosen": Rush Limbaugh, T.V., February 23,
1994, quoted in "Big Fat Lies," *Mother Jones*, May/June
1995, 39.

33 ". . . sphere by herself": Nathaniel Hawthorne, *The Scarlet
Letter* (New York: Penguin, 1986), 77, 81.

34 ". . . of three hours": Ibid., 89.

34 ". . . sort of scaffold": Ibid., 82.

34 ". . . upon her bosom": Ibid., 89.

34 ". . . upon her tombstone": Ibid., 90.

34 ". . . and our culture": Robert Pear, "Dole Courts
Conservatives with Changes on Welfare," *New York Times*,
August 10, 1995.

34 ". . . skyrocketing illegitimacy rate": Lisa Schiffren, "Penalize
the Unwed Dad? Fat Chance." *New York Times*, August 10,
1995.

35 with their father: Arlene F. Saluter, *Marital Status and Living
Arrangements: March 1993*, U.S. Bureau of the Census,
Current Population Reports, Series P20–478, U.S.
Government Printing Office, Washington, D.C., 1994, XI.

35 ". . . as a whole": Robin L. Jarrett, "Living Poor: Family
Life Among Single Parent, African-American Women,"
Social Problems, Vol. 1, No. 1, February 1994: 30–49.

36 ". . . used to be": Sue Woodman, "How Teen Pregnancy

Has Become a Political Football," *Ms.*, January/February 1995, 90–92.

37 ". . . outbursts in class": Barbara Dafoe Whitehead, "Dan Quayle Was Right," *Atlantic Monthly*, April, 1993, 47–84.

37 "reasonably happy intact": Ibid.

38 ". . . idea of fatherhood": David Blankenhorn, *Fatherless America: Confronting Our Most Urgent Social Problem* (New York: Basic, 1995), 2.

38 ". . . their children's lives": Ibid., 2.

39 ". . . will be gone. . . .": Senator Bill Bradley, Speech on Violence in America, National Press Club, Washington, D.C., May 11, 1994.

40 ". . . in 1990 and 1991": Adam Walinsky, "The Crisis of Public Order," *Atlantic Monthly*, July 1995, 39–54.

41 ". . . black city neighborhoods": Ibid.

42 ". . . with one parent": Arlene F. Saluter, *Marital Status and Living Arrangements*.

43 ". . . and for men, 26.5": Ibid., VII.

43 ". . . a never-married parent": Ibid., XII.

45 ". . . resident parent remarries": Sara McLanahan and Gary Sandefur, *Growing Up with a Single Parent* (Cambridge, Mass.: Harvard University Press, 1994), 1.

45 ". . . adolescence to adulthood": Ibid., 39.

46 ". . . the child's welfare": Ibid., 3.

46 grossly inadequate schools: Jonathan Kozol, *Savage Inequalities: Children in America's Schools* (New York: HarperCollins, 1992).

47 ". . . and, sometimes, abuse": McLanahan and Sandefur, *Growing Up with a Single Parent*, 28.

47 ". . . *themselves during interviews*": Ibid., 35.

51 "support a family": Christopher Jencks and Kathryn Edin, "Do Poor Women Have a Right to Bear Children?" *The American Prospect*, Winter 1995, 43–52.

51 "*get good jobs*": Ibid.

52 ". . . their earnings alone": Ibid.

52 ". . . of industrious whites": Andrew Hacker, "The Crackdown on African-Americans," *The Nation*, July 10, 1995, 45–49.

54 ". . . a drug addict": Katherine Q. Seelye, "Gingrich Looks to Victorian Age to Cure Today's Social Failings," *New York Times*, March 14, 1995.

54 ". . . things differently there": Michiko Kakutani, "If Gingrich Only Knew About Victoria's Secret," *New York Times*, March 19, 1995.

55 marriage and childbearing: Stephanie Coontz, *The Way We Never Were: American Families and the Nostalgia Trap* (New York: Basic, 1992), 23–29.

55 was 50 percent: Ibid., 29–30.

55 ". . . joked with them": Ibid., 30–31.

55 reached 1.15 million pounds: Ibid., 36.

55 ages fifteen to nineteen gave birth: Ibid., 39.

55 females in 1993: "Rate of Births for Teen-Agers Drops Again," *New York Times*, September 22, 1995.

56 ". . . Lord for Mama": "Who Is a Woman I Admire?" *New York Times*, March 25, 1995.

Chapter 3

Page

58 ". . . in American civilization": Newt Gingrich, "Renewing America," *Newsweek*, July 10, 1995, 26–27.

59 ". . . big, black zero": Ruth Sidel, *Women and Children Last: The Plight of Poor Women in Affluent America* (New York: Penguin, 1992), 27–28.

61 ". . . could survive economically": Ibid., 32–33.

61 ". . . a better life": Ibid., 35.

62 ". . . strong, productive lives": "Speaking for Themselves, House Members Talk Welfare," *New York Times*, March 26, 1995.

62 ". . . don't judge me": "Connecticut Lawmakers Approve Strict New Welfare Rules," *New York Times*, June 4, 1995.

63 in Los Angeles: Kenneth B. Noble, "Los Angeles Sweatshops Are Thriving, Experts Say," *New York Times*, August 5, 1995.

63 $2.50 an hour: Alan Finder, "Despite Tough Laws, Sweatshops Flourish," *New York Times*, February 6, 1995.

63 ". . . will fire me": Ibid.

64 ends meet financially: Ruth Sidel, *Battling Bias: The Struggle for Identity and Community on College Campuses* (New York: Penguin, 1995), 187–95.

64 ". . . I was pregnant": Ruth Sidel, *Women and Children Last*, 41.

65 ". . . up with this?": Ibid., 41–42.

65 ". . . to economic fears": Ibid., 43–44.

66 ". . . protest or revolt": Michael B. Katz, "Introduction: The Urban 'Underclass' as a Metaphor of Social Transformation," in *The "Underclass" Debate: Views from History*, Michael B. Katz, ed. (Princeton, N.J.: Princeton University Press, 1993), 4.

66 ". . . for social expenditures": Ibid.

66 ". . . behavior seems aberrant": Ken Auletta, *The Underclass* (New York: Vintage, 1983), xiii.

66 ". . . those it designates": Katz, *The "Underclass" Debate*, 21.

67 ". . . America's inner cities": Ibid., 445.

67 the labor force: Ibid.

67 ". . . and/or welfare dependency": William Julius Wilson, *The Truly Disadvantaged: The Inner City, the Underclass, and Public Policy* (Chicago: University of Chicago Press, 1987), 8.

67 ". . . norms of behavior": Ibid.

70 their poverty rates: *Despite Economic Recovery, Poverty and Income Trends Are Disappointing in 1993*, (Washington, D.C.: Center on Budget and Policy Priorities, October 1994), 1–10.

70 in the United States: Ibid.

70 that of whites (9.9 percent): Ibid.

70 poverty in 1992: *Young Children in Poverty: A Statistical Update*, (New York: National Center for Children in Poverty, 1994), 1–6.

70 married-couple families: Center on Budget and Policy Priorities, *Despite Economy Recovery*.

71 city's poor people: *Low-Income Populations in New York City: Economic Trends and Social Welfare Programs, 1994* (New York:

United Way of New York City/City of New York, Human
Resource Administration, April 1995), 2–5.

72 whites were poor: Ibid., 6.

72 poor and near-poor: Ibid: 7.

72 exclusively on welfare: *Young Children in Poverty: A Statistical
Update.*

73 the food budget: John E. Schwarz and Thomas J. Volgy, *The
Forgotten Americans* (New York: W. W. Norton, 1992),
35–36.

73 would be $20,700: Ibid., 42.

74 ". . . with a fee": Ibid., 43.

74 for other purposes: Ibid., 43.

74 ". . . work, is astounding": Ibid., 53.

75 ". . . Boston and Seattle": Ibid., 65.

75 living in poverty: Ibid., 92.

75 than 19 percent: William O'Hare, Taynia Mann, Kathryn
Porter, and Robert Greenstein, *Real Life Poverty in America:
Where the American Public Would Set the Priority Line*
(Washington, D.C.: Population Reference Bureau and
Center on Budget and Policy Priorities, 1990), vi.

76 ". . . receive public assistance": Robert Pear, "A Revised
Definition of Poverty May Raise Number of U.S. Poor,"
New York Times, April 30, 1995.

76 of the population: Ibid.

77 income of $13,300: Louis Uchitelle, "For Many, a Slower
Climb Up the Payroll Pecking Order," *New York Times*,
May 14, 1995.

77 Schwarz and Volgy: Ibid.

77 was 76.4 percent: "Facts on Working Women,"
(Washington, D.C.: Women's Bureau/U.S. Department of
Labor (No. 95-1), May 1995.

77 87 percent female: "Education and Training: The Path Out
of Poverty for Women," American Association of University
Women *Outlook*, Summer 1995, 19–24.

77 poverty increased significantly: "The Largest Gap Between
Rich and Poor," *New York Times*, January 15, 1995.

78 ". . . best they can": Steven A. Holmes, "Low-Wage Fathers
and the Welfare Debate," *New York Times*, April 25, 1995.

78 white family income: Claudette E. Bennett, *The Black Population in the United States: March 1994 and 1993*, U.S. Bureau of the Census, Current Population Reports, P20–480, U.S. Government Printing Office, Washington, D.C., 1995, 19.

78 non-Hispanic white families: Ibid., 11.

78 families with children: Ibid., 25.

79 ". . . outright discrimination": Robert D. Hershey, Jr., "Bias Hits Hispanic Workers," *New York Times*, April 27, 1995.

79 to be unemployed: Ibid.

79 ". . . has employers panicked": Ibid.

79 30.6 percent in 1993: *Despite Economic Recovery*.

Chapter 4

Page

81 ". . . and the disabled": Robin Toner, "A Day of Anger as Republicans Are Put on the Defensive," *New York Times*, March 23, 1995.

86 ". . . but deeply stigmatized": Linda Gordon, *Pitied But Not Entitled: Single Mothers and the History of Welfare* (New York: Free Press, 1994), 5.

86 of fatherless children: Ibid., 37.

86 ". . . support its recipients": Ibid., 45.

87 ". . . debates began here": Ibid., 37.

87 were children: *Overview of the AFDC Program: Fiscal Year 1993*, U.S. Department of Health and Human Services, June 1994, 2.

87 total U.S. population: Ibid., 6.

87 17.8 percent were Hispanic: 1994 Green Book (Washington, D.C.: House Committee on Ways and Means, 1994), 400.

87 income of $4,524: Ibid., 2.

88 in the state: *The State of America's Children Yearbook 1995* (Washington, D.C.: Children's Defense Fund, 1995), 108.

88 to 79 percent: "HHS News," U.S. Department of Health and Human Services, June 1994, 1–3.

88 1972 and 1992: Ibid.

88 3.2 persons to 2.9: Ibid.
89 1.1 percent in 1992: Ibid.
90 ". . . spend on welfare": Mary Jo Bane and David T. Ellwood, *Welfare Realities: From Rhetoric to Reform* (Cambridge, Mass.: Harvard University Press, 1994), 36.
90 and African Americans: Ibid., 40–50.
90 ". . . with moderate earnings": Ibid., 59.
91 work and welfare: *Combining Work and Welfare: An Alternative Anti-Poverty Strategy* (Washington, D.C.: Institute for Women's Policy Research, 1992), iii.
91 two and five: *Few Welfare Moms Fit the Stereotype*, (Washington, D.C.: Institute for Women's Policy Research, January 1995).
92 least work experience: *Combining Work and Welfare*, iv.
92 child care workers: *Few Welfare Moms Fit*.
92 out of poverty: *Combining Work and Welfare*, 31–32.
93 ". . . for its actions": *Summary of AFDC Waiver Activity Since February 1993* (New York: Center on Social Welfare Policy and Law, Publication No. 169-2, October 1994), 1–10.
93 ". . . no federal standards whatsoever": Robert Pear, "A Welfare Revolution Hits Home, But Quietly," *New York Times*, August 13, 1995.
94 stay in school: Ibid.
94 with two parents: *Summary of AFDC Waiver Activity*.
94–95 ". . . room to experiment": Mark Greenberg, *On Wisconsin? What's Wrong With the "Work Not Welfare" Waiver* (Washington, D.C.: Center for Law and Social Policy, February 1994), v.
95 ". . . a good balance": Jason DeParle, "States' Eagerness to Experiment on Welfare Jars Administration," *New York Times*, April 14, 1994.
96 ". . . want to do": Robert Pear, "A Welfare Revolution Hits Home, But Quietly," *New York Times*, August 13, 1995.
96 ". . . harm to families": Jason DeParle, "States' Eagerness to Experiment."
96 of the family: Michael C. Laracy, *The Jury Is Still Out: An Analysis of the Purported Impact of New Jersey's AFDC Child*

Exclusion (aka "Family Cap") Law (Washington, D.C.: Center for Law and Social Policy, March 1994), 1–8.

97 an "obvious" success: Ibid.

97 to AFDC recipients: Melinda Henneberger, "State Aid Is Capped, but to What Effect?" *New York Times*, April 11, 1995.

98 ". . . comforted my soul": Ibid.

98 ". . . what I'll do": Ibid.

99 for an exception: Mark Greenberg, *On Wisconsin?*, i–ii.

99 the welfare rolls: Ibid., iii–iv.

100 the poverty line: Peter T. Kilborn, "Michigan Puts Poor to Work but Gains Appear Precarious," *New York Times*, October 24, 1995.

100 ". . . is just appalling": Peter T. Kilborn, "Steps Taken on Welfare in Michigan," *New York Times*, November 1, 1995.

101 ". . . means to travel": James Dao, "Welfare Rules Created for Cities Cause Trouble in the Countryside," *New York Times*, August 9, 1995.

101 ". . . situation is like": Ibid.

101 "week after week": Ibid.

102 ". . . in New York City": Ibid.

103 or mental disabilities: Robert Pear, "House Backs Bill Undoing Decades of Welfare Policy," *New York Times*, March 25, 1995.

103 ". . . legislative child abuse": Robin Toner, "Senate Approves Welfare Plan That Would End Aid Guarantee," *New York Times*, September 20, 1995.

104 ". . . to their graves": Alison Mitchell, "White House Held On to Study of Senate Bill's Harm," *New York Times*, October 28, 1995.

104 ". . . lost to principle": Bob Herbert, "Welfare Stampede," *New York Times*, November 13, 1995.

104 ". . . its own indifference": Bob Herbert, "Asleep at the Revolution," *New York Times*, November 6, 1995.

105 "What a record!": Robert Pear, "Welfare Bill Cleared by Congress and Now Awaits Clinton's Veto," *New York Times*, December 23, 1995.

105 ". . . tears it to shreds": Ibid.

105 ". . . hardest on children": Robert Pear, "Clinton Vetoes G.O.P. Plan to Change Welfare System," *New York Times*, January 10, 1996.

106 "profits as well": Frances Fox Piven and Richard A. Cloward, *Regulating the Poor: The Functions of Public Welfare* (New York: Vintage, 1993), 177.

106 have been black: Ibid., 139–40.

107 ". . . pockets of millionaires": Michael Wines, "House Votes to Cut Taxes by $189 Billion Over 5 Years As Part of G.O.P. 'Contract,' " *New York Times*, April 6, 1995.

108 ". . . as security guards": Peter T. Kilborn, "Up From Welfare: It's Harder and Harder," *New York Times*, April 16, 1995.

108 ". . . that way anymore": Ibid.

108 ". . . most welfare recipients": Ibid.

110 office Christmas party: Stephen Moore and Dean Stansel, *Ending Corporate Welfare As We Know It*, Cato Institute (Draft Report), March 6, 1995, 2–23.

110 ". . . next seven years": Kevin Phillips, "Corporate Welfare Lives," *USA Today*, October 31, 1995.

110 ". . . compete without it": Michael Wines, "Where the Budget Ax Turns Dull," *New York Times*, August 30, 1995.

111 their food budget: Dirk Johnson, "Risky G.O.P. Politics of Farm Cuts," *New York Times*, March 19, 1995.

111 "I think so": "What, Us Worry?" A Conversation, moderated by Todd S. Purdom, *New York Times Magazine*, March 19, 1995, 38–43.

112 ". . . off your table": Ibid.

113 ". . . against government handouts": David S. Broder, "Gramm's Entitlements," *Boston Globe*, March 1, 1995.

114 ". . . it feels like": Melinda Henneberger, "Welfare Bashing Finds Its Mark," *New York Times*, March 5, 1995.

Chapter 5

Page

116 ". . . like it or not": Donna Gaines, *Teenage Wasteland: Suburbia's Dead End Kids* (New York: Pantheon, 1991), 54.

120 ". . . of their attractiveness": Michael A. Carrera, "A Holistic View of Adolescent Sexuality," Newsletter of the Bernice and Milton Stern National Training Center for Adolescent Sexuality and Family Life Education, The Children's Aid Society, Winter 1994, 1–4.

120 "It just happened": Mireya Navarro, "The Threat of No Benefits: Will It Deter Pregnancies?" New York Times, April 17, 1995.

120 pregnancies are unintended: Sex and America's Teenagers (New York: The Alan Guttmacher Institute, 1994), 43.

120 ". . . talk to her": Jan L. Hagen and Liane V. Davis, Another Perspective on Welfare Reform: Conversations with Mothers on Welfare (Albany, N.Y.: The Nelson A. Rockefeller Institute of Government, 1994), 31.

121 some young people: Ruth Sidel, On Her Own: Growing Up in the Shadow of the American Dream (New York: Penguin, 1991), 132.

121 ". . . would get pregnant!": Ibid., 132.

122 age of eighteen: Sex and America's Teenagers, 19.

122 the late 1980s: Ibid., 27.

122 had sex involuntarily: Ibid., 22.

122 ". . . element of violence": Shari Roan, "The Invisible Men," Los Angeles Times, July 10, 1965.

123 ". . . tainted and spoiled": Ibid.

123 medical contraceptive services: Sex and America's Teenagers, 33.

123 ". . . often is no": Sidel, On Her Own, 134.

123 the poverty line: Sex and America's Teenagers, 35.

124 ". . . plan for sex": Sidel, On Her Own, 134–35.

125 ". . . think about sex": Shari Roan, "The Birth Control Bust," Los Angeles Times, July 11, 1995.

125 twenty- to twenty-four-year-olds: Sex and America's Teenagers, 41.

125 end in miscarriage: Ibid., 45.

125 to choose abortion: Ibid.

126 ". . . to support them": Shari Roan, "A Sign of the Times," Los Angeles Times, July 9, 1995.

126 ". . . much to lose": Sidel, On Her Own, 126.

126 states above $350: Patricia Donovan, *The Politics of Blame* (New York: The Alan Guttmacher Institute, 1995), 25.

127 just 267 women!: Ibid., 34.

128 not given birth: *Sex and America's Teenagers*, 58.

128 age of nineteen: Ibid.

128 four times higher: Claudette E. Bennett, *The Black Population in the United States: March 1994 and 1993*, U.S. Bureau of the Census, Current Population Reports, P20–480, U.S. Government Printing Office, Washington, D.C., 1995, 1.

129 to become parents: Roan, "A Sign of the Times."

129 ". . . a woman now": Ibid.

130 ". . . control and pregnancy": Sidel, *On Her Own*, 121.

130 ". . . of her life": John Berger, *Ways of Seeing* (London: Penguin, 1972), 46.

131 ". . . to them again": Sidel, *On Her Own*, 122.

131 pregnancies every day: Mike Males, "Unwed Mothers: The Wrong Target," *New York Times*, July 29, 1994.

132 ". . . black men": William Julius Wilson, *The Truly Disadvantaged: The Inner City, the Underclass, and Public Policy* (Chicago: University of Chicago Press, 1987), 104–5.

132 on to college: *Sex and America's Teenagers*, 60.

132 age twenty-five and older: Ibid., 61.

133 26 percent in 1992: *Families on Welfare: Sharp Rise in Never-Married Women Reflects Societal Trend* (Washington, D.C.: United States General Accounting Office, May 1994), 62.

133 the poverty line: *Families on Welfare: Teenage Mothers Least Likely to Become Self-Sufficient* (Washington, D.C.: United States General Accounting Office, May 1994), 2–3.

133 lack of prenatal care: *Sex and America's Teenagers*, 62–63.

135 ". . . part of you": Gaines, *Teenage Wasteland*, 158–59.

136 ". . . or reconstructed identity. . . .": Rickie Solinger, *Wake Up Little Susie: Single Pregnancy and Race Before* Roe *v.* Wade (New York: Routledge, 1992), 105.

136 ". . . made to disappear": Alice McDermott, *That Night* (New York: Farrar, Straus and Giroux, 1987), 90.

Chapter 6

Page

141 Every Day in America: *The State of America's Children Yearbook 1995* (Washington, D.C.: Children's Defense Fund, 1995), back cover.

142 ". . . a violent death": Walda Katz-Fishman and Jerome Scott, "Welcome to Washington," Society for the Study of Social Problems Newsletter, Summer 1995, 4–8.

142 lived in poverty: *Despite Economic Recovery, Poverty and Income Trends Are Disappointing in 1993*, (Washington, D.C.: Center on Budget and Policy Priorities, October 1994), 1–10.

143 the same year: *The State of America's Children Yearbook 1995* (Washington, D.C.: Children's Defense Fund, 1995), 18.

143 non-Hispanic white children: Ibid.

143 year round: Ibid.

144 two-parent families (12 percent): Ibid.

144 ". . . injury, and indignity": Arloc Sherman, *Wasting America's Future: The Children's Defense Fund Report on the Costs of Child Poverty* (Boston: Beacon, 1994), xvi–xvii.

144 ". . . from other diseases": Ibid., xvii.

144 fatal accidental injuries: *The State of America's Children Yearbook 1995*, 19.

144 ". . . contract rheumatic fever": Sherman, *Wasting America's Future*, 64.

145 twenty years earlier: *The State of America's Children Yearbook 1995*, 18.

145 of black women: Ibid., 111.

145 1,000 live births: Ibid., 113.

146 of white babies (5.8 percent): Ibid., 112.

146 areas are underimmunized: Ibid., 7.

147 all family members: *Community Childhood Hunger Identification Project: A Survey of Childhood Hunger in the United States* (Washington, D.C.: Food Research and Action Center, July 1995), v–vi.

147 children to eat: Ibid., vii.

147 ". . . non-hungry families": Ibid., viii.

148 was 2.6 persons: *The State of America's Children Yearbook 1995*, 45.

148 one employed worker: Ibid., 46.

149 from these programs: Ibid., 48–49.

149 by that group: Ibid., 63.

150 from domestic violence: "The New Poverty: A Generation of Homeless Families," Homes For the Homeless Newsletter, June 1992, 1–7.

155 ". . . erased by time. . . .": Jonathan Kozol, *Rachel and Her Children: Homeless Families in America* (New York: Crown, 1988), 28.

156 ". . . is my birthday": Ibid., 62–66.

157 480,000 in 1994: Steven A. Holmes, "G.O.P. Seeks Shift in Child Welfare," *New York Times*, March 13, 1995.

157 ". . . always poor institutions": Richard Wexler, "A Warehouse Is Not a Home," *New York Times*, March 18, 1995.

158 ". . . hell for Donald": G. Robert Hohler, "Two Views From the Orphanage," *Boston Globe*, December 22, 1994.

159 as in families: Ann Hartman, *Out of the Arms of Mothers: What Will Happen to Children If Proposed Family Income Support Cuts Leave Some Parents Unable to Care for Them?* (New York: Center on Social Welfare Policy and Law, June 1995), 1–35.

160 average AFDC grant: Ibid.

161 due to guns: *The State of America's Children Yearbook 1995*, 54.

161 ". . . neighborhoods, and schools": Ibid.

161 carries a gun: Ibid., 55.

161 among young people: Ibid., 58.

162 ". . . on the street": Adam Walinsky, "The Crisis of Public Order," *Atlantic Monthly*, July 1995, 39–54.

162 maintained for adults: Joseph B. Treaster, "Hard Time for Hard Youths: A Battle Producing Few Winners," *New York Times*, December 28, 1994.

163 children, to play: Sara Mosle, "Who's Playing Games?" *New York Times*, June 4, 1994.

Chapter 7

Page

166 ". . . a good education": President Franklin D. Roosevelt, Annual Message to Congress, 1944, *The Annals of America 1940–1949: The Second World War and After* (Chicago: Encyclopaedia Britannica, Inc., 1968), 211–14.

169 over $10 billion: "The Billionaires," *Forbes*, July 17, 1995, 110–36.

169 designated the "overclass": "The Overclass," *Newsweek*, July 31, 1995, 32–46.

169 other industrialized countries: Keith Bradsher, "Widest Gap in Incomes? Research Points to U.S., *New York Times*, October 27, 1995.

170 "retreat from caring": Roger Lawson and William Julius Wilson, "Poverty, Social Rights, and the Quality of Citizenship," in *Poverty, Inequality and the Future of Social Policy: Western States in the New World Order*, Katherine McFate, Roger Lawson, and William Julius Wilson, eds. (New York: Russell Sage, 1995), 703.

173 ". . . lack of values": *Meet the Press*, July 23, 1995. (Transcript prepared by Burrelle's Information Services.)

173 ". . . the common good": Hugh Heclo, "The Social Question," in *Poverty, Inequality and the Future of Social Policy*, 678.

175 ". . . families with children": Sheila B. Kamerman, "Gender Role and Family Structure Changes in the Advanced Industrialized West: Implications for Social Policy," in *Poverty, Inequality and the Future of Social Policy*, 239.

175 Western European countries: Ibid., 233.

175 were virtually identical: Ibid., 236–37.

176 ". . . system of production": Katherine McFate, "Introduction: Western States in the New World Order," in *Poverty, Inequality and the Future of Social Policy*, 1.

176 ". . . wages and salaries": Stanley Aronowitz and William DiFazio, *The Jobless Future: Sci-Tech and the Dogma of Work* (Minneapolis: University of Minnesota Press, 1994), 3.

178 ". . . the coal miners": Troy Duster, "Postindustrialism and Youth Unemployment: African Americans as Harbingers," in *Poverty, Inequality and the Future of Social Policy*, 465.

178 were persistently poor: Ibid., 463.

178 ". . . ethnic urban cores": Ibid., 473.

179 that of whites: Ibid., 474.

179 the prison population: Andrew Hacker, *Two Nations: Black and White, Separate, Hostile, Unequal* (New York: Charles Scribner's Sons, 1992), 197.

179 or university full-time: Duster, *Poverty Inequality*, 476.

180 a fourfold increase: Kamerman, Ibid., 235.

180 remain the same: Katherine McFate, Timothy Smeeding, and Lee Rainwater, "Markets and States: Poverty Trends and Transfer System Effectiveness in the 1980s," in *Poverty, Inequality and the Future of Social Policy*, 31–32.

181 than 9 percent: Ibid., 38–39.

182 the required amount: Kamerman, Ibid., 248–54.

183 ". . . care for children": Lydia Morris, *The Underclass and Social Citizenship* (New York: Routledge, 1994), 134.

184 ". . . are opting out": Lester C. Thurow, "Companies Merge; Families Break Up," *New York Times*, September 3, 1995.

185 or after school: Ibid.

186 most in need: Peter Dreier and John Atlas, "Housing Policy's Moment of Truth," *The American Prospect*, Summer 1995, 68–77.

188 to additional workers: For a more complete discussion of these issues, see Sheila D. Collins, Helen Lachs Ginsburg, and Gertrude Schaffner Goldberg, *Jobs for All: A Plan for the Revitalization of America* (New York: Council on International and Public Affairs, 1994).

191 ". . . now in existence": Holly Sklar, *Chaos or Community? Seeking Solutions, Not Scapegoats for Bad Economics* (Boston: South End Press, 1995), 171.

192 ". . . with 'family values' ": Thurow, "Companies Merge; Families Break Up."

192 and well-being: M. Harvey Brenner, "Estimating the Effects of Economic Change on National Health and Social Well-

Being," a study prepared for the use of the Subcommittee on Economic Goals and Intergovernmental Policy of the Joint Economic Committee (Washington, D.C.: U.S. Government Printing Office, 1984), 3.

192 the control group: Ramsey Liem and Paula Rayman, "Health and Social Costs of Unemployment," *American Psychologist* 37 (October 1982), 1116–23.

193 ". . . friends and neighbors": Elliot Liebow, *Tally's Corner: A Study of Negro Streetcorner Men* (Boston: Little, Brown, 1967), 210.

193 ". . . as a man": Ibid., 211–12.

196 next seven years: Seymour Melman, "Preparing for War (Against Ourselves)," *New York Times*, June 26, 1995; Eugene J. Carroll, "US Is in a Wasteful Arms Race With Itself," ECAAR News Network (The Newsletter of Economists Allied for Arms Reduction), Summer 1995, 3.

196 amidst "private opulence": John Kenneth Galbraith, *The Affluent Society* (New York: New American Library, 1958), 203.

197 ". . . were in 1980": Kevin Phillips, *Arrogant Capital: Washington, Wall Street, and the Frustration of American Politics* (Boston: Little, Brown, 1994), 206–8.

198 ". . . of American families": Edward N. Wolff, "How the Pie Is Sliced," *The American Prospect*, Summer 1995, 58–64.

199 "How long?": Michael Harrington, *The Other America: Poverty in the United States* (Baltimore: Penguin, 1963), 170.

Epilogue

Page

201 ". . . Bill Clinton has done.": Peter Edelman, "The Worst Thing Bill Clinton Has Done," *Atlantic Monthly*, March 1997, 43–58.

204 ". . . on hard times.": George Soros, "Legal Immigrants Deserve a Safety Net," *New York Times*, August 22, 1997.

204 . . . uninsured children: Peter T. Kilborn, "In Budget Bill,

President Wins Welfare Battle," *New York Times*, August 1, 1997.

204 . . . on this provision: Lizette Alvarez, "In New Retreat, Senate Restores Food Stamps for Legal Immigrants," *New York Times*, May 13, 1998.

204 Governor George Pataki: Material on the New York State Welfare Reform Act of 1997 can be found in *Putting New York City's Children at Risk: The Welfare Reform Act of 1997* (New York: Citizens' Committee for Children of New York City, January 1998), 1–37.

207 enacted in 1992: Tamar Lewin, "Report Tying Abortion to Welfare is Rejected," *New York Times*, June 8, 1998.

208 will be exempt: Rachel L. Swarns, "Giuliani To Place Disabled Mothers in Workfare Jobs," *New York Times*, June 8, 1998.

209 appealed this order: "New York City Ordered to Stop Unsafe and Dangerous Workfare Assignments," *Welfare News*, The Welfare Law Center, Vol. 2, No. 4, September 1997, 1–2.

210 of the demand: *Welfare Reform: Implications of Increased Work Participation for Child Care* (Washington, D.C.: United States General Accounting Office, May 1997), 3.

211 ". . . go find him.": Kathryn Edin and Laura Lein, *Making Ends Meet: How Single Mothers Survive Welfare and Low-Wage Work* (New York: Russell Sage, 1997), 134.

212 on waiting lists: Sara Rimer, "Children of Working Poor Are Day Care's Forgotten," *New York Times*, November 25, 1997.

213 two-year-olds: Tamar Lewin, "Fewer Children Per Care Provider Is Good for All, Study Finds," *New York Times*, March 7, 1998.

213 an animal caretaker: Tamar Lewin, "From Welfare Roll to Child Care Worker," *New York Times*, April 29, 1998.

213 than family members: Tamar Lewin, "Fewer Children Per Care Provider Is Good for All, Study Finds."

214 ". . . into the streets.": "Soup Kitchens Fill After Idaho Welfare Cuts," *New York Times*, December 7, 1997.

214 ". . . have to eat.": Rachel L. Swarns, "Denied Food

Stamps, Many Immigrants Scrape for Meals," *New York Times*, December 8, 1997.

214 ". . . so much confusion.": Somini Sengupta, "Hundreds Lose Food Stamps in Error Under U.S. Welfare Change," *New York Times*, March 9, 1998.

215 for-profit groups: Richard P. Nathan, "The Newest New Federalism for Welfare: Where Are We Now and Where Are We Headed?" (Albany, N.Y.: Nelson A. Rockefeller Institute of Government, October 30, 1997), 1–8.

215 two years earlier: James Bennet, "900,000 More Leave the Welfare Rolls," *New York Times*, May 28, 1998.

216 than other workers: John Pease and Lee Martin, "Want Ads and Jobs for the Poor: A Glaring Mismatch," *Sociological Forum*, Vol. 12, No. 4, 545–564.

217 "It's troubling.": Raymond Hernandez, "Most Dropped From Welfare Don't Get Jobs," *New York Times*, March 23, 1998.

217 ". . . the labor force.": *Life After Welfare: An Interim Report* (Baltimore, MD: Maryland Department of Human Resources and University of Maryland School of Social Work, September 1997), 1–46.

218 of their expenses: Edin and Lein, *Making Ends Meet*, 6.

218 ". . . go buy groceries.": Ibid., 75.

219 that of whites: *Poverty Rate Fails to Decline as Income Growth in 1996 Favors the Affluent* (Washington, D.C.: Center on Budget and Policy Priorities, October 14, 1997), 1–7.

219 69 percent in 1996: "Child Poverty Rate Alarms Advocates," *CDF Reports* (Washington, D.C.: Children's Defense Fund, November 1997), 4.

220 two-parent families: *Young Children in Poverty: A Statistical Update* (New York: National Center for Children in Poverty, March 1998), 1–12.

220 the mid-1980s: Kathryn Larin and Elizabeth C. McNichol, *Pulling Apart: A State-by-State Analysis of Income Trends* (Washington, D.C.: Center on Budget and Policy Priorities, December 1997), i.

220 total national income: *Poverty Rate Fails to Decline as Income Growth in 1996 Favors the Affluent*.

220 billions of dollars: David Cay Johnston, "Executive Pay
Increases at a Much Faster Rate Than Corporate Revenues
and Profits," *New York Times*, September 2, 1997.

221 1994 to 1996: *Pulling Apart*, ii–iii.

221 increased 53 percent: Ibid., 5.

222 "poverty rates increase": Wendell E. Primus, Kathryn Porter,
Margery Ditto, and Mitchell Kent, *The Safety Net Delivers:
The Effects of Government Benefit Programs in Reducing Poverty*
(Washington, D.C.: Center on Budget and Policy Priorities,
November 1996), 1–3.

223 ". . . that creates independence.": Jason DeParle, "As
Nation's Economy Hums, Welfare's Image Is Polished," *New
York Times*, September 1997.

223 And to train: Robert Pear, "Welfare Workers Rate High in
Job Retention at Companies," *New York Times*, May 27,
1998.

224 ". . . stayed at home.": Susan Chira, *A Mother's Place: Taking
the Debate About Working Mothers Beyond Guilt and Blame*
(New York: HarperCollins, 1998), 4.

225 ". . . mother should do.": Ibid., 3.

226 ". . . into the workforce.": Suzanne M. Bianchi and Philip
Cohen, "Marriage, Children, and Women's Employment:
Do We Know What We Think We Know?" Paper prepared
for an Invited Session on "Gender Inequality at Work" at
the annual meeting of the Eastern Sociological Association,
Philadelphia, PA, March 20, 1998.

226 out of poverty: Kathryn Porter, Wendell E. Primus, Lynette
Rawlings, and Esther Rosenbaum, *Strengths of the Safety Net:
How the EITC, Society Security and Other Government Programs
affect Poverty* (Washington, D.C.: Center on Budget and
Policy Priorities, March 1998), 20–21.

Selected Bibliography

Mimi Abramovitz, *Regulating the Lives of Women: Social Welfare Policy from Colonial Times to the Present* (Boston: South End Press, 1988).

Stanley Aronowitz and William DiFazio, *The Jobless Future: Sci-Tech and the Dogma of Work* (Minneapolis: University of Minnesota Press, 1994).

Ken Auletta, *The Underclass* (New York: Vintage, 1983).

Mary Jo Bane and David T. Ellwood, *Welfare Realities: From Rhetoric to Reform* (Cambridge, Mass.: Harvard University Press, 1994).

John Berger, *Ways of Seeing* (London: Penguin, 1972).

David Blankenhorn, *Fatherless America: Confronting Our Most Urgent Social Problem* (New York: Basic Books, 1995).

Patricia Hill Collins, *Black Feminist Thought: Knowledge, Consciousness, and the Politics of Empowerment* (Boston: Unwin Hyman, 1990).

Sheila D. Collins, Helen Lachs Ginsburg, and Gertrude Schaffner Goldberg, *Jobs for All: A Plan for the Revitalization of America* (New York: Council on International and Public Affairs, 1994).

Stephanie Coontz, *The Way We Never Were: American Families and the Nostalgia Trap* (New York: Basic Books, 1992).

Chandler Davidson, *Race and Class in Texas Politics* (Princeton, NJ: Princeton University Press, 1990).

Patricia Donovan, *The Politics of Blame* (New York: The Alan Guttmacher Institute, 1995).

Thomas Byrne Edsall and Mary D. Edsall, *Chain Reaction: The Impact of Race, Rights, and Taxes on American Politics* (New York: W. W. Norton, 1991).

Kai T. Erikson, *Wayward Puritans: A Study in the Sociology of Deviance* (New York: Macmillan, 1966).

Martha Albertson Fineman, *The Neutered Mother, the Sexual Family and Other Twentieth Century Tragedies* (New York: Routledge, 1995).

Donna Gaines, *Teenage Wasteland: Suburbia's Dead End Kids* (New York: Pantheon, 1991).

Herbert J. Gans, *The War Against the Poor: The Underclass and Antipoverty Policy* (New York: Basic Books, 1995).

Erving Goffman, *Stigma: Notes on the Management of Spoiled Identity* (Englewood Cliffs, N.J.: Prentice-Hall, 1963).

Erich Goode and Nachman Ben-Yehuda, *Moral Panics: The Social Construction of Deviance* (Cambridge, Mass.: Blackwell, 1994).

Linda Gordon, *Pitied But Not Entitled: Single Mothers and the History of Welfare* (New York: Free Press, 1994).

Andrew Hacker, *Two Nations: Black and White, Separate, Hostile, Unequal* (New York: Charles Scribner's Sons, 1992).

Michael Harrington, *The Other America: Poverty in the United States* (Baltimore: Penguin, 1962).

Nathaniel Hawthorne, *The Scarlet Letter* (New York: Penguin, 1986).

Philip Jenkins, *Intimate Enemies: Moral Panics in Contemporary Great Britain* (New York: Aldine de Gruyter, 1992).

Michael B. Katz, ed., *The "Underclass" Debate: Views from History* (Princeton, N.J.: Princeton University Press, 1993).

Jonathan Kozol, *Amazing Grace: The Lives of Children and the Conscience of a Nation* (New York: Crown, 1995).

———, *Rachel and Her Children: Homeless Families in America* (New York: Crown, 1988).

———, *Savage Inequalities: Children in America's Schools* (New York: Harper Collins, 1992).

Elliot Liebow, *Tally's Corner: A Study of Negro Streetcorner Men* (Boston: Little, Brown, 1967).

Katherine McFate, Roger Lawson, and William Julius Wilson, eds. *Poverty, Inequality and the Future of Social Policy: Western States in the New World Order* (New York: Russell Sage, 1995).

Sara McLanahan and Gary Sandefur, *Growing Up with a Single Parent* (Cambridge, Mass.: Harvard University Press, 1994).

Lydia Morris, *Dangerous Classes: The Underclass and Social Citizenship* (New York: Routledge, 1994).

Charles Murray, *Losing Ground: American Social Policy 1950–1980* (New York: Basic Books, 1984).

Elaine Pagels, *The Origin of Satan* (New York: Random House, 1995).

Kevin Phillips, *Arrogant Capital: Washington, Wall Street, and the Frustration of American Politics* (Boston: Little, Brown, 1994).

Frances Fox Piven and Richard A. Cloward, *Regulating the Poor: The Functions of Public Welfare* (New York: Vintage, 1993).

John E. Schwarz and Thomas J. Volgy, *The Forgotten Americans* (New York: W. W. Norton, 1992).

Sex and America's Teenagers (New York: The Alan Guttmacher Institute, 1994).

Arloc Sherman, *Wasting America's Future: The Children's Defense Fund Report on the Costs of Child Poverty* (Boston: Beacon Press, 1994).

Ruth Sidel, *Battling Bias: The Struggle for Identity and Community on College Campuses* (New York: Penguin, 1995).

———, *On Her Own: Growing Up in the Shadow of the American Dream* (New York: Penguin, 1991).

———, *Women and Children Last: The Plight of Poor Women in Affluent America* (New York: Penguin, 1992).

Holly Sklar, *Chaos or Community? Seeking Solutions, Not Scapegoats for Bad Economics* (Boston: South End Press, 1995).

Rickie Solinger, *Wake Up Little Susie: Single Pregnancy and Race Before Roe v. Wade* (New York: Routledge, 1992).

The State of America's Children Yearbook 1995 (Washington, D.C.: Children's Defense Fund, 1995).

William Julius Wilson, *The Truly Disadvantaged: The Inner City, the Underclass, and Public Policy* (Chicago: University of Chicago Press, 1987).

Maxine Baca Zinn and Bonnie Thornton Dill, eds., *Women of Color in U.S. Society* (Philadelphia: Temple University Press, 1994).

Index

260 INDEX